LES POISSONS—FISH

Scampis frits	fried scampi
Coquilles St. Jacques	scallops
Homard au naturel	cold lobster
Moules marinières	mussels cooked and served in a clear liquid
Fruits de mer	generally a dish of mixed shell fish
Plie frite	fried plaice
Plie frite à la tartare	fried plaice with tartare sauce
Sole frite	fried sole
Merlan frits	fried whiting
Sole bonne femme	sole cooked with a wine and cream sauce garnished with mushrooms and creamed potatoes
Sole Véronique	sole with grapes*
Poissons à la Provençale	fish with Provençale sauce (many dishes are served à la Provençale —the sauce should have onion, garlic and tomatoes)
Saumon poché	poached salmon
Truite à la meunière	trout with browned butter

*there are many ways of serving sole with classic garnishes (menus often interpret these)

LES VIANDES—MEAT DISHES

Often these are divided in a menu into Les grillades (grills), Les rôtis (roasts) or sometimes you will find two headings given, Entrées—savoury meat dishes, followed by Relevés (removes), which includes solid, straightforward meat dishes like roasts.

Escalope de veau	fried slice of veal, often called Wiener Schnitzel
Ris de veau frits	fried sweetbreads
Filet de boeuf	fillet steak
Bifteck	beef steak, but generally type is given, e.g.—
Tournedos	rolled fillet steak, generally given a second name according to garnish
Côtelettes de veau	veal cutlets
Côtelettes de mouton	mutton cutlets
Côtelettes d'agneau	lamb cutlets
Côtelettes de porc	pork cutlets
Blanquette de veau	veal blanquette* (creamy stew)
Boeuf à l'anglaise	roast beef with Yorkshire pudding etc.
Boeuf braisé	braised beef
Rôti de boeuf	roast beef
Rôti d'agneau	roast lamb, but generally cut is given, e.g.
Carré d'agneau rôti	roasted loin of lamb. etc.

Other meats are described in the same way.

Jambon grillé	grilled ham

*these French words have become the usual term in any language

METRIC CONVERSION CHART

Imperial Measure	Metric equivalent	Approximate equivalent
WEIGHT		
$\frac{1}{4}$ oz	7·09 g	7 g
$\frac{1}{2}$ oz	14·17 g	15 g
1 oz	28·35 g	30 g
$\frac{1}{4}$ lb	113·4 g (0·113 kg)	125 g
$\frac{1}{2}$ lb	227 g (0·227 kg)	225 g
1 lb	454 g (0·454 kg)	450 g
2 lb	907 g	900 g
3 lb	1361 g	1350 g (1 kg 350 g)
LIQUID MEASURE		
1 fl oz	28·4 ml	30 ml
$\frac{1}{4}$ pt (1 gill)	142 ml	150 ml
$\frac{1}{2}$ pt	284 ml	300 ml
1 pt	568 ml	600 ml
1 qt	1137 ml	1200 ml (1 litre 200 ml)
LENGTH		
$\frac{1}{4}$ inch	6·35 mm	6 mm
1 inch	2·54 cm (25·4 mm)	2·5 cm (25 mm)

g = gram; kg = kilogram (1000 g); ml = millilitre; 1 litre = 1000 ml

Note Strict application of approximate equivalents may produce unsavoury results. Teachers are advised to test those recipes in which the proportions of ingredients are critical, and to modify the quantities in the light of their tests.

Adventures in Cookery

3

MARGUERITE PATTEN

Ginn

INTRODUCTION

IN THIS, the third of the series *Adventures in Cookery*, you will find more advanced skills in cookery have been covered in detail, together with new and interesting recipes based on the processes you will already have learned or which may be found in the earlier books. In addition, this book gives advice to help in the feeding of various groups of people—from babies to the elderly, vegetarians, invalids and those who have limited cooking facilities.

There are menus for special occasions when, for example, you wish to entertain or, on the other hand, when you need to produce a meal just from the ingredients available in your store cupboard. In addition, there is a considerable amount of factual information on nutrition, the digestive system, the use and choice of domestic equipment, etc., which is essential knowledge for the good home-maker and which covers the requirements of many school external examinations.

I hope you will derive pleasure from following the recipes and that you will continue to enjoy using *Adventures in Cookery*. I would like to record my appreciation of the help, encouragement and advice given to me by Miss W. Hargreaves in preparing this series.

MARGUERITE PATTEN

Second impression 1970 157003
GINN SBN 602 20048 2
Published in Great Britain
by Ginn and Company Ltd
18 Bedford Row, London W.C.1.
Published in Australia by Cheshire
346 St. Kilda Road, Melbourne
142 Victoria Road, Marrickville, N.S.W.

(Title page) Cheese soufflé
(Left) Roast turkey

ACKNOWLEDGEMENT is made to the owners of coloured photographs used in this book as follows: Atora Suet (pp. 2, 160), Cheese Bureau (pp. 1, 213), Danish Food Centre (p. 214), Eden Vale (p. 19), Electricity Council (pp. 55, 56, 195), from their book *How to Cook Perfectly with Electricity*, Fruit Producers' Council (pp. 37, 142, 196, 232), Herring Industry Board (p. 74), Lard Information Bureau (p. 178), McDougalls (pp. 141, 159, 177), Marvel (p. 38), New Zealand Lamb Information Bureau (pp. 20, 91), Outspan (p. 231), Pig Industry Development Authority (p. 92), White Fish Authority (p. 73).

Thanks are due to the following for the use of black and white photographs and diagrams: Australian Home Cookery Service (pp. 86 right, 93, 146, 182, 190), Bacon Information Bureau (p. 81), Barnaby's Picture Library (p. 205), Bird's Dream Topping (p. 135), Blue Band (p. 174), Anne Bolt (p. 223), British Egg Marketing Board (pp. 123, 127, 155, 186), Cadbury's (pp. 147, 149, 156, 191, 192), California Prune Advisory Board (p. 99), Camp Coffee (p. 128), Cheese Bureau (pp. 63, 65, 75, 76, 79, 119, 120, 121), Chicken Information Bureau (p. 85), Colman's Mustard (p. 209), Council of Scientific Management in the Home (p. 44), Cranberry Kitchen (pp. 103, 104), Creda Domestic Appliances (pp. 47 left, 201 foot), Danish Food Centre (p. 117), Delrosa (p. 153), Electricity Council (pp. 8, 50, 57, 58 centre and right, 59 left and right, 60), Electrolux and Dordec (pp. 52, 53), Flour Advisory Bureau (pp. 26, 80, 100, 115, 144, 154, 175, 179, 183), Fowler's West Indian Treacle (pp. 138, 185, *Fresh Meat From Britain's Farmers* by F. M. C. (Meat) Ltd (p. 94), Jobling Housecraft Service (p. 225), Lard Information Bureau (p. 130), Mamade (p. 30), Marsh and Baxter (p. 90), New Zealand Lamb Information Bureau (pp. 83, 220, 221), George Newnes (pp. 129 picture 2, 139 foot, 176, 201), P.I.D.A. (p. 203), Philips Electrical (p. 58 left), Potato Marketing Board (p. 111), Prestige Ltd (p. 49), Radiation (pp. 22, 44, 47 right), Smith's Potato Crisps (p. 208), Spry (p. 134), Stork Cookery Service (pp. 136, 139 top, 184), Thorn Electrical Industries (p. 51), Unigate Double Devon Cream (p. 202), T. Wall & Sons (pp. 86 foot, 114, 143), White Fish Authority (pp. 68, 69, 72, 77, 78, 129 picture 1).

The author and publishers also gratefully acknowledge the expert advice given at all stages in the preparation of this course by Miss Winifred Hargreaves, formerly H. M. Staff Inspector, Home Economics.

CONTENTS

5

CHAPTER ONE

Learning about food and cookery

THE primary purpose of food is to provide the nourishment needed by the human body to enable it to grow, and to assist in maintaining health and energy. In stressing this, however, people sometimes forget that food is also there to be *enjoyed* and that good cooking should be appreciated like any other skill.

The basic principles of cooking are to be found in Book 2 (Book 1 covers the beginning of cookery) and therefore constant reference will need to be made to Book 2.

Some terms used in *preparing* food and others used in *cooking* food, which should assist in following any cookery book, are given on pages 239–41.

Consider these points when planning meals:

1. *Choose food carefully* so that it benefits all members of the family or the particular community. To do this, you need a knowledge of simple nutrition. Remember, too, that people's needs vary with their age and occupation. For example, a manual worker who uses a great deal of physical effort needs more energy-giving foods than someone in an office job.

The main purpose of the various groups of foods has been covered in Book 2, Chapter One, but the tables on pages 10–16 analyse the more usual foods and their nutritive values so that you can plan well-balanced as well as appetising meals. It is important to appreciate how the digestive system works and how food is assimilated by the body so as to give the maximum benefit (pages 18, 21–2).

2. *Buy food well.* This means developing a good shopping sense

(a) to shop wisely and economically,

(b) to be knowledgeable about new kinds of food, i.e. frozen, A.F.D., etc. (page 31).

(c) to look at food shops and supermarkets and judge whether the foods they sell are fresh and are marketed under the best conditions, described fully in Book 2, Chapter Two.

(d) to store food under the best conditions: in a refrigerator (Book 2, Chapter Four) or in a store-cupboard or larder (pages 33–5).

3. *Learn how to cook well*

(a) You must follow recipes with accuracy. If an incorrect temperature is used, food can be spoilt; if the balance of ingredients given in the recipe is changed, the results are often poor.

(b) Be sure to manipulate the ingredients and utensils correctly for various processes.

(c) Be imaginative in the choice and presentation of the food.

(d) Preserve the maximum nutritive value, flavour and texture of the food.

4. *Choosing menus*. Always choose a menu that is suitable for the particular occasion.

5. It is important to realise that many modern appliances can help the busy housewife and to assess the value of these turn to page 45.

6. It is important to make cooking, and indeed all work in the kitchen, as labour saving as possible, so always have a chair or stool available so you can sit when preparing vegetables, ironing or cleaning silver, etc. This is not inefficient. It saves the fatigue of standing and provided the stool or chair is the right height, often one has a better control over movement than when standing.

This is an admirable layout for a very small kitchen. (See Chapter Five.) In this there is no room for a table and a shelf has been built against one wall to take the place of a table. Stools fit under this and a skirting heater provides warmth.

Another feature of the design in this kitchen is the corner cupboard, which utilises all the space. The refrigerator has been built under the working surface

CHAPTER TWO

Menu planning, nutrition and digestion

WHEN planning menus, think of the foods that are needed, e.g. a dinner may include MEAT which provides protein and may give a certain amount of fat. With this will be POTATOES, providing carbohydrate (starch) and a certain amount of vitamin C. CARROTS add vitamin A; a GREEN VEGETABLE gives vitamins A and C; a SWEETENED RAW FRUIT SALAD provides additional vitamin C and sugar; or CHEESE AND BISCUITS WITH BUTTER gives more protein, calcium, carbohydrate (starch), and vitamins A and D.

It is easy to assess the essential foods *omitted* from this particular meal and adjust menus for breakfast, tea or supper on that day.

Ways in which students may be asked to analyse foods are:

1. To give the nutritive value of a certain food or dish, e.g. MILK, CHEESE, BREAD.

As shown in the table overleaf, *every* food, except pure sugar, provides *more than one* important nutrient.

2. To list the main PROTEIN or CARBOHYDRATE foods.

3. To plan a well-balanced menu for a family or one particular group.

This means a knowledge of simple nutrition is invaluable for meal planning.

Books 1 and 2 deal in detail with the function of various foods, so if you are unsure of these facts, check with one of these books.

Table of main nutrients

The table which begins on the next page enables the most usual foods to be analysed at a glance. Before using this table, here are some points to bear in mind:

1. The table deals with the main foods only. Obviously when foods are combined in a made-up dish, you are adding other nutrients. For example, the second item under Beef is 'Beef for stewing'. This refers only to the beef itself. When carrots are added, the dish has the nutrients of carrots too; with a thickened gravy, a very small amount of the nutrients of flour is included.

2. Some everyday foods will not be found in this table. It is because they supply relatively little of the main nutrients. This does not mean they should not be included in the diet, for they add interest, variety and probably colour to a dish.

Food values

Read pages 9 and 17 before using this table

Food	Protein	Fats	Carbohydrates		Minerals				Vitamins				Calories (per 1 oz. food unless stated)
			Starch	Sugar	Iron	Calcium	Iodine	Phosphorus	A	B Group	C	D	
MEAT													
Beef													Can vary between
good quality	X	X			x	x		X		x			52-90
stewing	X	X			x	x		X		x			75
Lamb	X	X				x		X					57-90
Mutton	X	X				x		X					Up to 75
Pork	X	X						X		x			lean 67 fat 112
Veal	X					x		X					36
Offal													
Heart	X	x			X								66
Liver	X	x			X			X	X	x			40
Kidneys	X	x						X	x	x			30-36
Tripe	X	X very little				x							17-29
Bacon, Ham	X	X								x			115-124
Sausages	X	X	x			X				x			beef 60 pork 72
Canned meat													
Tongue	X	X											72
Luncheon meat	X some fairly low	X	x varies			x				x			75-100
Corned beef	X	X			x	x							70
Frozen meat	as fresh												as fresh
POULTRY													
Chicken, Turkey	X	x								x			41-47
Duck	X	x											47-62
Frozen poultry	as fresh												as fresh

10

Food values (cont.)

Food	Protein	Fats	Carbohydrates		Minerals				Vitamins				Calories (per 1 oz. food unless stated)
			Starch	Sugar	Iron	Calcium	Iodine	Phosphorus	A	B Group	C	D	
FISH													
White Cod, Haddock, Plaice, etc.	X	x				x	X	X					22-29
Oily Herrings, Sprats, Mackerel, etc.	X	X				x	X	X	X			X	67
Smoked Haddock	X	X				x	X	X				x	30
Kippers, Bloaters, etc.	X	X			x	x	X	X	x	x		x	62
Shell Crab	X					x	X	X					37
Lobster, Prawns, Shrimps	X					x	X	X					14-16
Canned Salmon, Tuna	X	X				x	X	X	x			X	40
Sardines, Pilchards	X	X			x	x	X	X	x			X	75-80
Frozen	as fresh												as fresh
DAIRY FOODS													
Eggs Yolk, raw or boiled	X	X			X			X	X	x			1 small yolk 69
White, raw or boiled	X												1 small white 11
Whole egg, fried, scrambled	X	X						x	X	x			one: 140

Food	Protein	Fats	Carbohydrates		Minerals				Vitamins				Calories (per 1 oz. food unless stated)
			Starch	Sugar	Iron	Calcium	Iodine	Phosphorus	A	B Group	C	D	
DAIRY FOODS cont.													
Fats													
Butter		X							X			X	260
Margarine		X							X			X	220
Lard		X											240
Cooking fat		X											240—varies
Suet		X											260
Olive oil		X							x				Tablespoon 100
Corn oil		X							x				255
Cheese													
Cheddar and similar	X	x				X		X					120
Cream	X	x				X		X					145-232
Cottage	X					X		X					50
Milk													
Fresh	X	x	x			X		X	x			x	pint: 360
Dried, skimmed	X					X		X		x	x		pint: 135
Evaporated	X	x	x			X		X	x			x	1 oz.: 45
Condensed full cream	X	X	x	X		X		X	x			x	100
Cream													
Thin	X	x				x		x	x			x	¼ pint: 275
Thick	X	x				x		x	x			x	¼ pint: 275
Yoghourt	X	x				x		x	x				¼ pint: 100
FRUIT, NUTS													
Citrus (orange, etc.)				x		x			x		X		6-9
Soft (blackberries, raspberries, strawberries, etc.)				x		x					X particularly strawberries		6-8

Food values (cont.)

Food	Protein	Fats	Carbohydrates		Minerals				Vitamins				Calories (per 1 oz. food unless stated)
			Starch	Sugar	Iron	Calcium	Iodine	Phosphorus	A	B Group	C	D	
FRUIT NUTS cont.													
Apples, Pears, raw				x					x				11-15
Apricots, raw									x				11
Bananas			x	x					x				1 : 80-100
Blackcurrants				x					x		X		12
Peaches, Plums, Pineapples				x							x		10
Dried													
Apricots				x	X	x			x				50
Dates				x		x							75
Figs				x	X	x							57
Prunes				x	X	x			x				37
Raisins, sultanas				x	X	x							62
Cooked or canned fruit with sugar				X	x	x					X very little		20
Nuts (almonds, etc.)	X	x	x			x							170
Coconut, fresh	X	x	x										170
Dried (desiccated)	X	x	x										180
FRESH VEGETABLES AND SALADS													
Root and Bulbs													
Carrots			x	x		x			X		x		7
Celery, Chicory			x			x	x						3
Onions, Leeks			x			x	X						6
Potatoes			x			x					X*		boiled 24 fried 67
Turnips, Swedes, Parsnips			x			x					x		10

*This varies a great deal throughout the year, NEW potatoes containing a good amount of Vitamin C

Food values (cont.)

Food	Protein	Fats	Carbohydrates		Minerals				Vitamins				Calories (per 1 oz. food unless stated)
			Starch	Sugar	Iron	Calcium	Iodine	Phosphorus	A	B Group	C	D	
FRESH VEGETABLES AND SALADS cont.													
Green													
Sprouts, Cabbage, Greens, Cauliflower Broccoli								X			X		5
Spinach (Kale has same to less degree)					X	x			X		X		5
Fresh peas	X		x			x			X		X		19
Beans (Runner, French)	x little		x			x			X		X		4
Beetroot			x	x		x							7
Tomatoes						x			x		x		4-5
Watercress					X	x	X		X	x	x		4
Canned													
Baked beans, Peas	X		x			x			x				26
Carrots			x	x		x			x				as fresh
Frozen	Varies—green vegetables lose certain Vitamin C; carrots retain Vitamin A, starch												as fresh
PULSES													
Beans, haricot, butter, etc.	X		x		x	x							120
Peas—dried	X		x		x	x							85
Lentils	X		x		x	x							80
Soya bean (made into flour)	X	x			x	x				X			123

Food values (cont.)

Food	Protein	Fats	Carbohydrates		Minerals				Vitamins				Calories (per 1 oz. food unless stated)
			Starch	Sugar	Iron	Calcium	Iodine	Phosphorus	A	B Group	C	D	
CEREALS AND FOODS made from FLOUR													
Oatmeal			X		X	x				X			110
Wheat	see flour												see flour
Breakfast cereals	x		X							x			100-110
Rice													
cooked in milk and sugar	x	x	x	X									125
boiled in water	x		x	X									125
Canned creamed rice	x	x	x	X									75
Flour													
white	x		X		x	x added				X			99-100
wholemeal	x		X		X					X			91-100
Bread													
White, Brown (made with ½ white ½ wholemeal flour)	x		X		x	x				X			70
Wholemeal	x		X		x					X			70
Cake, with fat	x	x	X	X	x	x				X			75-90 varies
Sponge, no fat	x		X	X	x	x				X			67 varies
Iced cakes	x	x	X	X	x	x				X			112 varies
Biscuits													
plain	x	x	X		x	x				X			105
sweet	x	x	X	X	x	x				X			145
crispbread	x		X		x	x				X			97
starch-reduced	x		X		x	x				X			120
Pastry, short	x	x	X		x	x							75
Semolina	x		X		x	x							80
Macaroni, spaghetti	x		X		x	x							80 (dry)

Food values (cont.)

Food	Protein	Fats	Carbohydrates		Minerals				Vitamins				Calories (per 1 oz. food unless stated)
			Starch	Sugar	Iron	Calcium	Iodine	Phosphorus	A	B Group	C	D	
SWEETS													
Sugar				X									50
Honey				X		x				x very little			82
Golden Syrup				X	trace	x							84
Black treacle				X	X	x							84
Jams				x		x							120
Dairy ice cream		x		X		x							60
Chocolate													
plain	x	x	X	x	x				x	x			150
milk	x	x	X	x	x	x							120
BEVERAGES, ETC.													
Tea with milk and sugar	x Amount depends on milk used	x		x		x				x			1 cup: 75
Coffee with milk and sugar	x			x		x				x			1 cup: 85
Cocoa powder	x	x	x	x	X	x			x				128
Rose hip syrup (sweetened)				x							X		fluid oz. 95:
Beer						x				x			pint: 260-420
Yeast and yeast extract	x									X			neglible
Soups	Depending upon ingredients used												Average: Clear: 5 Thick: 16

3. Where the amount of a nutrient, e.g. mineral salts, etc., is very small, they are not marked on this particular table.

4. To read this table correctly and to differentiate between main and minor sources of nutrients, the following coding is given:

X means a good supply of that nutrient.

x means a *smaller* amount.

5. When assessing the nutritive value of foods one must also take into consideration their use. For example, parsley has a high vitamin C content, but one eats so little parsley that the amount actually eaten can contribute little vitamin C to the diet, whereas potatoes, which contain less vitamin C, are eaten so often and in such large quantities that they are known to contribute about one-third of the total vitamin C intake. This is why people who do not eat potatoes for fear of putting on too much weight must choose other foods rich in vitamin C. People often worry that they are not eating enough of certain nutrients, e.g. protein and vitamin C. This may be the case, but a normal well-balanced diet generally includes all the nutrients.

Water from food

The table does not mention the percentage of water in foods, but it is important to realise we must have a good amount of water in the diet since the body cannot exist without it. Not only the things we drink, coffee, tea, water itself, provide this liquid, but so do many of our foods.

Calories

The last column in the table shows the number of calories found in the particular foods. A calorie is a heat unit and it records the amount of energy given by food.

One calorie is the amount of heat required to raise the temperature of 1,000 grams (approximately 2 pints) of water by one degree centigrade.

Just as a car engine needs fuel to enable it to work properly, so the body needs food to give it energy. This energy is used in working; to create warmth; and even during sleep it is needed for breathing and to keep the heart beating. Foods vary a great deal. Some are very high in calories, e.g. fat and carbohydrate; others lower, e.g. green vegetables and certain fruits.

Slimming diets

When good slimming diets are worked out, they are planned in such a way that they give fewer calories than the body needs to maintain its present weight. This causes a gradual loss of weight.

It is essential that any drastic slimming diets are followed under doctor's orders for many people are foolish enough to cut down the calories to such an extent that they harm their health. The ideal slimming diet provides the *essential* foods, i.e. protein, vitamins, etc.

Diets for underweight people

When people are very thin and underweight, it may well be they are not eating enough foods with a high calorie content.

Often, however, people are very thin because they cannot digest food easily (see the descriptions of the digestive system below).

When planning menus for somebody who is very thin, bear in mind the points raised in Section 27 on cooking for invalids.

When working out calories per ounce, remember it is a 1 oz. *edible* portion and does not include the food you leave, e.g. bones in meat and tough stalks in vegetables.

The B group vitamins

The column of vitamin B in the table is headed 'B group', for, as given in Book 2, this vitamin is divided into

Thiamine—B_1, Riboflavine—B_2 and Nicotinic acid.

Digestive system

In order for food to have the maximum value it must be digested properly and the following pages give a simple explanation of digestion.

The process of digestion comprises the changes to which molecules in food are subjected from the time the food is eaten until it is absorbed into the body.

Considerable chemical changes have to take place in this food to make it either soluble in water or divided into such fine particles that it may pass through the walls of the alimentary tract (food canal) and capillaries (small blood vessels).

Here are the stages in the digestion of food:

1. *Mouth.* The food is chewed by the teeth and thorough chewing enables the food to be easily swallowed and so helps the process of digestion. The tongue and cheeks mix the food with saliva and the ptyalin (starch-splitting enzyme) in the saliva begins the digestion of the starch.

2. *Pharynx (the throat cavity).* The food is swallowed by muscular action and enters the oesophagus (the muscular tube connecting the pharynx and stomach). Solid foods are guided by the epiglottis (the cartilage at the root of the tongue), but more liquid foods are swallowed with little muscular effort.

3. *Oesophagus.* Small lumps of solid food, often known as bolus, have to be propelled along this tube by the contractions of the muscles to guide the food into the stomach.

4. *Stomach.* The muscles of the stomach are

A slimming diet me

seldom completely at rest even when the stomach is empty for they tend to contract giving a sensation which is interpreted as hunger. When solid food enters the stomach these contractions complete the disintegration of the food and then propel it into the duodenum; liquid foods do not need this aid and can begin to pass into the duodenum at once.

The time food remains in the stomach varies —fat and carbohydrates remain longer than other foods, which is why one often hears that they are 'difficult to digest'. When food enters the stomach, the gastric juices, which are secreted after eating and while food remains in the stomach, begin their work.

Starch digestion begins as the acid in the stomach neutralises the alkali of the saliva. This is continued in the small intestine.

Protein digestion begins due to the action of pepsin and hydrochloric acid. Pepsin also coagulates milk and the cassein separates out. In the young, another enzyme known as rennin fills this function.

5. *Duodenum (first part of the small intestine).* The food enters the small intestine and the digestive juices and sodium bicarbonate secreted by the pancreas (large gland across the back of the stomach) complete the process of digestion.

In the small intestine, the digestive juice amylopsin (amylase) converts cooked starch and dextrins into maltose, then to glucose, after which it is absorbed.

In this part of the digestive tract

(a) Starch and digested sugar finish forming glucose.

(b) Protein forms amino acids.

(c) Fats are attacked for the first time. Some fats are absorbed as fat. The rest are absorbed as fatty acid and glycerol (glycerine).

The bile from the liver helps to emulsify fats; this bile is alkaline and slightly antiseptic.

After this the digested foods, which are now in a solution, begin to be absorbed through capillaries into the blood stream. The absorption of the food occurs mostly in the small intestine, for the entire surface is covered by tiny 'villi' which are very small muscles which absorb the food. Food not needed by the blood is rejected by the body as waste products.

Chemical changes in food
(This will be covered in greater detail in your biology lessons.)

Carbohydrates. Taken into the body as starch and sugar, are converted into simple sugars, of which glucose is the most important. Much of this is passed to the liver, then into circulation to produce energy. The rest is stored by the liver

Kebabs

in the form of glycogen. When the amount of sugar in the blood falls, the liver changes some of the glycogen into glucose to keep the blood sugar content steady.

Proteins. Taken into the body as animal proteins (meat, fish, etc.), vegetable proteins (lentils, beans, etc.) and converted into amino acids. These are passed into the liver then into circulation, where they are used for building new cells in growth or for the repair of tissues.

Fats. Taken into the body in the form of butter, margarine, oily fish, fat from meat, etc. and converted into glycerine and fatty acid.

Most of these are absorbed into the blood stream but some are stored as fat deposits.

This is a more luxurious kitchen than the one shown on page 8, with well planned kitchen cabinets. The cooker is the 'split level' type, the oven being installed at working height apart from the top of the cooker. (See Chapter Five)

Buying food wisely

WHEN shopping for food, consider the following:

Price
Compare the prices in different shops, for they may vary quite considerably. Remember, however, that you must also compare
(a) *the quantity offered* for the money (particularly with pre-packed foods)
(b) *the quality*—inferior food is rarely cheaper than better quality food, in the long run.

Freshness
Perishable foods—meat, fish, vegetables, and fruit in particular—*must* be fresh, otherwise the flavour is bad and the food is wasted. Bad food can also cause food poisoning.

Suitability
Consider the purpose for which the food is needed, for example:
cheaper cuts of meat are excellent for slow methods of cooking, but quite unsuitable for quicker cooking;
cheaper fish such as cod, and fresh haddock are not only more economical than plaice, sole, etc. in made-up fish dishes such as fish pie and fish cakes, but also better, as they have a more pronounced flavour;
cheap tomatoes, if of reasonable quality, are suitable for cooking, but you may need the better quality and firmer tomatoes for salads;
single cream, when available, is ideal for serving with fruit and is cheaper than thick (often called 'double') cream. Double cream whips easily, but no cream will whip if it has been homogenised. For economy, mix equal quantities of double and single cream which will whip to produce a light result.

Watch the shops carefully and you will find that special offers are made on certain proprietary foods. This is the time to buy them, particularly if they are non-perishable. It is important not to be unduly swayed by too persuasive advertising.

Ask yourself:
(a) do you *need* the goods?
(b) if perishable, can they be used at once or stored satisfactorily?

Bulk buying
Much is written about buying in bulk to save money, but before doing this, consider if it is wise economy.

Selection of peas

Amount purchased to give 4 servings. Prices quoted do not necessarily represent one particular brand
—they are an average price based on various brands and different shopping areas

| | Fresh | | Canned | | Dried Ordinary | A.F.D. | Frozen |
	A	B	Garden	Processed			
Price	1/6d. lb.	9d. lb.	1/3d.	11d.	1/10d. lb.	1/11d.	1/11d.
Weight bought or used	2 lb.	1½ lb.	15 oz.	15 oz.	6 oz.	2¼ oz.	10 oz.
Average weight when cooked or heated	10 oz.	12 oz.	nearly 10 oz.	nearly 10 oz.	10½ oz.	9 oz.	9½ oz.
Preparation time	10-15 mins.		1 min.	1 min.	*12 hours soaking	1 min.	1 min.
Cooking or heating time	15-20 mins.		few mins.	few mins.	*1½ hours	15 mins.	5 mins.
Cost per person to nearest ½d.	9d.	3½d.	4d.	3d.	2d.	3d.	6d.

Note : Batch A of peas were bought at the very beginning of the season
Batch B of peas were bought at the height of the season

*unless using pressure cooker

COST At the height of the season, fresh peas compare favourably in cost with frozen, A.F.D. and better-grade canned peas. At the beginning of the season they are the most expensive because of the high percentage of waste. Ordinary dried peas and processed peas are the cheapest, followed by canned garden peas. A.F.D. and frozen peas are very similar.

TIME TAKEN Fresh peas take the longest to prepare ; ordinary dried peas the longest to cook, and they have a long soaking period. Both of these, therefore, would be less practical for a busy housewife than canned, A.F.D. or frozen.

FLAVOUR Although flavour is a matter of personal choice, most people prefer good fresh peas.

Interesting comparisons can be made, on similar lines, for
(a) Home-made cake ; shop-bought cake ; cake mixes
(b) Fresh and frozen fish ; and some forms of canned fish
(c) Instant coffee ; ground coffee ; coffee essence

Detergents and cleaning materials are generally cheaper to buy in larger quantities. This is wise economy as they will not deteriorate.

Flour is often slightly cheaper to buy in 3 lb. bags, rather than 1 lb. bags. This is sensible buying in a household where a reasonable amount of baking is done.

Canned fruit, etc.

Large cans are cheaper; a double size may cost only 1½ times the amount of the half quantity. Consider, however, if the whole can will be needed or if some may be left over and, if it is left over, whether it can be used for another meal or if it would be wasted. If this is the case, then it would be wiser to buy the smaller size.

Storage space must also be considered when buying in large quantities.

Bulk buying can save time as well as money. Some perishable foods *must* be bought fresh, particularly if no refrigerator is available, but when food can be stored, bulk buying minimises daily shopping.

Selection of food

In certain foods you have a wide selection, i.e. food may be purchased fresh, canned, frozen or dried. To shop wisely it is important to compare the various advantages. For example, peas can be purchased in some form throughout the year.

The table opposite gives the ways in which they may be bought, and an assessment of the value and advantages of each kind.

Although they cannot be compared in quite the same way as peas, other foods are available in different forms and guidance on some common foods is given below.

Flour

Most of the flour used in this country, especially in bread, comes from *wheat*. In many Continental countries, *rye* is used.

A recent government survey showed that flour and bread provide about one fifth of the energy value, protein, iron, calcium and essential B vitamins needed each day.

The diagram of the grain of wheat is given overleaf.

Wholemeal flour, 100% of the wheat; sometimes a little of the coarse bran removed in milling.

Wheatmeal flour, this is 85–95% of the wheat; contains the germ and some bran.

Brown flour is a mixture of white and wholemeal.

White flour has a far greater percentage of the bran and germ removed so it is very white in colour and fine in texture. It is enriched with calcium, iron and vitamin B nutrients.

In addition certain flours are made that are mixed with varying amounts of wheatgerm,

A grain of wheat cut lengthwise through the crease

Note — this is magnified more than 250 times

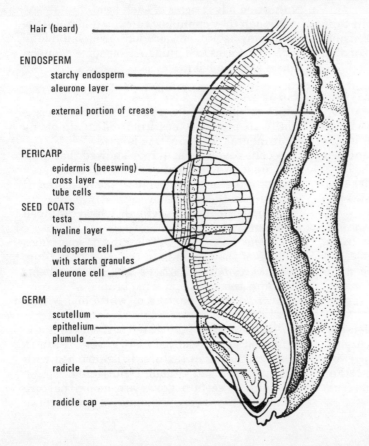

Hair (beard)

ENDOSPERM
    starchy endosperm
    aleurone layer

    external portion of crease

PERICARP
    epidermis (beeswing)
    cross layer
    tube cells

SEED COATS
    testa
    hyaline layer

    endosperm cell
    with starch granules
    aleurone cell

GERM
    scutellum
    epithelium
    plumule

    radicle

    radicle cap

A wheat grain is a seed fitted for reproducing the plant from which it came.

THE GERM is an embryo plant, with a radicle which can grow into a root system and a plumule which can develop into stems, leaves and ears.

THE PERICARP is a tough skin which protects the inner seed from soil organisms which may attack it.

The inner SEED COATS control the intake of water by the seed.

THE ENDOSPERM is the food reserve on which the young plant lives until it has developed a root system.

bran, soya flour, malt flour, and such cereals as rye and barley.

Purpose of gluten in flour

It is the gluten in flour which holds the shape of the cake, bread, etc. There are two main types of flour available: high gluten (strong flour) or low gluten (weak flour).

Strong flour is better used for bread making and any recipes using yeast; for puff pastry and pancake batters, but gives tougher cakes and other pastries. Strong flour is sold without a raising agent, i.e. plain.

Weak flour is better for cakes, other types of pastry, particularly short crust, biscuits.

Weak flour can be sold both as plain flour or self raising.

It must be remembered that different makes of flour vary, which is why you find in bread-making you need more liquid with some flours than others and in cake making different brands of flour give varying results.

There is a limited amount of 'high ratio' or very light flour—mostly used in cake mixes. This has about 50% of the bran, germ, etc. removed. This type of flour gives a particularly light cake.

Bread

Wholemeal (see flour), brown (see flour), white (see flour). There are often differences of opinion as to the relative merits of wholemeal and white bread, but modern nutritionists find that, used in conjunction with a well planned diet, people are equally healthy on either.

In addition, shops sell many fancy breads, rolls, etc. Malt bread, milk bread, fancy rolls and fruit loaves, are a few of the most usual.

Wrapped bread and sliced bread have become extremely popular in recent years. This is because wrapped bread keeps moist for a longer time than unwrapped bread, and sliced bread is convenient and saves time.

Starch reduced bread is also sold in many shops. It has a slightly lower carbohydrate content than ordinary bread.

Starch reduced rolls and crispbread, as well as ordinary crispbread, are readily available; these are generally sold in packets.

Cake mixes

Some cakes are sold frozen, which means they must be defrosted before being used. Cake mixes are available in a variety of flavours and these are interesting to try for they save time and in most cases give an acceptable result.

Pastry

Pastry is obtainable as frozen pastry, which saves much time, particularly with puff pastry. Follow the directions for handling.

It is also possible to buy packets of pastry mix.

Oils

In many Continental countries—which grow olives—olive oil is used a great deal in cooking. Various oils, e.g. olive and corn oil, are available and are excellent for frying, salad dressings, etc.

Fats

Butter, produced from cream. There is a choice of unsalted or lightly salted, called fresh butter, or more salted varieties. Butter is home produced, but also imported from Australia, New Zealand and Continental countries.

Butter gives an excellent flavour in cooking; see it does not get too hot if used for frying, for it burns easily. Equal quantities of oil and butter give excellent results and burn less easily due to the high smoking point of oil.

Margarine, made from various types of vegetable oils, etc. It varies in price and quality. Some margarines are given the name 'luxury', or 'super', and may be mixed quickly, rather than creamed for a long time, but as little creaming takes place, air is not introduced, so extra baking powder must be used for light cakes (recipe page 183). Margarine is used in many types of dishes: cakes, pastry, etc.

Cooking fats, also made from oils, etc., some-times called 'shortening'. Many are aerated like some margarines so they cream or blend quickly. Cooking fats are used in many types of dishes, some cakes, pastry, etc. and are excellent for frying.

Lard, produced from pig's fat. Excellent for frying as well as in certain types of baking, i.e. short crust, rough puff pastry, and mixed with margarine or butter for other pastry.

Suet, the best is beef suet, as it has a high fat content. Sold by butchers, when it needs skinning and chopping; or in packets, shredded and mixed with flour, for prolonged storage. Used in puddings, suet crust pastry, etc.

Milk

Book 2 pages 42–43 gave detailed imformation on the method used to pasteurise milk and on the types of milk available today: fresh, sterilised, canned, dried.

Sugar

See next chapter, page 35.

Meats

Since so much meat is used, much has to be brought from abroad. It comes in specially refrigerated ships and is often frozen, which means that it has to be defrosted by the butcher, so that it may be cut into joints. Some imported meat is called 'chilled' which means it has been kept at carefully selected cold temperatures and does not deteriorate in storage, but has not been frozen. Most people feel this is an advantage as it retains more flavour. Frozen meat is also available for sale and this must be defrosted as instructed before use.

Cuts of meat are given in full in Book 2.

Bacon

Cuts of bacon are given in Book 2, but today there are the following types of bacon sold:

Cured bacon, smoked and salted. Until fairly recently this was the type of bacon most often seen, since it keeps best, but with modern cold cabinets and refrigerators green or sweet cured also keep well. Soak cured bacon before boiling.

Green bacon, a milder curing, not smoked. It does not need soaking before boiling. Found a lot in country districts in the past.

Sweet cured bacon, a modern form of curing which makes the bacon very tender and sweet in taste; needs no soaking. Often wrapped and dated, so it must be used by the date given.

Chickens

These have become much cheaper, due to increased production.

The types of chicken you can buy are:

Boiling fowl, an older bird that is best for boiling and casserole dishes. This can be distinguished from a roasting chicken by the fact that the wish bone is rigid instead of flexible; it has far more fat under the skin, and the legs tend to look more sinewy.

Roasting chicken, sold either as fresh or frozen. The latter should be defrosted slowly before using. Free range chickens are those that are not kept in close confinement and many people feel they have more flavour.

Spring chicken, young chickens often no more than 10 weeks old. Sold fresh, frozen (either whole or jointed); often they are described as *broiler* (a word used a great deal in America) which means suitable for grilling, or they are called frying chicken (recipe, page 84).

Coffee and tea

Ground coffee is available in various roasts; the darker the roast the stronger the coffee flavour.

Coffee beans, freshly roasted, are the ideal way of buying coffee, as they can be ground freshly when needed. The coarser the beans are ground the less flavour is extracted; for most methods of making coffee use a medium ground type.

Coffee essence, with sweetening added, is used in cooking as well as making a beverage.

Instant coffee is a very fine powdered coffee that dissolves completely when mixed with water

Marmalade making

or milk. It can also be used in cooking.

Tea, see next chapter, page 35.

Preserved foods

There are many ways to preserve food, e.g. bottling (pages 193–8) and making into jam, chutney, etc. (Book 2). Here are some more ways:

Salting: Used for some meats, runner beans— enables food to be kept for a long period.

Smoking or curing: This has been in existence for a long time—it was one of the earliest methods of preservation. Used for fish—smoked haddock, cod, salmon, etc.—for pork in the form of bacon and ham, and many continental delicacies, including cheese.

Freezing: This is a comparatively modern method of food preservation—see pages 31–2 and pages 198–9.

Drying: A form of preservation that is changing. Drying of vegetables and fruits in the past meant they needed soaking and long, slow cooking. This form of dried food is still available, but the modern accelerated freeze dried foods (A.F.D.) (see opposite page) need no soaking and relatively short cooking periods. Cake mixes, etc. are not specially treated, but save some time in weighing, etc.

Canning: A very popular form of preserving food. Canned food can be stored in an ordinary cupboard, providing the temperature is not unduly high. The picture on the left shows marmalade made with canned prepared Seville oranges, an excellent idea when fresh oranges are out of season.

Storing preserved food
Always store as directed. When once the food is cooked or defrosted or the can is opened, the food is highly perishable and must be used quickly.

Accelerated freeze dried foods
This modern method of drying has made a big improvement in the flavour and colour of dried foods. The best way to visualise the process is to think of clothes drying on a line when the temperature is below freezing—the clothes freeze, but they are also drying at the same time. In this process the food is first quick frozen, then dried and becomes extremely light in weight, so taking up very little space in packing. When you want to cook A.F.D. foods, soaking is *not* necessary and the cooking or reheating time for complete meals is short. Accelerated freeze dried foods can be stored in an ordinary larder or dry cupboard.
The most usual foods obtainable today are:
Vegetables
   peas; beans; some green vegetables; etc.

Complete meals
   chicken in sauces; meat and vegetables; shell fish in sauce; etc.
Soups
   many varieties of soup are available in this form of drying. It is important to add the right amount of liquid and cook for the recommended time, so that the soup is not too thick or thin when ready to serve. Seasoning is generally added to this soup, so do not add seasoning before tasting.
   If you use less water, you can use the soup as a sauce.

Frozen foods
There is a very wide range of frozen foods available. Follow directions for storing, cooking, etc. It is essential, as stressed in Book 2, to buy from shops where frozen foods are stored correctly, i.e. below the line in a frozen food cabinet.
There is a short section beginning on page 198 on home freezing.
Vegetables: In order to freeze well these must be young. Because the vegetables are 'blanched' before freezing they need less cooking than fresh vegetables so *do not over-cook.*
Fruit: Only a limited number of fruits freeze well—and they are at their best if eaten when *just* defrosted. Concentrated fruit juice in cans

must be stored in the freezing compartment as instructed.

Meats: See the section on meat and poultry, pages 81–100.

Fish: Some fish can be cooked while still frozen, others need defrosting before cooking and this should be done at room temperature or hastened by putting the packet into cold water (see packet). Because fish is frozen very quickly after it is caught it has a good flavour.

Ready cooked meals: Store most carefully for no longer than the time specified.

Pastry: This is very good, particularly puff pastry, and best used while fairly firm.

Cakes: Allow to defrost as recommended—eat when just defrosted.

Canned foods

Canned foods have been available for many years, but the variety available is increasing. With the exception of fruit they can be stored in the cans which are now treated to be quite suitable for short storage.

Always transfer any left-over canned fruit to another container, since the syrup becomes cloudy if kept in the can.

Remember that, in the process of canning, foods are cooked or partially cooked, so re-heating time is short. Follow directions on the can as to whether you should heat in the can, or re-move the contents. When advised to heat contents *in* the can it is advisable to pierce a small hole in the can for excess steam to escape. When opening the can, take care to protect your hands so they are not burned by the hot food.

Never use the contents of a can if it has 'blown', i.e. if the ends bulge badly. Sometimes cans are dented in storage-the contents of the can may be unharmed, but Public Health Authorities advocate that they shouldn't be sold, as the seam may have been weakened or damaged and this would allow bacteria to enter the can.

The concentrated frozen fruit juice cannot be treated like other canned foods; it must be stored in a deep freeze for any period of time.

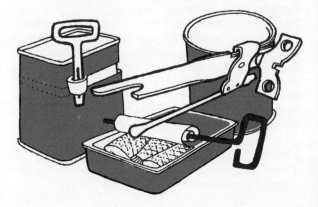

A well-planned store cupboard

A well-planned store cupboard should enable you to produce an appetising meal in an emergency without difficulty.

Many people buy a great variety of canned or dried foods, imagining they have a well-stocked store cupboard, but often there is little planning in their buying.

It is a good idea to have a variety of non-perishable foods in a size suitable for family needs or unexpected entertaining.

Menus based on food in the average store cupboard are given on pages 207–9.

Include the following in your store cupboard:

Non-perishable foods

Blackcurrant or rose hip syrup—for drinks, sauces, etc.

Bouillon cubes—to make a quick gravy.

Breadcrumbs—packets of dried breadcrumbs to use for coating (page 239), known as raspings.

Cheese: Processed cheese (sold in slices or portions) keeps well. Canned Camembert cheese is sometimes obtainable.

Cocoa or chocolate—used for making drinks and in cooking.

Coffee: Directions for making coffee have been covered fully in Book 1 and Book 2. It is essential to buy coffee either freshly ground, in sealed cans or in the form of coffee beans to put through a coffee grinder. If coffee is kept in an open packet or can it deteriorates quickly, so seal can again firmly or transfer coffee to screw top or covered jar.

Instant coffee is useful to prepare coffee in a very short time.

Cornflour—for the quick thickening of sauces, etc. (N.B. If recipe says 1 oz. flour, use $\frac{1}{2}$ oz. cornflour.) Used to make moulds (blancmange, etc.). Ingredient in some types of biscuits.

Custard powder—for custard sauce, etc.

Dried fruit—to use in cakes, puddings, etc.

Fish: Canned sardines, tuna or salmon to serve in salads, sandwiches or in a hot dish (pages 79 and 208).

Flour: If storing plain flour only, you need baking powder. For self-raising, etc, see pages 25 and 27.

Fruit: One or two cans of fruit to serve with ice cream or to make into a quick sweet (pages 171–2).

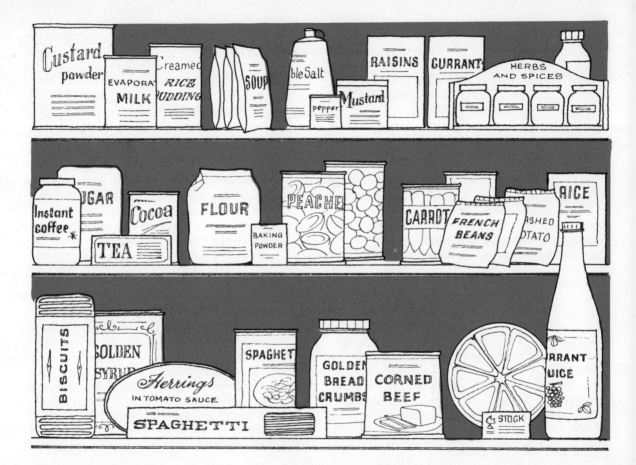

Golden syrup or treacle—used in sweetening and cooking.

Meat: Corned beef, luncheon meat, and/or canned ham or tongue for salads, sandwiches or to use in a hot dish (page 207).

Milk and cream: Canned milk (non-sweetened evaporated or sweetened condensed) can be used as substitute for cream, or diluted with water; dried milk (generally skimmed milk for household purposes or full cream as baby food); sterilised milk is treated and sealed to last several days; canned or bottled cream.

Milk puddings: Canned ready prepared puddings to heat or use in cold sweets (Book 2 pages 219–21).

Pasta: Canned spaghetti—to serve as a snack or instead of potatoes; dry spaghetti—for spaghetti Bolognese (Book 2, page 204); dry macaroni for macaroni cheese (Book 1, pages 148–9).

Rice—round (Carolina) for rice pudding; long grain (Patna) for savoury dishes, e.g. Kedgeree (page 79), Risotto.

Soups: One or two cans or packets of dried soup. These can be used for a first course, or could make a quick and easy sauce in a casserole dish.

Spices and herbs—to add flavour (see the tables pages 36, 39–43).

Sugar: Castor sugar is best for light cakes and puddings since it has a finer texture. Granulated sugar is cheaper than castor and can be used in cooking fruit, etc.

Brown sugar is obtainable in (a) Demerara—a light, dry brown sugar used for sweetening in place of granulated or in some recipes (page 137); (b) Moist dark brown used for *rich* fruit cakes and Christmas or similar puddings.

Icing sugar—for icing and decorating cakes, etc.

Loaf sugar—for table use.

Sugar (particularly moist brown and icing) should be kept well covered, since it has a tendency to form into hard lumps when it becomes slightly damp.

Tea: This keeps well in a dry place. Some people prefer China to Indian or blended teas which come chiefly from India and Ceylon. China tea is generally served with slices of lemon rather than milk. Do not keep tea too long.

Vegetables: Canned or A.F.D. peas or beans and carrots; packet dehydrated potato to make mashed potatoes; canned mixed vegetables to use hot or mixed with mayonnaise in a salad; baked beans for quick snacks or as a vegetable (Book 2, page 203).

In addition you will need *plain biscuits or crispbread* to use instead of bread.

Spices

These are the aromatic parts of plants which are generally dried. The following list gives the most usual and most useful.

Name	How available	How to use
ALLSPICE (from dried fruit of pimento tree) This is not a mixture of spices, but its flavour is very like a combination of cinnamon, cloves, nutmeg.	Generally ground in powdered form	In cakes, puddings, some drinks Add a little allspice to creamed potatoes Top a milk pudding with this Stir a pinch into a stew
ANISE from very tiny seeds of plant	Generally the oil of aniseed used, NOT the seed	In sweetmeats (aniseed balls), cakes, puddings, pickling Add a few drops of oil to drinks.
CARAWAY seeds of plant	Either in seed form or ground into powder form	Used chiefly for cakes, biscuits, but in Scandinavia in particular, the seeds are added to meat dishes and to cooked cabbage. Try cooking red or green cabbage in the usual way, then toss in butter and caraway seeds There is a delicious Danish cheese with caraway seeds called DANBO.
CARDOMAN seeds of plant	Either in seed form or ground into powder form	One of the principal ingredients in curry powder Add a little to the vinegar when pickling
CELERY seeds of plant	In seed form	Add to pickles, excellent in soused fish.
CINNAMON from the bark stripped from the young branches of the tree	Either in rather large pieces (generally called 'stick') or ground in powder form	In cakes, puddings, drinks Add a little cinnamon to apples, pears or rhubarb when cooking these.
CLOVES unopened flower buds of the tree	Either as whole cloves or ground in powder form	The most usual spice to put with apples in a pie Onion is studded with cloves when making bread sauce Excellent in stews, soups
CORIANDER seeds of plant	Generally ground in powder form	Used mainly as a curry ingredient
CUMIN seeds of plant	Generally ground in powder form	Used mainly as a curry ingredient Add to soups, particularly lentil soup for a new taste
GINGER from the root of the plant	Fresh (rather rare)—known as green ginger Crystallised (in sugar) Preserved (in syrup) Ground in powder form	Used in cakes, parkin, gingerbread being the most famous, biscuits, pudding, icing Add a little to hamburgers; also to curries Used in making homemade gingerade

Salad using rice and fru

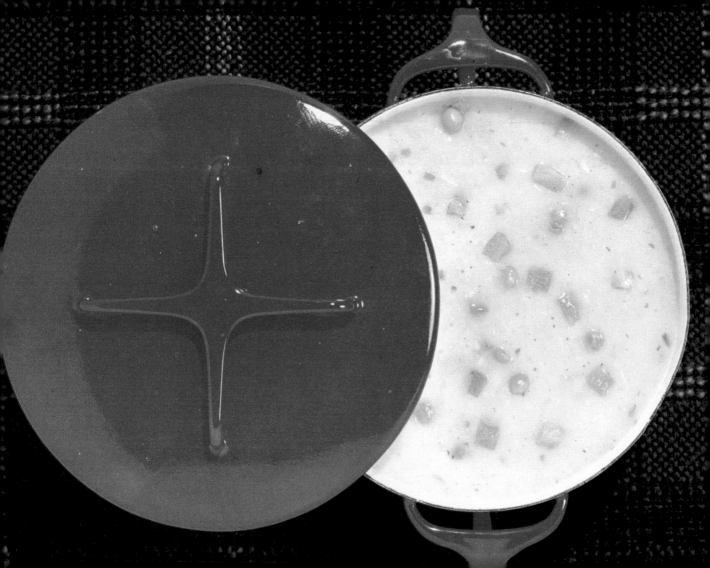

Spices (cont.)

Name	How available	How to use
MACE covering of nutmeg	Ground in powder form	As nutmeg, see below
MIXED PICKLING SPICE	Mixture of peppercorns, mustard seed, chili, etc.	In pickling or preparing vinegar
MUSTARD seeds of plant	Either as seeds or ground in powder form or ready-mixed (English, French mustard, etc.)	As a condiment Used as a flavouring in many meat dishes, pickles, etc.
NUTMEG seeds of plant	Either whole (grate to use) or ground in powder form	As flavouring for puddings (particularly baked custards), cakes, biscuits, drinks, soups Add grated nutmeg to mashed young turnips, swedes, etc.
POPPY seeds of plant	Seeds	Used in bread making as a topping
PEPPER black—dried immature fruit (stronger) white—dried mature fruit with hull removed. Paprika—not true pepper plant—dried sweet pepper (capsicum) Cayenne—not true pepper plant—dried hot pepper (capsicum) Chilli powder or pepper—from the very hot chillies (type of capsicum)	As peppercorns or ground in powder form Ground in powder form Ground in powder form In form of whole dried pods or ground in powder form	One of the most usual condiments; as seasoning in all savoury dishes An interesting colour (red) for garnish; not hot but rather sweet Used in sauces, etc. and in goulash, see page 94 An interesting colour (red); can be used VERY sparingly as garnish to flavour dishes, especially cheese pastry, see page 121 and Book 2 As cayenne; most famous use of this is Chilli con carne
SAFFRON dried stigma of a crocus-like plant	As strands (soak these in water and strain) or ground in powder form	Used to flavour cakes and biscuits, rice, etc.
SESAME seeds of plant	As seeds	Used as a topping for breads, biscuits, and sometimes used in sweetmeats
TURMERIC root of ginger family	Dried in powder form	Used in pickles; an ingredient in curry
VANILLA pod of plant	As dried pod, or ready prepared with sugar (vanilla sugar) or as an essence	Cut pod through centre, put into jar of sugar, store, and use this sugar as flavouring in cakes, biscuits, etc. Or put pod into milk for puddings, heat gently, remove pod, rinse in cold water, allow to dry and store. Pods keep for a long time Add a few drops of vanilla essence to cakes, puddings, sweetmeats

Vegetable soup

Herbs

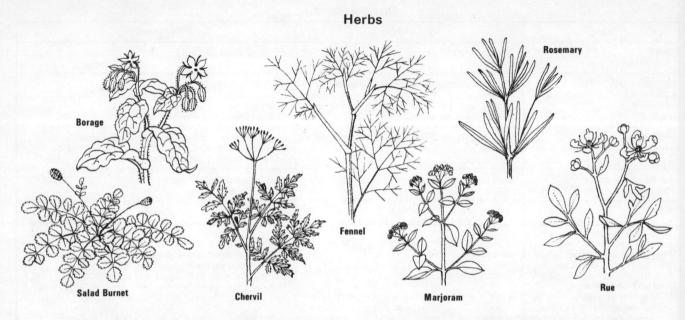

Borage

Rosemary

Salad Burnet

Chervil

Fennel

Marjoram

Rue

Many herbs can be grown at home in a window box or garden, so instructions for growing are given.

An annual means the seeds have to be planted each year.

A biennial means the seeds are planted one year, the herb grows the following year, and generally lasts for two years.

A perennial is a plant that comes up every year.

A few spices are also included in the following table since it is possible to grow the non-tropical ones.

Dried herbs: These are obtained from grocers in drums or packets, but many herbs can be dried at home, see page 199. Unless stated to the contrary, the dried herbs are in a very fine, almost powder-like, form.

Herbs

Name	How available	How to use
ANISE	Sow from seed in the spring	Liquorice flavour. Dry seeds, crush, sieve. See spices
ANGELICA	Already crystallised Biennial, sown from seed in August, but it is a difficult process to crystallise	Stems and leaf stalks used in sweet dishes, or for decoration
BALM	Dried Easily grown perennial. Raise from root divisions in March or seeds or cuttings in April or May	Slight lemon flavour Used in stuffings Add to drinks
BASIL (a) Bush (b) Sweet	Dried Half hardy annual. Sow from seed under glass in March or April and plant out in May	Rather like bay leaf and used for same purpose (see below) A mild, clove flavour
BAY laurel	Dried whole leaves Plant in April. Bay trees can be grown in tubs or pots. Wise to move to sheltered position in autumn	Put into stews, soups or even custard. Use about two leaves for a stew and one for custard. Use fresh or dried. Dried leaves stronger in flavour than fresh
BORAGE	Dried Hardy annual. Sow in April	Slight cucumber taste. Leaves excellent in salads, pickles, or if put into custards, then removed Flower and leaves in drinks, fruit cups, see page 225
BURNET or SALAD BURNET	Rarely obtained—dried Perennial. Propagate by seed or root division in the spring or autumn	Slight taste of cucumber Use leaves only when young Add to salads
CARAWAY	Biennial. Sow in April	Gather seeds, dry. Use for cakes, etc. See spices
CELERY	In seed form Sow annually	Dry seeds from celery flowers Use for pickles. See spices
CHERVIL	Dried A hardy annual which is best sown several times in the year, starting in April	Fine parsley-like leaves, useful for soups, salads, egg and fish dishes As it withers quickly, it is not so useful for garnishing as parsley
CHIVES	Rarely obtained—dried Perennial. Grass-like tops which can be cut again and again from March to October	Has a more delicate flavour than onion and can be chopped finely and used in omelettes and savoury dishes

Herbs (cont.)

Name	How available	How to use
CLARY	Rarely obtained—dried Perennial. Can be grown originally from seeds	Very good dried herb for winter use in salads with vegetables The fresh leaves can be put into salads
CORIANDER	In seed form Sow annually in the spring or autumn	Hard seeds used in curries or cakes See spices
CUMIN	In seed form Sow annually, first in pots, then planted out. Needs warmth and sun	Use ripe seeds in curry or with home-made cheese See spices
DILL	Rarely obtained—seeds Sow annually; tall plants; the seeds drop quickly	Chopped leaves can be used in white sauce like parsley, but chiefly grown for seeds which are dried when ripe and used in pickling vinegar. Used in Scandinavia in fish dishes
FENNEL	Rarely obtained—dried Perennial. Sow in April from seed	Add a little chopped leaf to sauce to serve with fish Use seeds for flavouring pickles and soups
FLORENCE (SWEET)	Sow annually; thin out as they grow very tall and bulbous	Has an aniseed-like taste. Use the thick stalk as a raw vegetable in salads, or cook like celery
GARLIC	Can be purchased fresh or in the form of garlic salt, powdered garlic or garlic juice Cloves should be planted annually in sunny, enriched ground in February or March	Use sparingly to give a strong onion flavour in salads, stews, etc., e.g. skin one clove (segment), cut and rub round salad bowl. When crushed garlic is needed put skinned clove on to board with a very little salt and crush with the tip of a strong knife
HORSERADISH	Purchased in the form of ready-made cream or sauce and shredded horseradish or buy whole roots from the green-grocer Plant annually from pieces of root. If left, it spreads and becomes uncontrollable	The grated root has a 'hot' flavour and is used for sauces for meat and fish
MARJORAM Italian (wild marjoram is known as oregano)	Dried Perennial. Sow first in April	These delicate flavoured leaves are ideal for soups, stuffing and sauces Sprinkle on lamb The most famous use of oregano is in a pizza. Cultivated marjoram can be substituted
Sweet	Annual. Sow seeds towards end of April	As marjoram

Herbs (cont.)

Name	How available	How to use
MINT	Dried and fresh Perennial. Sow first in February or March	The perfect accompaniment to lamb A little sprig can be put into fruit drinks, and chopped in salads There are several varieties of mint, each of which has a slightly different flavour, including, of course, peppermint
PARSLEY	Dried and fresh Although biennial, sow annually several times a year to ensure a continuous supply. Very slow growing. Move to a cold frame for the winter	The most useful herb of all to give flavour and provide a gay garnish Add to sauces
ROSEMARY	Dried Propagated by soft cuttings in May or heeled cuttings in autumn, in sandy soil. Seed can be sown in April or May	A sprig put inside a roasting fowl instead of stuffing, gives a delicate flavour to the flesh Use also with rabbit, lamb and chopped in salads
RUE	Rarely obtained Perennial. Seeds should originally be sown in April	Generally used as an old-fashioned herb tea. The leaves are very bitter
SAGE	Dried Perennial. Buy plants rather than sow seeds. Cuttings can be taken in April or May	Chopped fresh sage leaves are perfect for sage and onion stuffing or for giving flavour to savoury dishes
SAVORY	Dried Winter savory is an almost evergreen perennial. New plants are raised from divisions or heeled cuttings or seeds in April Summer savory is sown in April and is an annual	Use when cooking broad beans, in stuffings and in soups
SORREL	Rarely obtained Perennial. Raised from seed sown outdoors in April or by the division of roots in early spring	The acid tasting leaves are cut up for use in omelettes, soups and salads Could be cooked like spinach, especially to make a Cream of Sorrel soup, which is delicious
TARRAGON	Obtainable dried but often the whole sprig is put into vinegar to give tarragon flavoured vinegar	The chief use of this herb is for making tarragon vinegar Add a little chopped tarragon to mayonnaise with fish or chicken A few leaves can be added to a salad
THYME	Dried, or fresh Perennial. Renew every few years by divisions or cuttings or seeds sown in March or April	There are several varieties of thyme including a very delicious lemon thyme Use in stuffings, add to soups, to mayonnaise, to salads, etc.

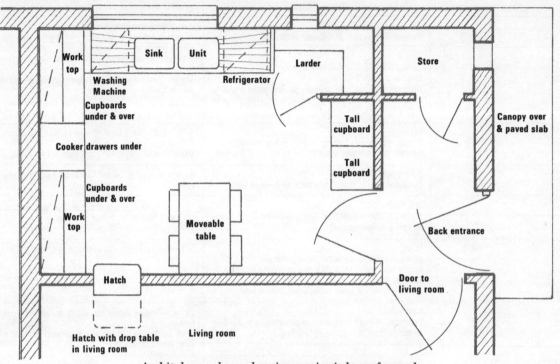

Work top

Sink

Unit

Larder

Store

Washing Machine

Refrigerator

Cupboards under & over

Canopy over & paved slab

Cooker drawers under

Tall cupboard

Cupboards under & over

Tall cupboard

Work top

Moveable table

Back entrance

Hatch

Door to living room

Hatch with drop table in living room

Living room

A kitchen plan showing principles of good design. Various authorities, those who have prepared this kitchen and the British Standards Institution have found that, although most people plan a kitchen of one uniform height, it is practical to include a second height, since beating for most people is more comfortable at a lower level, while pastry rolling is better at a greater height.

CHAPTER FIVE

Kitchen planning

THE kitchen is the work room of the home, and care should be taken to plan it so that it is as labour saving as possible.

The kitchens illustrated on pages 8 and 22 show how to arrange the equipment so as to minimise movement and make the best use of space.

A kitchen should also be a gay, colourful place so the family enjoy being in it, especially if it is used for family meals.

Working surfaces

Ideally these should be covered with laminated plastic to facilitate cleaning, etc.

Working height

Since some people are taller than others there is now a choice in working height of tables, working surfaces, etc.

The higher is 3 feet—36 inches.

The lower is 2 ft. 9 ins.—33 inches.

Take time to choose the right height when planning a kitchen.

If working surfaces are too high then you have less control over movements and in time your arms will ache.

If working surfaces are too low you will stoop, which is tiring and bad for your posture.

The cooker

Book 1 gave full information on using various types of cookers; how to pack the foods for correct cooking; the right way to clean the cookers, etc. Some of this information is repeated in Book 2.

When choosing a cooker there are certain points to consider:

Split level cookers

Do you want a standing cooker or a split level cooker? See pictures pages 8 and 22.

The latter has the advantage that the electric hotplates or gas burners can be placed in a convenient position, which need not be next to the oven, and the oven can be installed higher than usual so that there is no need to bend when putting food into it. Since the space below and above the oven, and below the hotplates or burners can be used for cupboards, there is no wastage of space. This type of cooker is, however, more expensive to install.

Types of grill

The grill can be eye level or under the hotplates or burners. Sometimes it is at the top of the oven (see pictures). Each type has its own advantages.

Automatic cookers

Would you find an automatic cooker an advantage? It is possible to leave food in the cold oven and set the oven to switch on and off at the selected temperature and given time. This is useful when women are working or shopping. The following menu is analysed to show the problems (if any) of an automatic oven.

Note: When roasting meat, the size of the joint determines the suitability of the rest of the menu, e.g.

Roast beef: Put in the tin as usual, but select a piece that needs the same cooking time as the Yorkshire pudding and potatoes, i.e. a small piece. If you wish to have a large joint of beef, then the Yorkshire pudding must be omitted as it would be left for too long a period in the oven; and it would be unwise to choose a fruit pie, for it would burn in the tin.

Yorkshire pudding: Bake in a fairly deep dish to increase the cooking time, and put in the cooler part of the oven. Grease the dish well before putting in the batter. The pudding will rise, but not as well as when using the normal method, i.e. putting the batter into a hot oven.

Roast potatoes: If left peeled, they will go black, so they should be thoroughly coated in a little hot fat before being put into the oven. If roasting a moderately large piece of beef, choose very large potatoes.

Fruit pie: Choose short rather than the richer pastries, which, though they *may* be put into a cold oven, are less satisfactory. Short crust pastry, on the other hand, is very good if 'cooked from cold'—an expression often used to denote that the food is put into the cold oven. Put a piece of foil lightly over the pastry to prevent overbrowning and stand on a baking sheet so the juice will not boil over.

Baked custard: This needs to be cooked in a very cool part of the oven, so would be more satisfactory in a gas than electric oven, since there is a greater contrast between the bottom (coolest) part of the gas oven and the rest of the oven than there is between the centre (coolest part) of an electric oven and the rest. Use a deep dish to delay cooking and stand it in a container of cold water.

It is possible to buy both gas and electric cookers with an automatic timing device, but the gas cooker will also need connecting to the electricity supply to operate the timing device.

Thermostatic control

The thermostat is a device fitted on many modern appliances to control temperature: refrigerators, water heaters, central heating systems, etc.

Modern gas and electric cookers have this device. The required temperature is set—in an electric cooker in degrees, in a gas cooker by

(Above) An electric cooker
(Right) A gas cooker

47

numbers or letters (see table below)—and when that temperature is reached, the gas heat goes down or the electricity is automatically switched off. When the temperature in the oven drops *below* the set temperature, the thermostat causes the gas heat to rise and remain high until the temperature is reached once more; in an electric oven the thermostat automatically switches the electricity on; when the desired temperature is regained it switches off again.

In this way the user can be sure the food is cooked at the pre-set heat throughout. When cooking a certain dish for the first time, however, it is important to check on cooking progress, for recipes can give approximate settings only—and all cookers vary.

The pressure cooker
Until the pressure weight is put on to a pressure cooker and the lid fixed in position, it is exactly the same as an ordinary saucepan. The tem-

	ELECTRIC	GAS	
		Number	Letter
Very cool or	225 or 250	0 or ½	A
Very slow	250 or 275	½ or 1	
Cool or slow	275 or 300	1 or 2	B
Very moderate	325 or 350	3 or 4	C - D
Moderate	350 or 375	4 or 5	D - E
Moderately hot	375 or 400	5 or 6	E - F
Hot	425 or 450	7 or 8	G - H
Very hot	450 or 500	8 or 10	I - J

perature of water boiling is 212°F.—as in a saucepan. When once the lid is fixed into position, the weight put on and the pressure built up inside, *then* the temperature is greatly increased; for example when the pressure inside the cooker has built up to 15 lb. the boiling point of water is raised to 250°F.

This means that cooking time when using a pressure cooker is very much shorter than in a saucepan.

A pressure cooker can be used for:

(a) Preparing stock from bones, for soups, etc.

(b) Cooking most vegetables. Careful timing is essential to preserve colour, texture and vitamins.

(c) Meat dishes, e.g. stews, where tough meats can be made more tender.

(d) Preserving. The *only safe* way to bottle

The same cooker with the lid and pressure weight in position

vegetables is in a pressure cooker at 10 lb. pressure which destroys harmful bacteria present. Fruit may be bottled at 5 lb. pressure and the first stage of jam or marmalade making, i.e. softening the fruits is done quickly.

(e) Cooking some puddings—Christmas pudding is a good example (see page 150).

Most pressure cookers are sold with a recipe book, and this must be followed carefully.

The problem of a pressure cooker is that food may easily be over-cooked. For example, even 1 minute over-cooking can spoil green vegetables.

Instructions for using the pressure cooker to make soup are given on page 63.

A typical modern pressure cooker before the lid is placed in position

A refrigerator small enough to fit under a work-ing surface in a small room

The refrigerator

The main purpose of a refrigerator is to store foods at the correct temperature and humidity and so produce the hygienic conditions to slow the growth of harmful bacteria that cause food to spoil. The ideal temperature in the main storage part of the cabinet should be between 40–45°F. (4–7°C.) although 1 or 2 degrees lower or higher is often given in information. If the refrigerator is too warm foods will deteriorate more quickly; if too cold then foods will become hard and could freeze, so adjust the control correctly. It is essential to store foods correctly and to defrost and clean the refrigerator regularly. Information on these points is given very fully in Book 2.

The temperature in the freezing compartment (the evaporator) is at least 25°F. lower than in the rest of the cabinet, but will vary with modern star markings. When freezing ice cream, it is important that the temperature control is set to the coldest position and naturally this lowers the cabinet temperature, so as soon as the ice cream is frozen, the temperature control should be returned to the normal setting.

Other advantages of owning a refrigerator

1. Time may be saved in shopping, since perishable foods can be purchased in larger quantities. But remember that even in a refrigerator there is a very definite limit to the time fish, meat, etc. should be stored.

2. A refrigerator enables preparations for meals to be made in advance, so giving greater leisure. It is of particular value to a working housewife as she may prepare the meals early in the day before going to work.

3. It is possible to save money on shopping with a refrigerator as perishable foods may be bought when they are cheaper, and any food left over may be stored at a safe temperature to be used again later. Care, however, must be taken that left-over foods are not kept too long; cover to prevent drying or evaporation.

How a refrigerator works

The freezing compartment (evaporator) is designed not only for storing frozen foods, making ice, ice cream, etc., but to extract heat from the food stored in the cabinet. Inside the tubes of the evaporator—one cannot see these as they are in a steel frame—is a chemical liquid known as a 'refrigerant'. The heat extracted from the food in the cabinet is sufficient to make this boil. Naturally, refrigerants must be able to boil at a very low temperature. It would be no good, for example, using water, as this needs 212°F. to bring it to boiling point, and this amount of heat could never be extracted from food alone.

When the refrigerant boils, it turns into vapour (normally called 'steam'). This vapour is condensed (the processes by which this can be done are shown on pages 52–3).

When it is condensed it becomes a liquid; the liquid once more goes into the tubes of the evaporator.

The mechanism of this is done in two ways: Either by (1) a compressor cycle—this needs a motor and is only suitable for working on electricity or by (2) an absorption cycle. This has no motor—in fact no moving parts and is suitable for electricity, gas (including bottled gas) or oil.

A refrigerator with a finish that looks like wood for use in a living-room

The compressor cycle

A *compressor* (No. 1 on diagram) is a type of pump, operated by an electric motor. This motor is under the refrigerator cabinet and is hermetically sealed.

The *compressor* forces the heated vapour from the *evaporator* (No. 4 on diagram) into the *condenser*—situated at the base and back of the refrigerator cabinet (No. 2 on diagram).

When the boiling vapour is pumped to the *condenser* its heat is dissipated into the room and it cools to become a liquid once again.

This liquid is regulated to flow through the *small expansion valve*—also described as a *capillary tube*—(No. 3 on diagram) to the evaporator and the cycle is complete. In order to operate this cycle the refrigerator is fitted with a thermostat (temperature control). When the temperature inside the cabinet rises slightly, the thermostat causes the motor to operate and the compressor cycle begins; when once the temperature has dropped the motor automatically stops.

This is why it is unwise to leave a refrigerator door open longer than necessary as it allows the cabinet to become too hot and, as well as being a danger to the food inside, it causes the motor to operate for an unnecessarily long period.

The average consumption of electricity in

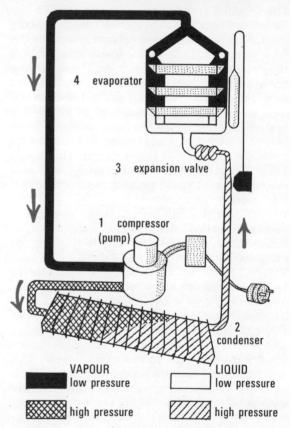

THE COMPRESSOR CYCLE

4 evaporator

3 expansion valve

1 compressor
(pump)

2
condenser

| | VAPOUR low pressure | | LIQUID low pressure |
| | high pressure | | high pressure |

operating this type of refrigerator is from $\frac{1}{2}$ unit for 24 hours. This is economical as the refrigerant generally used boils at an exceptionally low temperature—21°F.

The absorption cycle

This is easier to understand if one visualises the method of operation beginning with the refrigerant—in this case ammonia plus water—being heated by a *generator* (boiler) (No. 1 on diagram)—situated at the base of the refrigerator. This means that ammonia gas is liberated and driven through various pipes into the *condenser* (No. 2 on diagram), where it once again becomes a liquid due to air circulating over the fins of the condenser. This liquid flows towards the *evaporator* and hydrogen is introduced at this stage to stabilise the pressure. Remember that the evaporator is the freezing compartment. Here the liquid ammonia absorbs latent heat from the contents of the refrigerator, cooling them and becoming a gas once again. The ammonia and hydrogen gases flow from the evaporator (No. 3 on diagram) to the *absorber* (No. 4 on diagram) but here they separate—the hydrogen rising to the evaporator, the ammonia returning in solution to the boiler.

This type of refrigerator also has a temperature control (thermostat). When the temperature inside the cabinet rises slightly, the thermostat

THE ABSORPTION CYCLE

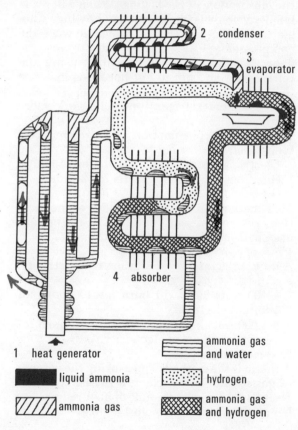

1 heat generator

ammonia gas and water

liquid ammonia

hydrogen

ammonia gas

ammonia gas and hydrogen

causes the boiler to come into operation and the absorption cycle begins. When once the temperature has dropped, the heating automatically ceases. This is why, as with the compressor type, it is wise economy to close the door as quickly as possible after using the refrigerator and not to put hot foods in, since they not only cause an intermingling of smells, but make the refrigerator cycle work more frequently.

The average consumption in operating this type of refrigerator is:

Electricity from about $1\frac{1}{4}$ units for 24 hours.

Gas from 0.13–0.2 of a therm for 24 hours.

Oil from 0.75 to 1 pint for 24 hours.

This method of operation is less economical than the compressor cycle as the refrigerant used boils at a higher temperature.

Units of electricity

A unit is the rate of calculation for electricity, e.g.

a 100 watt bulb will burn for 10 hours for 1 unit of electricity

a 1,000 watt or 1 kilowatt fire will burn for 1 hour for 1 unit of electricity.

Thermal units of gas

A therm is the method of measuring the amount of gas used or to be exact, a British Thermal Unit (B.T.U.) is the amount of heat required to heat 1 lb. of water through 1°F., e.g.

1 therm of gas would bring 64 gallons of cold water to the boil,

1 therm of gas would run an average-sized air heater for 4–5 hours.

The deep freeze

The temperatures in a deep freeze are completely different from those in an ordinary domestic refrigerator.

For freezing, set the home freezer at the lowest setting.

For storing, the temperature can be somewhat higher, up to 0°F. (-17°C.).

Home freezing is covered more fully on pages 195–9.

A deep freeze is of great value for

(a) country housewives in preserving home-grown or cheaply purchased fruit and vegetables.

(b) for working housewives to preserve ready cooked foods.

(c) for storing large quantities of commercially frozen foods.

It is important to appreciate the difference that the lower temperature makes in preserving food and also conserving nutrients. The lower the temperature the longer food can be stored and remain nearly perfect in flavour, colour and food value.

Vitamin C is the nutrient most likely to be lost

Cheese dream

during any process of preservation and in freezing. Some is destroyed in the initial process of 'blanching' vegetables, i.e. cooking for a short time in boiling water. A certain amount of this vitamin, as well as flavour, could be lost if fruit is kept for a period before freezing.

In storage the lower the temperature the less the loss of vitamins and flavour (see page 54).

The electric mixer

These are obtainable in various sizes and the pictures overleaf show (a) a large model and (b) a small hand model.

The standard fitments in all mixers are beaters and/or whisks.

The purpose of these attachments is to:

(a) cream fat and sugar, page 174;

(b) whisk egg whites or other light mixtures, page 125;

(c) cream vegetables, page 109. The small mixer is particularly useful here since it may be put into the saucepan of vegetables;

(d) it is possible to use these beaters for incorporating fat into flour for pastry but this is a less usual purpose.

The whisk or beaters work by revolving at varying speeds to give the effect of beating, whisking, etc.

(Above) A neat, compact deep freeze   (Colour) Scotch eggs

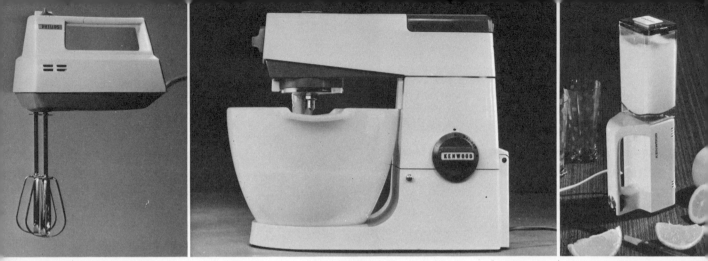

Small hand mixer

Larger type of mixer

*A liquidiser or blend
on a small mixer*

The liquidiser or blender

This gives a smooth mixture of vegetables for soups or sauces, e.g. mayonnaise (page 104) or purées of fruit. It will not take the place of a sieve in removing pips and every particle of skin. It enables ingredients for certain stuffings, breadcrumbs, etc. to be prepared quickly. It makes milk shakes and other drinks.

It works by means of blades which revolve at a very great speed.

In addition to these two main attachments, larger mixers have other attachments such as a mincer.

A mixer is of great value to a housewife in:

(a) saving time. While mixtures are being creamed, etc. she is released for other jobs.

(b) saving hard work. Creaming, beating need a certain amount of energy.

(c) saving money by enabling the housewife to prepare soups, etc. quickly. It is possible that she may not make them without a mixer, since sieving by hand takes a long time.

The dishwasher

There are various types of dishwasher. Some need to be 'built in' and attached to the existing plumbing. This means that they will draw water automatically without hoses, etc. Other smaller dishwashers can be put on the working surface and filled from hoses.

Dishwashers will wash cutlery, china and certain saucepans, etc. if pre-soaked. They then rinse the articles which dry automatically in the hot air left inside the dishwasher.

The method of operation varies, but generally when the dishwasher is switched on, it automatically covers all the processes above.

To many people a dishwasher may seem a waste of money as it takes time to pack the plates, etc. into it, but washing up after meals takes a great

The type of dish washer that is generally installed permanently into the kitchen

deal of time and many busy housewives feel this is money well spent.

Since the temperature of the water when washing up in a dishwasher is hotter than the hands can bear, the china, glasses, silver, are hygienically cleaned, and dry without smears.

The type that can be put on to the working surface

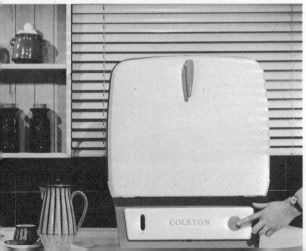

A waste disposal unit

This is fitted into the waste pipe under the sink. It works in very much the same way as the liquidiser or blender, i.e. blades revolve at a very great speed and make vegetable peelings, etc. into a fine powder that may be easily flushed away with running water.

The vegetable peelings, etc. are put into the sink, the waste disposal unit is switched on and the cold tap turned on. The food is then swept into the unit, ground down and flushed away.

The advantages of a waste disposal unit are:

(a) *Hygiene.* There is never any food left in the outlet pipe from the sink which could cause the sink to clog or smell unpleasant.

(b) *Time is saved.* Vegetable peelings, etc. do not have to be taken to a dustbin.

The only disadvantage is that a waste disposal unit must be used with care, since spoons, etc. which slip down into it can be spoiled and can also damage the unit.

Children must be taught NEVER to put their hands down the sink outlet where a waste disposal unit is installed as the power is considerable and they could permanently damage their hands. Even when the machine is not in operation, the blades are sharp.

Note: Appliances illustrated in this chapter are a general guide only; they are not necessarily available in the shops.

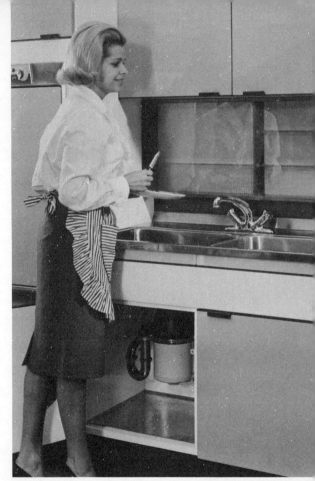

Waste disposal unit fitted under the sink

1. HORS D'OEUVRE

HORS d'oeuvre is the name given to the first course of the meal; it precedes the soup if soup is being served. It is also the name for the mixture of ingredients given below.

Hors d'oeuvre

Try to have a good selection of ingredients— one or more from each group, i.e. fish, meat, salad, egg.

Fish: Sardines, anchovies, rollmop herrings, mussels, prawns, smoked salmon, fresh salmon, fish salads of any kind, cod's roe, cooked roes.

Dress the fish with mayonnaise or oil and vinegar and garnish it with chopped parsley, etc.

Salads: Potato, Russian, tomato, sliced cucumber, corn on the cob, lettuce, watercress, celery, rice mixtures.

The salad should be mixed with mayonnaise or French dressing.

Meat: Diced salami, chopped cooked sausages, small cubes or rolls of ham, tongue, chicken —these to be mixed with dressing—also portions of pâté.

Eggs: Sliced hard-boiled, hard-boiled and stuffed (pages 114 and 115).

In addition, use some of the ready prepared savoury ingredients which are such a good standby in the cupboard—pickled gherkins, cocktail onions, olives, pickled walnuts, etc.

Fruit and tomato juice

Fresh or canned fruit juices are served as an hors d'oeuvre. Chill if possible. Allow approximately $\frac{1}{4}$ pint canned juice per person.

Tomato juice is obtained in cans or bottles. Either serve with a teaspoon and bottle of Worcestershire sauce so everyone may add sauce as wished, or add a *few drops* of sauce and a pinch of celery salt for extra flavour. Allow a small bottle or $\frac{1}{4}$ pint tomato juice per person. Serve in small tumblers.

Fresh fruit

Grapefruit: halve; separate the segments; remove any pips and pith. Decorate with glacé, canned or maraschino cherries or mint leaves. Serve sugar separately.

Melon: Cut the melon into slices. Either serve with a dessertspoon and fork or cut the flesh into fingers and arrange these on the skin. Decorate with a cherry or twisted orange slice on a cocktail stick. Serve with a small or special fruit knife and fork.

Avocado pear: often served as an hors d'oeuvre (see fruit table page 159).

Vegetable hors d'oeuvre

Serve cooked asparagus; globe artichokes—hot with melted butter or cold with a French dressing (page 105). See vegetable table Book 2. Stuffed tomatoes, hot or cold, are excellent too.

Egg hors d'oeuvre

Small omelettes, hard-boiled egg salads and poached eggs on spinach with cheese sauce (opposite) make excellent hors d'oeuvres.

Fish hors d'oeuvre

The fish given in the mixed hors d'oeuvre can be served separately.

Smoked salmon, smoked trout, smoked eel are garnished with lemon and served with brown bread and butter and paprika or cayenne pepper. Horseradish sauce can be served with trout or eel.

Half portions of cooked fish dishes can also be served, the most suitable being fried scampi, small fillet plaice or other white fish, fish soufflé, etc.

Meat hors d'oeuvre

Sliced salami and salad, thin slices of ham rolled round asparagus tips or pâté are a good choice, particularly if serving fish as the main course. Pâté is garnished with lemon and lettuce and served with hot toast and butter.

Fish cocktails

2–3 oz. shelled shrimps or prawns—or 1 pint fish with shells 4–6 lettuce leaves	*To garnish:* lemon *Cocktail sauce* (see below) ④

While shell fish is generally selected for this recipe, a more economical dish is prepared by using half shell and half white fish.

If using frozen fish, allow to defrost at room temperature. To shell shrimps and prawns easily, put into hot water for 1 minute.

Shred the lettuce very finely. Put at the bottom of 4 sundae or small glasses. Make the sauce and toss the fish in it. Pile on top of the lettuce. Stand glasses on small plate, with wedge of lemon. Serve with a small fork and teaspoon.

Cocktail sauce

3 tablespoons mayonnaise 1 tablespoon tomato purée (fresh or canned) or tomato ketchup	few drops Worcestershire sauce 1 tablespoon cream or top of the milk ④

Mix all the ingredients together. A little lemon juice can be added.

2. SOUPS

HOME made soups are divided into 2 main headings: clear soups, e.g. consommé, etc. and thick soups. The latter includes vegetable soups, purée soups, creamed soups, broths, chowders and bisques.

Vegetable soups: Diced or grated vegetables are simmered until tender. For 2–3 allow approximately $\frac{3}{4}$ pint water or stock to 8 oz. vegetables. Choose mixed vegetables or one variety only. For a richer flavour the vegetables may first be tossed in $\frac{1}{2}$–1 oz. butter or margarine. Most vegetables are suitable. Recipes are given in Books 1 and 2.

Oeufs à la Florentine
(eggs on spinach with cheese sauce)

Purée soups: In these the cooked vegetables or meat are sieved then reheated to give a moderately thick purée. A thin white sauce may be added. Many vegetables are suitable, the most usual being potatoes, lentils, split peas—recipes Book 2.

Creamed soups can be similar to purée soups in that a white sauce or milk blended with flour or cornflour is added to the purée, which can be vegetable, poultry or meat. Where the purée is very thick allow $\frac{1}{2}$ pint *thin* white sauce to approximately 1 pint purée, but $\frac{1}{2}$ pint *coating* white sauce to a thinner purée. An easier way is just to add cream to the soup instead of white sauce. A cream of tomato soup presents special difficulties due to the risk of curdling (recipes page 65).

Broths, chowders and bisques are thick soups in which meat, vegetables, fish, etc. are left in the liquid.

Most soups are served hot but Vichyssoise is an ideal summer soup which can be served cold or is excellent before a hot main course.

Making soups in a pressure cooker
Any ordinary soup recipe may be used, but since there is far less evaporation of moisture, use half the amount of liquid given in the recipe

for a long cooking soup, but reduce the amount by one-third only for a quick cooking soup. Reduce cooking time by 75%, i.e. 1 hour in a saucepan means 15 minutes at 15 lb. pressure. When making soup, never fill a pressure cooker more than two-thirds full and allow pressure to drop at room temperature.

To use a liquidiser for soups

This makes a purée of the mixture, but does not get rid of pips or some skins. Warm the liquidiser (often called a blender) goblet before putting in the soup. The liquidiser should be no more than two-thirds full and the lid on tightly before switching on, for the mixture rises in the goblet owing to the speed of the blades. To start, use the lowest speed, then work up to maximum until the mixture is smooth.

To season soups

Always taste before serving and add extra seasoning if necessary.

Convenience soups

Canned or dehydrated soups can be prepared within a very short time. They can be given a more individual flavour by adding various garnishes, additional herbs, a little milk or cream, etc.

Minestrone soup

3 oz. haricot beans	chopped celery
1 large onion	8 oz. tomatoes
2 tablespoons olive oil	(bottled or fresh)
	8 oz. shredded cabbage
1 clove garlic	2 oz. macaroni
1–2 oz. diced bacon	*To garnish:*
seasoning	1 tablespoon chopped
1½ pints water or	parsley
stock	grated Parmesan
1 large diced carrot	cheese
2 tablespoons	④–⑥

Soak the haricot beans overnight in water. Chop onion finely and toss in the hot oil, together with the crushed garlic and bacon. Add haricot beans, seasoning and water and simmer gently for about 1½ hours. Put in rest of vegetables, except the cabbage, and cook for a further 20 minutes, adding a little more water if necessary. Add cabbage and macaroni and cook until both are just tender. Serve with chopped parsley and top with the cheese.
Note: ¼ pint red wine can be substituted for the same amount of stock.

Cream of mushroom soup

Cook 8 oz. mushrooms or mushroom stalks in 1 pint water or stock, season well. Sieve and add to a moderately thick white sauce made with 2 oz. butter, 2 oz. flour, ¾ pint milk. ④

Cream of tomato soup

1 lb. tomatoes	*bouquet garni*
1 onion	½ oz. cornflour or
1 carrot	1 oz. flour
1 stick celery	½ pint milk
little fat bacon	pinch sugar
1½ pints stock	*To garnish:*
salt	chopped white of egg
pepper	or croûtons ④—⑥

Method No. 1
Slice the vegetables. Fry the bacon slowly to extract the fat, then add the vegetables and fry for about 10 minutes. Add the stock (or water), seasoning and *bouquet garni*, bring to the boil and simmer gently until tender—about 1 hour. Remove the *bouquet garni* and bacon, rub the soup through a fine sieve, and add the cornflour blended with the milk. Return to the pan and cook gently, stirring well until very hot. DO NOT BOIL otherwise the mixture will curdle. Add the sugar and top with the garnish or serve the croûtons separately.

Method No. 2
Cook the bacon, etc., sieve as above, return to the saucepan and heat. Make a white sauce with 1 oz. margarine or butter, 1 oz. flour and ½ pint milk; season lightly. Whisk the hot sauce into the hot tomato purée and serve.

French onion soup

1–2 oz. butter or good beef dripping	4 slices toast or French bread
1–1½ lb. onions	2 oz. grated cheese
2 pints brown stock	(preferably Gruyère)
seasoning	④

Melt the fat in a saucepan. Slice the onions thinly and fry in the hot fat until a pale golden brown. Add the liquid and seasoning. Bring slowly to the boil, lower the heat and simmer gently for ½ hour. Put each slice of hot toast on a soup plate; pour the soup over and sprinkle with cheese. (See picture above.)

Beef consommé

12 oz. shin of beef	sprig parsley ④
2 pints good stock	bay leaf
seasoning	1 dessertspoon sherry
1 onion	(optional)
1 carrot	*To clear the soup:*
small piece celery	1 egg white and shell

Cut the meat into small pieces and put these into a saucepan together with the other ingredients. Simmer very gently for 1 hour, then strain through several thicknesses of muslin. Add sherry if desired. To clear the consommé, put in a stiffly beaten egg white and clean egg shell, simmer gently for a further 20 minutes, then re-strain.

Other consommés

The garnish gives the name to the consommé.
Consommé Celestine: garnished with match-sticks of cooked pancake.
Consommé au vermicelli: garnished with cooked vermicelli.
Consommé jardinière: garnished with finely diced cooked vegetables.
Consommé julienne: garnished with match-sticks of cooked vegetable.
Game consommé: Game bones and carcase can be used in place of beef.
Veal consommé: Use half beef and half veal.

Vichyssoise

2 oz. butter	1 tablespoon chopped
8 large leeks, chopped	parsley
2 pints chicken stock	seasoning
2 large potatoes,	¼ pint cream
peeled and chopped	3–4 tablespoons
2 tablespoons	white wine *or* extra
chopped chives	cream ⑥–⑧

Heat the butter and toss the chopped leeks in it until pale golden colour—do not allow them to brown. Add the stock, the chopped peeled potatoes, half the chopped chives and all the parsley. Season well and simmer gently for 30 minutes. Rub through a fine sieve. When the purée is cool, gradually add the cream and wine. Serve very cold, topped with the remaining chopped chives.
This soup can be served hot, in which case add a chopped onion to the leeks.

Scotch broth

1 oz. pearl barley	8 oz. diced swede
8 oz. stewing beef or	salt and pepper
mutton	2 oz. sliced cabbage
2 pints water	*To garnish:*
3 oz. sliced leeks or	1 tablespoon chopped
onion	parsley
8 oz. diced carrot	④–⑥

To blanch the barley, add to 2 pints cold water, bring the water to the boil, then strain the barley and throw away the water. This process whitens the barley. Put the barley, diced beef* and water into the pan, bring to the boil, skim, and simmer gently for 1 hour. Add all the prepared vegetables except the cabbage, plenty of seasoning and cook for a further 1½ hours. Add the cabbage and allow another 15 minutes cooking. Skim off any superfluous fat from the broth, pour into a hot dish or soup cups and garnish with the parsley.

*If desired the meat can be left in one piece and removed from the soup whole so that it can be used for a separate dish.

Kidney soup

8 oz. kidney (ox kidney can be used)*	2 pints stock or water
1 small onion	seasoning
2 oz. butter	sprig of parsley
1 oz. flour	a little port or Burgundy ④–⑥

*If using lambs' kidneys the cooking time will be 30 minutes only, so reduce the amount of stock to 1¼–1½ pints.

Chop the kidney and onion very finely and fry in the hot butter for 3 minutes—over-cooking will harden the outside of the meat. Blend in the flour, and gradually add the stock. Bring to the boil, stir until smooth, add seasoning and a sprig of parsley, then simmer gently for about

1½ hours. Remove the parsley, add wine and serve.

Creamed chicken soup

Carcase of a chicken or boiling fowl	1 oz. flour or ½ oz. cornflour
2 pints water or chicken stock*	½ pint milk
seasoning	1 oz. butter ④–⑥

*If you are using the remains of a boiling fowl, you will have some stock left over too. If not, use 2 pints water with 1–2 chicken stock cubes.

Simmer the carcase and stock for 1 hour. Season lightly. Strain, remove any tiny pieces of chicken flesh and chop finely or sieve. Return stock and chicken to the pan, add the flour blended with the milk, bring to the boil, add the butter and extra seasoning.

Chicken broth

Add 1–2 oz. blanched barley (see Scotch Broth page 66) and 8 oz. diced vegetables to the chicken stock after removing carcase, and simmer for approximately 30 minutes. Garnish with chopped parsley.

Variations

Vegetables may be added to the liquid and sieved with the chicken, or finely diced vegetables may be put into the clear chicken stock.

3. FISH

A TABLE giving all types of fish and simple methods of cooking is given in Book 2. The following recipes are more unusual, but are still based on the familiar cooking processes.

BAKED FISH

BAKED fish is cooked in the oven—often with a stuffing or in milk or some other liquid. Care must be taken that the fish does not become over-cooked or dry.

When liquid of any kind is added, grease the dish well and cover the fish with greased foil, greaseproof paper or a casserole lid, unless the recipe states to the contrary.

Stuffed mackerel

4 medium-sized mackerel	seasoning
2 oz. cooked long grain rice	2 oz. butter
1 small onion	*To garnish:*
2 oz. mushrooms	2 oz. mushrooms
2 teaspoons chopped fennel or parsley	1 oz. butter
	1 lemon
	④

Clean and remove the backbones, heads and tails from the fish. Mix the rice with the finely chopped onion, the chopped mushrooms, the fennel or parsley and the seasoning. Bind together with the melted butter. Stuff the fish with this mixture, fold over and wrap each fish in a piece of foil. Put into an ovenproof dish and bake for 30 minutes above the centre of a moderately hot oven, 400°F.—Gas Mark 5–6, until the fish is tender. Unwrap the foil carefully and place the fish on a hot serving dish. Spoon any liquid retained in the foil round about the fish. Serve with the rest of the mushrooms fried in the butter and with slices of lemon. (See picture.)

Plaice fillets with asparagus

1 medium-sized packet frozen or 1 medium can asparagus	seasoning
	1 oz. butter
	To garnish:
4 large fillets of plaice	1–2 oz. blanched almonds
juice of 1 lemon	④

If using frozen asparagus spears, cook as directed on the packet and drain; if using the canned variety, simply drain. Wrap each fillet of plaice around several spears of asparagus. Arrange in a shallow baking dish, sprinkle with lemon juice and season to taste. Top with the butter and cover with foil. Bake in the centre of a moderate oven, 375°F.—Gas Mark 4–5 for 20–25 minutes. Place on serving dish and top with the almonds, which can be toasted under the grill. Serve with a white or cheese sauce.

Sole bonne femme

4 large or 8 small fillets sole	1 oz. butter
seasoning	1 oz. flour
	$\frac{1}{4}$ pint milk
1 dessertspoon chopped parsley	2–3 oz. mushrooms
$\frac{1}{2}$ pint white wine or fish stock (page 76)	1$\frac{1}{2}$ oz. extra butter to grease dish and fry mushrooms ④

Skin the fillets of fish (see page 71) and butter an ovenproof dish. Put the fillets into this,

either folding or rolling them. Add seasoning, parsley and wine or fish stock. Cover the dish with greased foil or paper and cook in the centre of a moderate oven 375°F.—Gas Mark 4–5 for approximately 15–20 minutes until the fish is cooked, but unbroken. Meanwhile, prepare a thick sauce of the butter, flour and milk, and fry the mushrooms in the extra butter. Lift fillets on to a hot dish and arrange mushrooms round them and strain the wine liquid into the sauce. Stir briskly until very smooth, then pour over the fish. Serve in a border of mashed potato.

The fish is often served in a border of piped creamed or duchesse potatoes as shown in the picture, page 78.

Herring crumb bake

4 large herrings	2 oz. fine
Stuffing:	breadcrumbs
1 tablespoon made	*Topping:*
mustard	1 tablespoon oil or
1 teaspoon sugar	melted butter
1 teaspoon vinegar	1 oz. fine
seasoning	breadcrumbs (4)

Clean and bone the herrings. Mix stuffing ingredients together and spread inside the fish. Fold over and arrange fish in a greased oven-proof dish. Brush with oil or melted butter and sprinkle with the crumbs. Bake above the centre of a moderate oven, 375°F.—Gas Mark 4–5, for 20 minutes. Serve with grilled tomatoes and toast.

Fish Portuguese

4 cutlets or portions	1 medium-sized (4)
of fillet of white fish	onion
—cod, haddock, etc.	3 large tomatoes
1 oz. butter	seasoning
	1–2 oz. grated cheese

Arrange the washed portions of fish in a fairly shallow buttered ovenproof dish. Peel and slice the onion *very thinly* so it can be cooked within a short time. Skin and slice the tomatoes thickly. Season the fish, then put the onion over this, topped with the sliced tomatoes, then the cheese and small knobs of butter. Do not cover the dish. Bake for approximately 30 minutes just above the centre of a moderate oven, 375°F.—Gas Mark 4–5. As the fish is kept moist during cooking, no sauce is needed.

Variations
1. Add 2–3 tablespoons milk or white wine.
2. Rub the dish with a cut clove of garlic.

FRIED FISH

FRYING is one of the most popular methods of cooking white fish. It is also suitable for cooking scampi—the large-sized prawns.

Fish for frying may be coated with seasoned flour, egg and crumbs or coating batter (page 71).

Another interesting coating is made by mixing finely grated cheese with the crumbs (picture page 76). There is another method of frying fish in which it is not coated. The fish is fried in butter and then the butter is allowed to brown (see Trout meunière page 71).

Fried scampi

Approximately 16–32	1–2 oz. crisp bread-
large prawns	crumbs (raspings)
½–1 oz. seasoned flour	Fat or oil for frying
1–2 eggs	*To garnish:*
coating batter	lemon
(page 71) or	parsley (4)

Use a smaller quantity than that given if the scampi are to be served as hors d'oeuvre.

If using frozen scampi allow these to defrost at room temperature. Some frozen scampi has been cooked with the shells on and these need removing. Other scampi is frozen shelled but uncooked. Dry the fish well on kitchen paper before coating with the seasoned flour and beaten egg and crumbs, or the coating batter. Test the fat (page 75–6) then fry the fish in the hot fat, allowing 2 minutes for ready cooked prawns but approximately 4 minutes for the uncooked kind. Drain on absorbent kitchen paper or crumpled tissue paper and garnish with lemon and parsley. Serve with tartare sauce (page 105).

If wished, the parsley may be fried for garnish. Put well dried parsley for a few seconds only in the hot fat. In this way the parsley becomes crisp but remains green.

Sole or plaice is often fried to look like scampi. Fillet the fish, skin (see below) then cut each fillet across into half-inch ribbons. Dry, coat and fry as scampi.

To skin fish

Make a slit at the base of the fish or fillet of fish. Gradually lift the fish away from the skin with a really sharp knife. If the knife is dipped in salt this makes it easier to remove the skin.

Never hurry over this job or you may break the flesh.

Coating batter

4 oz. flour	$\frac{1}{4}$ pint plus 4 table-
pinch salt	spoons milk *or* milk
1 egg	and water

Sieve the flour and salt together, beat in the egg and gradually add the liquid. This will coat 4 portions of fish or 32 scampi.

Trout meunière

4 medium-sized trout	2 teaspoons chopped
3–4 oz. butter	parsley
1 tablespoon lemon	2 teaspoons capers
juice or vinegar	seasoning ④

Remove the heads from the trout, wash and dry the fish thoroughly. Heat the butter in a large pan and fry the trout on both sides until just cooked—approximately 10 minutes. Lift on to a hot serving dish, then heat the butter until golden brown; add the rest of the ingredients, then pour over the fish and serve at once.

Other fish suitable for cooking by this method: sole or plaice—either filleted or whole; skate (steam the portions of fish for 5 minutes before frying).

GRILLED FISH

GRILLING fish is a quick method of cooking and it retains the flavour well. White and oily fish are excellent cooked this way. Always pre-heat the grill so the fish cooks quickly.

The picture shows grilled fresh haddock topped with anchovy fillets which give extra flavour and interest to the dish.

Flétan Provençal—halibut with Provençal sauce

3 halibut steaks	*Sauce:*
seasoning	1 oz. butter
1 oz. melted butter	1 onion
2 tablespoons thick	½ oz. flour
cream	½ pint water *or*
2 oz. grated cheese	fish stock
3 slices French bread	3 tablespoons con-
	centrated tomato
	purée
Garlic butter:	a few sliced black
1–2 cloves garlic	and green olives
2 oz. butter	seasoning ③

Sprinkle fish with seasoning, brush on one side with melted butter, cook under hot grill for 4–5 minutes. Turn, season fish and brush second side with rest of butter, add cream and cheese. Grill until fish is well cooked.

Crush cloves of garlic (page 42), press into the butter. Heat in a frying pan then fry the bread on both sides. Arrange in the serving dish with the fish on top. Keep hot.

Meanwhile, melt butter and fry sliced onion until soft and transparent, add flour and cook the 'roux' for a few minutes. Gradually stir in the water or the stock and tomato purée, add olives. Bring to the boil, stirring well, and cook for a few minutes. Season and pour over hot fish steaks.

Serve hot with salad or green beans.

Variation

Use cod, fresh haddock or hake.

Halibut with Provençal sauce

STEAMED FISH

STEAMED fish retains its flavour and is easy to digest, which makes it an ideal method of cooking white fish for invalids. A little cream or milk, lemon juice and/or a pinch of freshly chopped herbs may be added to the fish, together with margarine or butter and seasoning. Steaming is also an excellent method of cooking fish for fish cakes, croquettes (below) as it keeps the fish firm.

Fish and cheese croquettes

6 oz. white fish (cod, haddock, etc.)	1 teaspoon chopped parsley
½ oz. margarine or butter	*To coat:*
seasoning	½ oz. seasoned flour
4 oz. mashed potatoes	½ beaten egg
½ beaten egg	2 tablespoons bread-
2 oz. grated Cheddar cheese	crumbs (raspings)
	Fat or oil for frying ④

Put the fish on to a heat-resisting plate with margarine and seasoning, and cover with a saucepan lid or foil. Steam for approximately 10–15 minutes over a pan of boiling water. Remove any bones and skin and flake the fish. Add the potatoes, egg, grated cheese, chopped parsley and extra seasoning if wished. Divide the mixture into 8 equal portions and form into

finger shapes. Coat first in seasoned flour and then in egg and crumbs. Fry in hot deep fat or oil (see below) for approximately 3 minutes. Drain on crumpled tissue or kitchen paper. Garnish with parsley and serve with white, tomato or cheese sauce.

Variation
Omit the cheese and use 8 oz. fish instead of 6 oz.

To test fat or oil for deep frying
It is essential for good frying that the fat or oil should be the correct temperature. If it is too cool, the food absorbs the fat and is greasy; if too hot, the outside is burned before the food is cooked. It is possible to purchase thermometers to test the temperature which may vary from

Herring crumb bake

75

Fried cod in a coating of egg, crumbs and cheese

360–390°F. for oil and 350–380°F. for lard. Chickens which need a fairly long cooking time should be put into a slightly lower temperature than onion rings which are cooked within 2–3 minutes.

For most frying purposes, however, the fat is the correct temperature if a cube of day-old bread turns golden brown within 1 minute. Oil may be heated to a greater temperature without fear of it burning so the bread should change colour within 30 seconds. Foods will cook more quickly in oil than in fat.

POACHED FISH

POACHED fish is cooked in liquid at a temperature just below boiling. Do not cook too quickly or over-cook, otherwise the fish will break. The liquid can be seasoned milk, water or fish stock (recipe below). This method is used for white fish, smoked haddock, etc.

Fish stock
Put the bones and skin—or shells if using shell fish—into a saucepan. Cover with cold water, add seasoning, *bouquet garni* or a sprig of parsley and simmer for 10–15 minutes. Strain and use in place of water. A sliced onion, carrot and small piece of celery may be added to give additional flavour, but take care this stock does not become too strong as it may spoil the taste of the fish.

Poached salmon cutlets—or portions of salmon
Method 1
Season the salmon, add a little lemon juice and tie carefully in a neat 'parcel' of buttered paper. Put into cold salted water with a little lemon and oil in the water. Bring slowly to the boil, simmer gently, allowing 10 minutes per lb.; alternatively, bring just to boiling point, cover with tightly fitting lid, turn heat off and leave until water is quite cold.

This is an ideal way of poaching salmon if it is to be served cold.

Method 2
Put the salmon into cold water with a little lemon juice, or into cold fish stock. Bring to the boil and simmer gently, allowing 10 minutes per lb. A few drops of oil may be added to help keep the fish moist.
To serve with salmon
With a cold salmon dish, serve mayonnaise and salad; with a hot dish, serve Hollandaise or tartare sauce.

Smoked cod with duchesse potatoes

1 lb. smoked cod (or haddock)	*White sauce:*
	1 oz. butter
¼ pint milk	1 oz. flour
1 oz. butter	½ pint milk
4 oz. cooked peas	seasoning
duchesse potato made with 8 oz. potatoes, etc. (page 113)	④

Divide the fish into two or four neat portions and poach in the milk with butter for 10 minutes. Add the peas and heat for a further 5 minutes. Keep warm.
Meanwhile, prepare the duchesse potatoes, pipe into rosettes in the heatproof serving dish

A summer fish salad

and brown under a hot grill. Lift the fish and peas from the milk, flake the fish and put into the serving dish, then top with the sauce.

To make the white sauce
Melt the butter in a saucepan, then stir in the flour and cook for several minutes, stirring well, until it becomes a dry 'roux'. Gradually blend in the milk, bring to the boil and cook until smooth and a coating consistency. Season well. Any milk left from cooking the fish may be strained and added to the sauce if wished.

Variations

1. $\frac{1}{2}$ teaspoon fresh or dried fennel or chopped parsley may be added to the sauce.
2. 2 oz. sliced fried mushrooms may be added to the sauce.

Scallops

4 scallops	1 oz. flour
$\frac{1}{2}$ pint milk	1 tablespoon sherry
seasoning	(optional)
1 oz. butter	④

These are quite economical when in season and can be served either as a main dish or first course of a meal. Allow one medium-sized scallop per person for a light course.

Remove the scallops from the shells and wash and dry the fish. If serving on the shells, wash and dry these also. Put the fish into the milk with seasoning and simmer gently for 10 minutes until tender. If wished, each scallop may be cut into 3–4 neat pieces. Leave the orange roe in one piece to give a good touch of colour. When the fish is cooked lift out of the milk and put into a hot dish or on to the heated shells. Keep warm. Heat the butter in a pan, stir in the flour, then continue as for white sauce, using the strained milk from cooking the scallops to give a thick coating consistency. Add the sherry if wished, taste and re-season if necessary. Coat the fish with the sauce.

Smoked cod with duchesse potatoes

Variations

1. Pipe or form a border of mashed potato round the edge of the dish or scallop shell and brown this in the oven or under the grill before adding fish and sauce.
2. Top the fish and sauce with a little grated cheese and breadcrumbs, then brown under the grill or in the oven for a short time.
3. Serve the fish in a cheese sauce instead of a white sauce.

Prawns or shrimps may be served in the same way; if using frozen fish allow to defrost at room temperature. As these are generally already cooked they should be heated for a few minutes only in the milk. Never over-cook shellfish otherwise it becomes tough.

RECIPES USING PRE-COOKED FISH

Kedgeree

2 oz. butter or margarine	6 oz. cooked long grain rice (page 108)
8–12 oz. flaked cooked smoked haddock (page 76)	2 hard-boiled eggs seasoning
	1–2 beaten eggs
	⅛ pint cream ④–⑥

Melt the butter. Put the fish in and shake over the heat until thoroughly hot. Add rice, chopped hard-boiled eggs and seasoning. Shake and stir over the heat with a fork for a few minutes. Add beaten eggs and cream. Reheat, stirring with a fork and, while still creamy, turn into a dish and serve very hot.

Variations

1. For a less extravagant recipe, omit the cream and raw eggs, and bind with a small quantity of milk.

Cheese kedgeree

Garnish with fried rings of onion. Serve with crisp fried bacon rolls.

2. *Mushroom kedgeree*
Fry 3–4 oz. sliced mushrooms in extra 1 oz. butter and add to rice and fish at the last minute.

3. *Salmon kedgeree*
Use flaked canned salmon or flaked cooked salmon in place of smoked haddock.

4. *Cheese kedgeree*
Stir 6–8 oz. grated Cheddar cheese into the fish mixture just before serving—do NOT overcook.

Fish pies

These may be found useful for packed meals or to use up fish that is already cooked, but apart from the dangers of eating left-over fish (which might have deteriorated, especially if not kept in a refrigerator), twice cooked fish loses much of its flavour.
Two of the best known fish pies are American and Russian fish pie.

American fish pie

Blend approximately 12 oz. flaked cooked fish with ½ pint coating white sauce (page 77), 1–2 chopped hard-boiled eggs and 1 oz. cheese. Put into a pie-dish and top with 12 oz. mashed

79

Fishy pie

potatoes and 1 oz. grated cheese, then bake for approximately 30 minutes above the centre of a moderately hot oven, 400°F—Gas Mark 5–6.

Russian fish pie

In Russia, uncooked salmon or smoked haddock are used. This gives an excellent flavour. Roll out 8 oz. flaky pastry (recipe page 133) into a 9 inch square. Cut approximately 12 oz. uncooked fish into neat pieces, blend with 2 chopped hard-boiled eggs, $\frac{1}{4}$ pint thick white sauce (panada) (Book 2, page 50) and 2 teaspoons chopped parsley. Pile this into the centre of the pastry. Moisten the edges then fold each corner to the centre, forming an envelope. Seal firmly, leaving a small central incision for the steam to escape, and decorate with pastry leaves. Glaze and bake above the centre of a very hot oven, 475°F.—Gas Mark 8–9, for 10 minutes, then lower heat to moderately hot, 400°F.—Gas Mark 5–6, for a further 30 minutes.

Variations

1. Use rough puff pastry (Book 2, page 188).
2. Use cooked flaked smoked haddock or white fish.
3. Add a few prawns or shrimps.
4. Add 1–2 oz. cooked macaroni.
5. Add 2 oz. grated cheese.

Fishy pies ⑥

Make 12 oz. short crust pastry. Roll out half the pastry and form into neat round or fish shape as picture. Fill with mixture as Russian Fish Pie—using cooked fish. Cover with remainder of shaped pastry as shown in the picture and bake in the centre of a hot oven, 425°F.—Gas Mark 6–7 for about 20 minutes, then lower the heat to very moderate, 350°F.—Gas Mark 3–4, for a further 20 minutes.

4. MEAT AND POULTRY

BOOK 2 gives a great deal of detailed information on the cuts of meat to choose for every basic method of cooking and it is important, therefore, that this is consulted, as the recipes in this chapter, while a little more elaborate than those in Book 2, are adaptations of basic methods of cooking.

FRIED MEAT AND POULTRY

Meat which is to be fried must be tender.

Beef
Choose fillet, rump or other steaks—see Book 2.

Bacon chops

Lamb and mutton
Choose lamb cutlets or chops. Before frying mutton cutlets or chops, steam them for approximately 10 minutes.

Pork
Cook chops or cutlets steadily to make sure the meat is adequately cooked.

Veal
Never under-cook veal. Choose cutlets, chops, or slices of veal, generally called fillets or escalopes.

Chicken
Choose young jointed frying chicken and brown well then lower the heat to cook through to the centre.

Bacon
Ordinary rashers of bacon are fried with no fat. The picture shows thick back rashers of bacon being prepared for frying. These are often called bacon chops.

Timings for all fried meats are given in Book 2.

Tournedos of steak

A fillet steak made into a round is called a tournedos. If you ask the butcher he will tie pieces of fillet steak into neat rounds with string and all you need do is to remove the string before serving. If he has not done this for you, simply press the meat with your hands into a circle and then tie it yourself.

The steaks can be fried or grilled.

Each type of garnish gives its name to a tournedos of steak.

Tournedos Africaine—serve with fried banana and horseradish sauce.

Tournedos maître d'hôtel—top the tournedos with maître d'hôtel butter, recipe below.

Tournedos Niçoise—serve with cooked French beans and tiny tomatoes.

Tournedos Othello—top with fried or poached egg.

Tournedos d'Orsay—top with stuffed olives and mushrooms.

Maître d'hotel butter

This is another name for parsley butter.

Blend a squeeze of lemon juice and 1–2 teaspoons finely chopped parsley with 1 oz. butter. Form into a neat shape, chill, then cut into four neat portions.

Steak Diane

1 onion or shallot	little Worcestershire
2–3 oz. butter	sauce
4 very thin slices of	little brandy
sirloin or rump	(optional)
steak*	chopped parsley ④

*Fillet steak is rarely used because it is not quite big enough.

Chop the onion or shallot very finely, and fry in the butter for 1–2 minutes. Add the thin slices of steak and cook on either side. Lift the meat out on to plates or hot dishes. Add the Worcestershire sauce and the brandy, if used, to the butter. Ignite if wished, and pour over the steaks. Garnish with chopped parsley.

Note: This dish needs last-minute cooking.

Hamburgers

1 lb. minced beef	1 heaped teaspoon
1 large onion, grated	chopped parsley
seasoning	1 teaspoon
½ teaspoon mixed	Worcestershire sauce
herbs	8 baps or large bread
1 good-sized grated	rolls
potato	⑧

Mix all the ingredients together thoroughly. Form into large flat cakes and place on a well greased tin. Bake in a moderately hot oven, 400°F.—Gas Mark 5–6, for 25–30 minutes. If preferred, fry in a little fat for approximately 10 minutes. Serve between sliced rolls.

Coated cutlets

Often lamb, veal or mutton cutlets or chops are coated before frying. The pictures opposite give the various stages. 1. Brush with beaten egg 2. Coat in the crumbs 3. The finished cutlets.

1

2
3

Garnishes for cutlets or chops

Both grilled and fried lamb or mutton cutlets and chops can be served with various garnishes which give the name to the dish. Unless stated to the contrary, they can be fried or grilled according to personal taste. Where the word 'coat' occurs, it means the chops are prepared as page 239. (See also the pictures on the left.)

Aux concombres—serve with rings of peeled fried cucumber.

Duchesse—coat and serve in a border of green peas cooked and sieved to a smooth purée, and with Espagnole sauce (page 103).

Jardinière—coat and serve with a colourful garnish of mixed spring vegetables.

Nelson—(particularly suitable for mutton cutlets). After steaming (page 81) spread with a veal stuffing (recipe page 90), top with grated cheese and bake in the oven till tender. Serve with a purée of onions.

Réforme—coat, but mix the crumbs with very finely diced bacon or chopped ham. Garnish with cooked strips of ham, mushrooms and hard-boiled egg. Often these are served with a tomato-flavoured brown sauce (page 103).

Escalope of veal

4 thin fillets veal	4 oz. butter *or* 2 oz.
flour	butter and 2 table-
seasoning	spoons oil or fat
1 beaten egg	*To garnish:*
little water	lemon slices or
crisp crumbs for	wedges
coating	(4)

Coat the fillets of veal with the seasoned flour. Brush with the beaten egg diluted with a little water and press the crisp crumbs firmly on to meat with a palette knife. Heat the butter or butter and oil or fat. The purpose of mixing the butter is explained on page 28. Put in the fillets of veal and cook fairly quickly on either side until crisp and brown. Lower the heat and cook for a few minutes to ensure that the meat is thoroughly cooked and tender right through to the middle. Drain well on kitchen paper and serve on a hot dish, garnished with lemon slices or wedges.

Fried sweetbreads

1–1¼ lb. sweetbreads	butter or butter and
salt	oil or fat for frying
1 egg, beaten	*To garnish:*
crisp breadcrumbs	parsley
	wedges of lemon (4)

Soak the sweetbreads in cold water. Lift out and drain. Put into a pan of cold water, bring to boil to blanch, then discard the water. Cover with fresh cold water, salted, and simmer for 20 minutes. Cool and remove thin skin from the sweetbreads. If wished, put the sweetbreads on to a plate or board with another plate and weight on top, then slice before coating, otherwise coat each portion separately with beaten egg and crisp crumbs. Fry in hot butter until crisp and golden brown. Drain well on kitchen or absorbent paper.

Serve with tartare sauce (page 105) or thickened gravy or tomato sauce (page 103) garnish with parsley and lemon.

Chicken Maryland

1 small frying	salt
chicken	cayenne pepper
1 egg	3 tablespoons milk
4 oz. breadcrumbs	4 oz. cooked or
fat for frying	canned corn, drained
2 bananas	fat for frying
Corn fritters:	*Garnish:*
1 beaten egg	watercress
2 oz. flour	tomatoes (4)

Cut the chicken into 4–6 joints as shown in the picture and coat each joint with egg and breadcrumbs. Fry joints quickly until golden brown in depth of ½ inch of hot fat, turning once. Reduce heat and cook gently until tender on both sides. Split the bananas in half lengthways and fry.

To make the fritters: Make a batter with the beaten egg, flour, seasonings and milk. Beat well and mix in the drained corn. Gently fry tablespoons of the mixture in a little hot fat, turning once, for 4–5 minutes until golden brown.

Serve the chicken with bananas and fritters on a large flat dish, garnish with watercress and fried tomatoes. Tomato sauce could be served separately.

Variation

Chicken and bananas can be coated in batter, then fried in deep fat or oil. For batter, see page 71.

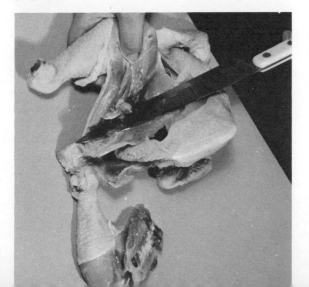

GRILLED MEAT AND POULTRY

THE times for grilling meat and poultry are given in full in Book 2, and the same cuts of meat are selected for grilling as for frying. With the exception of thick slices of bacon, the grill must be pre-heated before putting the food underneath so that the outside is browned quickly. This keeps the meat moist. The reason for not pre-heating the grill for bacon is to prevent the fat curling.

Mixed grill

Choose all or some of the following:	4–6 oz. liver
4–8 sausages	fat for frying
4 small cutlets lamb	tomatoes
1–2 fillet steaks or	mushrooms
piece of rump steak	eggs
cut into four	*To garnish:*
4 rashers bacon	watercress or sprigs
4 lamb's kidneys	of parsley ④

The order of cooking depends on the size of the grill pan. With a fairly small pan, many people prefer to cook the sausages in the oven.

Start with the foods that need a lot of cooking, i.e. sausages (unless cooking them in the oven), then tiny chops, steak and lastly those foods that are cooked quickly. Keep lean meat well brushed with melted fat or butter. Tomatoes and mushrooms can be cooked in the grill pan, brushed with melted fat or butter. If serving eggs, fry them in a little fat.

Arrange neatly on a dish or serving plates and garnish with watercress or parsley.

Kebabs

An interesting method of serving grilled meat is in the form of Kebabs. This type of cooking is found in Turkey and adjoining countries— where the meat is put on to large skewers and cooked over a fire or charcoal burner. It is possible to cook it under a gas or electric grill or over a barbecue fire. Metal skewers must be used and only tender cuts of meat are suitable.

Easy Kebabs. Small sausages, pineapple, mushrooms, quartered tomatoes and (at right) diced steak, onions, mushrooms and courgettes

Dice the meat and season lightly, dust with mixed herbs if wished. Put on to metal skewers with vegetables if wished (see pictures). Brush with melted butter and cook under the grill until the meat is tender—approximately 8–10 minutes. Turn the skewers during cooking. Serve with boiled rice (page 108) and a green salad or green vegetables.

ROAST MEAT AND POULTRY

VERY detailed instructions for roasting meat are given in Book 2, together with accompaniments. Additional poultry recipes follow. Instructions for carving are on page 238.

Roast duck

2 small duckling,* fresh or frozen sage and onion stuffing (page 89)	*To garnish:* watercress orange rings ④

*Since the breast of duckling is very thinly covered with meat, allow 1 small duckling for 2 people or one good-sized duck for 4.

1. If using frozen duckling, defrost.
2. Make the stuffing and put inside the ducks. Some people find this makes them a little fatty and prefer to cook it in a separate dish in the oven.
3. Put the ducks into an uncovered roasting tin. Allow approximately 1 hour for a small duckling, or 15 minutes per lb. and 15 minutes over, in a hot oven, 425–450°F.—Gas Mark 6–7. If using frozen duckling, cook rather more slowly, i.e. in a moderate to moderately hot oven, 375–400°F.—Gas Mark 4–5, allowing about 25 minutes per lb. and 25 minutes over.

4. To get a very crisp brown skin and allow fat to escape, prick skin lightly halfway through the cooking time.
5. Garnish with watercress and orange rings and serve with apple sauce (Book 2, page 124) and thickened gravy.

Roast goose

Goose is roasted in the same way as duck, allowing 15 minutes per lb. and 15 minutes over. Never reduce the cooking time for goose. Prick the skin of the goose twice during cooking. Be careful in handling the meat tin, for a great deal of fat comes from goose. This is excellent in cooking.

Roast turkey

1 12–16 lb. turkey butter or fat for basting sausages—allow one per person bacon rolls veal stuffing (page 90) made with 8–12 oz. breadcrumbs, etc.	*Chestnut stuffing:* 1 lb. chestnuts stock 8 oz. chopped cooked ham (optional) little milk 2 oz. breadcrumbs 2 oz. butter *To garnish:* watercress ⑫–⑳ *

*The difference in servings is because most people like to have some turkey left to serve cold, but this will cut into at least 20 hot portions.

1. *Chestnut stuffing:* Split and boil the chestnuts for 10 minutes in water. Remove the skin and simmer in stock until tender. Rub the chestnuts through a sieve, then add to ham, milk, breadcrumbs and butter.

2. Put veal stuffing (page 90) into the neck of the turkey and the chestnut stuffing into the body.

3. Weigh the bird, including the stuffing. For a bird up to 12 lb. in weight allow 15 minutes per lb. and 15 minutes over. Any weight over 12 lb. means an additional 12 minutes per lb. It is advisable to start cooking the turkey in a hot oven, 425–450°F.—Gas Mark 6–7, but after the first 45 minutes to one hour the heat may be reduced to moderate, 375°F.—Gas Mark 4–5.

4. Either baste well during cooking to prevent drying, or cover the turkey with greased foil. This means adding 10–15 minutes to the cooking time. Some people like to wrap the bird completely in foil, which has the great advantage of keeping the oven very clean. In this case allow 15–20 minutes extra cooking time and open the foil to allow the bird to brown for the last 30 minutes of the time. A slow method of roasting meat and poultry is given in Book 2.

5. To add the sausages to the turkey, prick them and put into the oven for the last 45 minutes of the cooking time.

6. To make the bacon rolls, allow half a rasher of bacon per person, roll the halved bacon rashers neatly, put on to skewers and put in the oven for the last 15–20 minutes.

7. Serve the turkey garnished with the bacon rolls, sausages and watercress.

Roast game

1 pheasant, or	2 oz. fairly coarse
2 grouse or 4 wood-	soft breadcrumbs
cock or other game*	
fat bacon	*To garnish:*
fat or butter	game chips (see
1 piece toast	next page)
2 oz. butter	watercress ④

*Do not truss woodcock and golden plover. Other game is trussed like poultry.

1. Game is inclined to be dry so do cover the whole of the body either with fat bacon or with butter. It is a good idea to put a knob of butter inside the bird as well.

2. It is usual to put a piece of toast under the game, particularly smaller game such as woodcock, etc., to catch the flavour.

3. Allow approximately 35–45 minutes for small game. Start in a hot oven, 425–450°F.—Gas Mark 6–7, for 10–15 minutes and lower the heat to moderately hot, 400°F.—Gas Mark 5–6, for the rest of the time. For larger birds, such as grouse, etc. allow 15 minutes per lb. and 15 minutes over.

4. Heat the butter and toss the crumbs in this until crisp and brown.

5. *Game chips:* Cut peeled potato into wafer-thin slices, fry in deep fat until crisp and golden.

6. Serve the game garnished with the crisp crumbs, game chips and watercress.

You can use packet potato crisps instead for game chips. Heat for a few minutes only.

Pigeons

In some parts of the country these are both inexpensive and plentiful. If plump and young, i.e. the breast is well covered and the legs are not unduly sinewy, the pigeons may be roasted as other game—they must be kept well covered with fat. If older they should be braised.

CARVING POULTRY AND GAME

Turn to page 238 for other joints.

Chicken and duck: Small spring chickens—serve one per person. Slightly larger chickens or duckling are halved—cut firmly downwards slightly to one side of centre of breastbone with a sharp knife. Medium-sized chickens or ducks —joint. Cut away the legs. The breast meat may be cut away on either side of the breast bone with the wings to give four joints; both the leg and breast joints may be halved to give eight portions.

Turkey, large chicken (capon) or goose: Either cut or pull off the leg on one side. Cut long thin slices across the breast with slices of stuffing as well. Cut large slices from the leg, finally cut round the bone into narrow thick pieces.

Game: Small birds are served whole or halved; larger birds—carve or joint as chicken. Venison—carve as lamb. Roasted hare and large rabbits—cut long slices on either side of backbone, then carve round bones of the legs.

JOINTS WITH STUFFING

Stuffing adds flavour and makes the poultry or meat 'go further'.

A well chosen stuffing also gives a good balance of flavour, e.g. sage and onion counteracts the richness and fat content of pork—it would also be excellent for breast of mutton. It would, however, be too strong to use with more delicate flavoured lean veal—use veal stuffing or one of the variations of this.

Sage and onion stuffing

2 large onions, peeled	4 oz. breadcrumbs
$\frac{1}{2}$ pint water	1 oz. suet
good pinch salt and pepper	1 teaspoon dried sage
	1 egg (or onion stock)

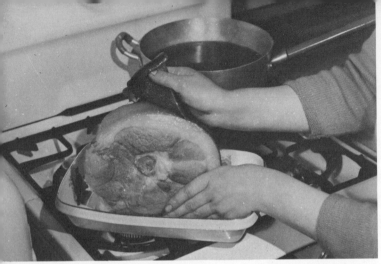

Removing skin from bacon joint before roasting

Cook onions with water and seasoning. Simmer steadily for 20 minutes to partially cook onions. Remove from water, cut finely on a chopping board. Transfer to basin and add all other ingredients. For a less firm stuffing, use some of the onion stock instead of egg.

Veal stuffing

2 oz. shredded suet	4 oz. breadcrumbs
½ teaspoon mixed herbs	1 egg seasoning
grated rind and juice ½ lemon	2–3 teaspoons chopped parsley

Mix all the ingredients together.

Stuffed breast of lamb

4 oz. pork sausagemeat	1 level teaspoon salt shake pepper
4 oz. soft white breadcrumbs	3 tablespoons water or milk
1 rounded tablespoon chopped parsley	1 breast lamb, approximately
1 level teaspoon dry mustard	1½–1¾ lb. in weight after boning
2 level teaspoons finely grated onion	little lard or dripping ④

1. Mix together sausagemeat, breadcrumbs, parsley, mustard, onion, salt and pepper and bind with the water or milk. If mixture seems a little dry add more liquid.
2. Spread lamb thinly with stuffing, roll up tightly and secure with string or skewers. Stand in baking tin, cover joint with a little lard or dripping. Bake in the centre of a moderate oven, 375°F.—Gas Mark 4–5, for 1¼ hours.
3. Transfer to a warm dish and serve with creamed potatoes, peas, garnished with raw or fried onion rings, and onion sauce (recipe page 102).

Glazed bacon

In this method, bacon is partially cooked by boiling then baked in the oven to give a more

Basting lar

interesting appearance. Choose one of the joints suitable for boiling—Book 2 gives these in great detail, but among the most suitable are collar and gammon. Soak overnight or for some hours in cold water, unless choosing a 'sweet-cure' bacon which does not need soaking. Put into fresh cold water and bring the water to simmering point, skim, then cover the pan.

The bacon should not be completely cooked, so allow only 20–25 minutes per lb. and 20–25 minutes over. Lift the bacon from the pan, remove the skin (picture page 90). Put into a roasting tin and cook in one of the following ways:

Allow 10 minutes per lb. and 10 minutes over in the centre of a moderately hot oven, 400°F.— Gas Mark 5–6.

(a) Score (mark) the fat and sprinkle lightly with brown sugar.

(b) Score the fat, sprinkle with sugar and spice.

(c) Score the fat, spread with a very little made mustard and sprinkle with sugar.

(d) Score the fat and spoon over syrup from canned apricots, peaches, pineapple. Cook as above, but cover with the fruit for the last 10 minutes (see picture).

(e) Prepare in any of the ways above, but press cloves into the fat at regular intervals.

If the bacon is very lean, wrap the sides of the meat in foil, leaving just the fat exposed to the

Bacon with apricots

dry heat of the oven. If preferred, put the bacon into a small quantity of stock, cider, or ginger beer (this is unusual, but very pleasant), so that the lean keeps moist but the fat is exposed and crisps.

STEWS AND CASSEROLES

SIMPLE stews and casseroles are in Books 1 and 2. The following recipes give more imaginative ways of using cheaper cuts of meat, etc. An interesting casserole dish is an excellent

ork pie

choice when entertaining, as there is little, if any, last-minute dishing up.

Carbonnade of beef

1½ lb. stewing beef (flank or chuck steak) seasoning	1–2 large onions 1 level teaspoon made mustard
1 oz. flour	¾ pint brown ale
2 oz. dripping or fat	1 bay leaf
1 tablespoon tomato purée	few sprigs of parsley seasoning (4)–(6)

1. Cut the meat into 1-inch cubes and toss in seasoned flour. Melt the fat in a pan and fry meat and chopped onions until lightly browned. Add the tomato purée and mustard and blend in the beer, add the bay leaf and parsley. Season again if necessary.
2. Bring to the boil, then simmer for 2½ hours. Alternatively, transfer to a casserole, cover and cook in a very moderate oven, 325–350°F.—Gas Mark 3, for the same amount of time; allow a little less liquid.
3. Serve with boiled noodles or cooked spaghetti and a green vegetable.

Pot roast

This describes the form of 'roasting' in a saucepan.

Brown the meat in a little fat in a large strong pan, lift out. Put a good layer of mixed vege-

Carbonnade of beef

tables into the pan, together with seasoning and enough water to cover the vegetables. Replace the meat then cover the pan. If the lid does not fit well put foil under this to make a good seal. Lower the heat and cook for 30–40 minutes per lb. and 30–40 minutes over.

Goulash

2 oz. fat or butter	pepper
12 oz. lean beef	¼–½ pint tomato pulp (recipe below)
12 oz. veal	
1 lb. onions	1 lb. potatoes, sliced
1 teaspoon salt	*To garnish:*
1–2 tablespoons paprika (sweet red)	chopped parsley (4)–(6)

4. MEAT AND POULTRY
4. MEAT AND POULTRY

Tomato pulp or purée: Skinned fresh tomatoes can be used, but the best tomatoes for cooking are the canned plum-shaped ones. Use either 1 lb. fresh tomatoes with ¼ pint water or a medium (15½–16 oz.) can of plum tomatoes. Simmer until soft, sieve if wished.

Heat the fat in a pan. Cut the meat into neat pieces. Slice the onions thinly. Fry the meat and the onions until pale golden. Add the seasonings and tomato pulp and simmer gently for 30 minutes. Add the sliced potatoes and more tomato pulp if necessary. Continue cooking gently for another 1–1½ hours until the meat and the potatoes are very tender. Lift carefully into a fairly deep serving dish and garnish with chopped parsley.

Goulash can also be cooked covered, in the centre of a very moderate oven, 325–350°F.— Gas Mark 3, for about 1½ hours.

Moussaka

3 oz. butter	*Sauce:*	④–⑥
8 oz. onions	1 oz. butter	
1½ lb. potatoes	1 oz. flour	
2 large aubergines	½ pint milk	
1 lb. minced beef	seasoning	
seasoning	1 egg	
2 tomatoes, sliced	2 oz. grated cheese	

This is a particularly interesting way of cooking minced meat, which originates from Greece and Turkey.

1. Slice aubergines, sprinkle lightly with salt, stand for 20 minutes, to prevent bitter taste. Pour off excess moisture.
2. Heat the butter and fry the sliced onions until just soft, but not broken. Remove onions then toss the sliced potatoes and aubergines in the butter.
3. Make a white sauce with the butter, flour and milk (page 101) season well, then whisk in the beaten egg and cheese, but do not cook again.
4. Arrange a layer of sliced potatoes and aubergines at the bottom of a deep casserole, then a layer of the meat, a layer of onion, then sliced tomato. Season each layer well. Pour a small quantity of sauce over each layer. Continue filling the casserole in this way ending with a layer of potato and aubergine.
5. Put the lid on the casserole and bake for 1½ hours in the middle of a very moderate oven, 300–350°F.—Gas Mark 2–3. Take off the lid, sprinkle with chopped parsley and serve at once.

Variation

Grated cheese may be sprinkled over the vegetables and meat to give a stronger flavour.

Sweet and sour pork

For the sauce:	1 lb. pork fillet
small can pineapple	$\frac{1}{2}$ tablespoon
1 level tablespoon	cornflour
cornflour	seasoning
1 tablespoon soy	1 clove garlic
sauce	1–2 spring onions or
2 tablespoons vinegar	1 small leek
or lemon juice	1 green pepper
1–2 tablespoons sugar	(capsicum)
or honey	2 tablespoons oil
$\frac{1}{4}$ pint chicken stock	
or water and chicken	
stock cube	④–⑤

The mixture of sweet and sour flavours is typical of some Chinese dishes and is very appetising; Chinese food is cooked for short periods only, so the food must be cut into small pieces and tender meat used.

1. Prepare the sauce first so it is ready when the pork is cooked. Strain the pineapple and chop more finely, then measure $\frac{1}{4}$ pint of the syrup or add a little water to give $\frac{1}{4}$ pint. Blend the cornflour with the rest of the ingredients, put into a pan and cook, stirring well, until thickened and clear, add the pineapple.
2. Cut the meat into small neat cubes, then coat with the seasoned cornflour. Chop the clove of garlic and spring onions or leek very finely, then cut the flesh of the pepper into small

pieces, discarding the core and seeds.
3. Heat the oil and fry the pork in this for 5 minutes, add the garlic, etc. and continue cooking for a further 5 minutes or until the pork is tender.
4. Put into a hot dish and top with the sauce.

Coq au vin

4 oz. mushrooms	1 clove garlic
4–8 small shallots or	1 oz. flour
onions	1 pint red wine
2–3 oz. butter or oil	*or*
4 oz. fat bacon or	$\frac{3}{4}$ pint chicken stock
pork	and $\frac{1}{4}$ pint wine
1 young chicken	seasoning ④

One of the classic French dishes is chicken cooked in wine. Most people prefer it cooked in red wine, but occasionally you will find a recipe with white wine. A young chicken is used in the following recipe, which means a relatively short cooking time. If using a boiling fowl, simmer for at least $1\frac{1}{2}$ hours instead of the 30 minutes, and add a little extra liquid so the sauce does not become too thick.

1. Slice the mushrooms and fry with the onions in butter until tender and the onions golden brown. Fry the diced bacon. Lift out and add the jointed chicken. Cook steadily for about 10 minutes until golden on the outside.

2. Remove from the butter and stir in the crushed garlic and the flour. Cook for about 3–4 minutes, then gradually add the wine. Add seasoning and bring just to the boil. Simmer until a smooth sauce.

3. Return the chicken, mushrooms and onions to the sauce, season well and simmer for approximately 30 minutes, until the chicken is tender.

Fricassée of rabbit

1 rabbit	Sauce:
water to cover	2 oz. butter
1 tablespoon vinegar	2 oz. flour
2–3 onions	$\frac{1}{2}$ pint milk
2–3 carrots	To garnish:
2 rashers bacon	4 oz. mushrooms
1 pint water	little butter
seasoning	3 rashers bacon
	few peas ④

1. Soak the jointed rabbit in the cold water and vinegar—this helps to whiten the flesh.
2. Lift out and dry well. Put into the pan with the chopped onions, carrots, bacon, water and the seasoning and simmer for 1½ hours until the rabbit is tender. Keep hot.
3. *Sauce:* Heat the butter in another pan, stir in the flour and cook for several minutes. Blend in the milk, then add ½ pint of the strained rabbit stock and cook until thickened and smooth. Taste and add seasoning if required.

4. Fry the mushrooms in the butter. Cut the rashers of bacon into neat pieces, form into bacon rolls, put on a skewer and grill or fry. Cook and drain the peas.
5. Put the rabbit on to a hot dish, coat with the sauce, garnish with the mushrooms, bacon rolls and the peas.
Variation: Add a little cream and/or sherry to the sauce.

Fricassée of veal
Use 1–1¼ lb. diced veal in place of rabbit.

Jugged hare

1 hare, cut into	little port wine
joints (save as much	1 tablespoon
blood as possible)	redcurrant jelly
1 onion, few carrots,	seasoning
chopped	veal stuffing (recipe
2 oz. dripping or lard	page 90)
2 oz. flour	④

1. Cook the liver of the hare for 30 minutes in 1½ pints salted water.
2. Soak the hare in cold water and little vinegar.
3. Fry the chopped onion and carrot in the dripping. Stir in the flour and add the liver stock. Bring to the boil, cook until thickened. Stir in blood of hare, port wine, redcurrant jelly and lots of seasoning.

4. Mash liver or rub through sieve, stir into sauce or put with sauce into electric blender. Switch on for few seconds until smooth.

5. Cover joints of hare with sauce and cook very slowly for about 3 hours in a saucepan or casserole.

6. Make stuffing, roll into balls and bake for 20 minutes in a very moderate oven, 300–325°F.—Gas Mark 2–3.

7. Arrange hare on dish unless serving in casserole. Coat with most of the sauce, serve the rest separately. Garnish with balls of stuffing and watercress and parsley if wished.

Variation: Leave out port wine for a less well-flavoured sauce.

BRAISING

BRAISING is a form of cooking that is often misnamed on a menu or in recipes. The dish that appears under 'braised beef' is frequently a rather ordinary beef stew—perhaps with a thicker sauce than usual or a little more flavour.

To braise meat is a complicated process, for the meat is browned then cooked *above* a bed of vegetables, etc. The correct name for the mixture used to give flavour to the meat is a mirepoise or mirepoix.

Braised beef

2 lb. beef—fresh brisket, topside, fillet	1 large onion ④–⑥
2 oz. fat bacon	1 stick celery
Mirepoix:	1 small turnip
1 oz. butter	*bouquet garni*
1 oz. bacon (fairly fat)	¼ pint stock ⎫ or ½ pint stock
2 large carrots	¼ pint red wine ⎬
	seasoning ⎭

1. Wipe the meat. Put the meat with the bacon into the pan and brown the meat gently on either side, then lift on to a dish.

2. Prepare the mirepoix: heat the butter, fry the chopped bacon and the thickly sliced vegetables then add the *bouquet garni*, stock, wine and seasoning.

3. Put the meat on top of this, cover with the bacon and a buttered paper, then put a tightly-fitting lid on the pan. Cook very gently for 1¼ hours for brisket or topside, but 1 hour only for fillet.

4. Lift the meat on to a hot serving dish, top with the bacon, then strain the liquid from the vegetables, etc. and serve this as a thin sauce. If preferred, the vegetables may be sieved and added to the liquid to give a thick sauce, or strain the liquid and use this as part of the stock in a brown or Espagnole sauce (page 103).

Variations

Chicken may be braised in the same way—a roasting chicken needs 15 minutes per lb. and 15 minutes over, a boiling fowl 30 minutes per lb. and 30 minutes over.

Sweetbreads: Blanch (page 84) then cook for 1 hour.

Game: Braising is particularly suitable for cooking older game, for it ensures it will be kept moist as well as being tender. Allow approximately 2 hours for small birds and $2\frac{1}{2}$–3 hours for larger birds, i.e. grouse, etc.

Beef olives

Cover thin slices of stewing steak or topside of beef with stuffing (veal stuffing or sage and onion are both suitable). Then form the meat into neat rolls or gather it into a round (hence the name olive) and tie it with string. Fry the meat in a little fat and cook as stewed beef (Book 2) or braised beef (page 98) with a selection of diced root vegetables, for approximately 2–$2\frac{1}{2}$ hours.

MEAT PIES

THE most popular of all meat pies is a steak and kidney pie (see picture overleaf) and this is given in Book 2. A raised veal and ham pie or a pork pie is an excellent choice for a picnic, and hot water crust pastry is used for both.

Hot water crust pastry

12 oz. plain flour	3–4 oz. fat
pinch salt	$\frac{1}{4}$ pint water

Sieve the flour and salt together. Melt the fat with the water, add to the flour, mix with a knife and knead gently with the fingers. Unlike other pastries, this should be used when warm, so roll out at once or keep in a warm place until ready to use.

California beef loaf

Veal and ham pie

12 oz. hot water crust pastry	7 tablespoons water or bone stock
1¼ lb. fillet of veal	beaten egg for glazing
6 oz. ham	1 level teaspoon gelatine
seasoning	
½ level teaspoon grated lemon rind	½ level teaspoon meat extract (optional)
1–2 hard-boiled eggs	④–⑥

1. Keep pastry warm in basin until ready to use.
2. Wash and dry the meats, removing any skin, and cut into 1-inch cubes. Roll the meats together in salt and pepper and lemon rind.
3. Line a 6-inch cake tin or 1 lb. loaf tin with two-thirds of the pastry and place half the meat in the bottom. Cut the eggs into halves, place on top of the meat, cover with remaining meat. Pour in three tablespoons of water or stock.
4. Turn the top edge of pastry-lining in over the meat, damp it all round, roll out remaining third of pastry to make a lid. Press down well all round the edge and cut at ½-inch intervals with a sharp knife to secure. Make a hole in the centre, brush over with beaten egg, decorate with pastry leaves and brush with egg again.
5. Place in the centre of a moderate oven, 375°F.—Gas Mark 4–5, for 2–2¼ hours. Cool.
6. Melt the gelatine in remaining water or stock and stir in the meat extract if wished. When the pie is cool and the gelatine mixture just setting, pour into the pie through the hole in the centre and leave to set before serving.

Pork pie

This is made by the same method as a veal and ham pie, but approximately 1½ lb. of fillet of pork is used instead of veal and ham. The pork may be flavoured with a little powdered sage. Traditionally no hard-boiled eggs are put into a pork pie. The lemon rind can be omitted.

Another way to make raised pies

Veal and ham pie, and pork pie are often called "raised" pies. The hot water crust pastry is moulded with the hands or round a container to the desired shape, the filling put in, the lid put on and the pastry baked as in the recipe. This method is more difficult than using a tin, but does give a rather crisper outside.

5. SAVOURY SAUCES

A GOOD sauce should be smooth and of the correct consistency and flavour for the dish in which it is being used or to which it is an accompaniment. Sauces can also provide extra nutrients to a meal in the form of milk, cheese, etc.

Condensed soups make good quick sauces, in particular tomato, mushroom and celery. It is also possible to buy dehydrated sauces which are quickly cooked. The term "a coating sauce" means a sauce which just coats the back of a spoon.

White sauce

The most usual sauce is a white sauce and detailed instructions for making this are in Book 2, but briefly the method is to heat the butter, stir in the flour and cook over a low heat, stirring well with a wooden spoon until a dry 'roux', and then gradually blend in the milk. A white sauce is given in several recipes in this book, for example, Smoked Cod with Duchesse Potatoes (page 113). The coating sauce here is made with 1 oz. butter (margarine could be used), 1 oz. flour and ½ pint milk and seasoning. If a thinner sauce is required—and this is used for soups, etc.—use ¾–1 pint milk.

If a really thick sauce or panada, for binding ingredients together as in fishcakes, etc, is required, use ¼ pint of milk.

A white sauce may be flavoured by adding anchovies, cheese, cooked mushrooms, chopped hard-boiled egg, parsley, etc., so is the basis for a very great number of sauces.

A rather better flavoured sauce is the following Béchamel sauce. Use it as a basic sauce instead of white sauce.

Béchamel sauce

½ pint milk	seasoning, or a few
small piece onion	peppercorns
small piece celery	1 oz. butter
small piece carrot	1 oz. flour

Put the milk with the vegetables, seasoning or peppercorns in a warm place and allow it to infuse for a time. Strain the milk off the vegetables and then make a sauce exactly like a white sauce. Cook until a coating consistency, add extra seasoning if wished. When pouring milk off the vegetables, it may be necessary to add a little extra fresh milk to make ½ pint again.

Onion sauce

3 onions	1 oz. flour
water	$\frac{1}{4}$ pint milk
1 oz. butter or	seasoning
margarine	

Boil the onions in water in a covered saucepan until tender. Large onions will take about 45 minutes. Chop the onions when cooked and keep $\frac{1}{4}$ pint of the liquid. If possible chop them on a laminated plastic surface rather than wood, since it is very difficult to get rid of the onion smell from a wooden surface. Heat the butter in a pan, stir in the flour and cook for several minutes. Remove from heat and add the milk, the onion stock and seasoning. Bring to the boil. Add the chopped onions and re-heat.

Brown sauce

1 oz. cooking fat or	$\frac{1}{4}$ pint brown stock
dripping	for panada or binding
1 oz. flour	sauce
$\frac{1}{2}$ pint brown stock	*or*
for a coating sauce	1 pint brown stock
or	for thin sauce
	seasoning

Heat the fat or dripping in a pan. Add the flour and cook steadily in the fat until brown. Be careful not to over-brown. Add stock, stirring all the time, and bring to the boil. Season and cook until thick and smooth.

A better flavour is given by using 2 oz. of fat, and frying a little chopped onion, celery and carrot and straining when cooked.

To make gravy

Gravy is so often lacking in flavour that it is worth taking time and trouble over it. The requirements are:

1. *Stock.* Made by simmering meat bones; by using vegetable water (this retains some valuable vitamins), by using stock cubes, gravy flavouring or gravy powder.
2. *Cooking the gravy sufficiently.* This may be done in a saucepan or when roasting meat it is better to use the meat tin, so that any sediment from the meat is incorporated into the gravy and gives an excellent taste.
3. Careful cooking of a gravy, like a sauce, is essential to make certain it is smooth.
4. If there are any particles or lumps in the gravy, it must be strained.

To make a thin gravy to serve with meat which is not stuffed, follow the proportions for a brown sauce, thin consistency.

For a thick gravy, follow the directions for brown sauce, using the coating consistency. Book 2 covers gravy making in detail, with step-by-step pictures.

Espagnole sauce

Brown sauce (page 102)	1 carrot
few mushrooms	little smooth tomato pulp
1 rasher of bacon	sherry
1 onion	

Add chopped mushrooms, bacon, onion and carrot to the brown sauce. Simmer until tender and sauce is very thick. Sieve and re-heat with little smooth tomato pulp and sherry.

Tomato flavoured brown sauce

Quite frequently a brown sauce has a distinct tomato taste. This is obtained by adding either ½–1 tablespoon of concentrated tomato purée or pulp (obtainable in cans or tubes), or 1–2 sieved tomatoes to the sauce.

Tomato sauce

2 rashers bacon (optional)	or 1 can tomatoes
1 small onion, finely sliced	seasoning
	good pinch sugar
8 oz. tomatoes, sliced	squeeze lemon juice
	1 small bunch parsley

Fry the bacon until just cooked. Fry finely sliced onion in fat until tender but not browned. Add sliced tomatoes and rest of ingredients and simmer until a smooth pulp. Rub through a sieve, then reheat gently. You can add a little water or stock to make a thinner sauce or, if you wish, you can serve the sauce without sieving it, in which case just remove the bunch of parsley.

Cranberry sauce

8–12 oz. cranberries	2–3 oz. sugar
¼ pint water	knob butter

Simmer the cranberries in the water. Rub through a sieve, add sugar to taste and little knob of butter.

For an unsieved sauce, make a syrup of the water and sugar, drop in the cranberries and cook until a thick mixture, then add the butter. If wished, a little port wine can be added to this sauce, in which case use slightly less water.

Unsieved cranberry sauce

Cranberries are very bitter in flavour so make sauce, taste, then add more sugar if wished.

Bread sauce

1 small onion	2 oz. breadcrumbs
2 or 3 cloves	salt
(optional)	pepper
½ pint milk	

Peel onion and if using cloves, stick these firmly into the onion. Put into the milk together with the other ingredients. Slowly bring milk to boil, remove from heat and leave in a warm place for as long as possible. Before serving, gently heat sauce, beating with a wooden spoon. Remove the onion.

Hollandaise sauce

2 egg yolks	lemon juice or white
pinch cayenne pepper	wine vinegar
salt and pepper	2–4 oz. butter
1–2 tablespoons	④

This sauce is excellent with cooked vegetables such as broccoli or with salmon. It can also be used as the basis for tartare sauce instead of mayonnaise. It is often considered a difficult sauce. This is not the case, the only difficulty being to prevent the egg mixture curdling due to excess heat, and to prevent the sauce separating when the butter is added. To avoid this, add the butter very slowly indeed.

Use a double saucepan or a basin over a saucepan. Put the egg yolks, seasoning and lemon juice or vinegar into the top or into the basin. Whisk over hot but *not boiling* water until sauce begins to thicken. Add butter in very small pieces, whisking in each pat and allowing to melt before adding the next. DO NOT ALLOW TO BOIL otherwise it will curdle. If too thick, add a little cream.

Mayonnaise

2 egg yolks	¼ level teaspoon
1 level teaspoon dry	paprika
mustard	4 tablespoons vinegar
1 level teaspoon salt	8 tablespoons (¼ pint)
good pinch pepper	salad or olive oil

Put the egg yolks into a basin. Add the mustard, salt, pepper and paprika and mix thoroughly together (the mustard helps to emulsify the dressing and prevent curdling). Add 2 table-spoons vinegar slowly and stir well. Add the oil drop by drop. Stir hard with a wooden spoon until the mayonnaise is thick and smooth. Add the remaining vinegar gradually and beat vigorously. To keep the basin firmly in position while making the mayonnaise, place it on a damp cloth and this will prevent it from slipping on the table.

Note: If using an electric mixer, the mayonnaise is made in the bowl and the oil added gradually as above, while the whisk rotates at slow speed. It is, however, possible to make it even more quickly in the blender and the oil is added steadily. The lid should be lifted very slightly from the goblet to add the oil, but should not be removed completely, otherwise the mayonnaise splashes badly.

This recipe provides a mayonnaise that is not too 'oily'. If wished, 1 egg yolk will absorb up to a good ¼ pint oil.

Ways to flavour mayonnaise

Green mayonnaise: Add chopped fresh herbs to mayonnaise. Serve with fish salads—if mint is used it is excellent with lamb salad.

Lemon mayonnaise: Add grated rind and juice of 1 lemon to ¼ pint mayonnaise. Serve with cheese or fish salads.

Tomato mayonnaise: Add 1 dessertspoon tomato ketchup or 1 teaspoon tomato purée to ¼ pint mayonnaise. Serve with shell-fish salad.

Tartare sauce

¼ pint mayonnaise or hollandaise sauce 2 teaspoons chopped parsley	1 teaspoon capers 2 teaspoons chopped gherkins ④

Mix all the ingredients together.

French dressing

½–1 teaspoon made English or French mustard shake of pepper pinch of salt pinch of sugar	3–4 tablespoons olive, salad or corn oil 1½–2 tablespoons white, brown or wine vinegar ④–⑥

Either put the seasonings on to a saucer or plate and gradually blend in the oil then the vinegar, or put them into an old clean mayonnaise bottle, add the oil and vinegar and shake vigorously.

These are the usual proportions of oil and vinegar, but naturally they may be varied to suit personal taste.

The dressing may be flavoured with chopped herbs or a crushed clove of garlic.

6. MAKING CURRIES

WHETHER one uses meat, vegetables, fish or eggs, a basic curry sauce is prepared in the same way.

Tastes vary as to how much flavouring is put into the sauce, so unless one knows the taste of the people to whom it is to be served, it is advisable to use a mild curry.

Mild curry

Sauce:	water with a little
2 oz. margarine or	yeast extract for
butter (the real	vegetable or egg
Indian curry uses	curries)
ghee—clarified	salt
butter)	pepper
1 onion	good pinch sugar
1 apple	1 dessertspoon
1 oz. flour	desiccated coconut
1 tablespoon curry	1 good tablespoon
powder, or less if	sultanas
desired	1 good tablespoon
1 teaspoon curry	chutney
paste (can be omitted)	squeeze lemon juice
¾–1 pint stock (use	or few drops vinegar
meat stock for meat	
curries, fish stock or	
water for fish curries,	④

1. Heat the butter or margarine and fry the finely chopped onion and apple until soft. Stir in the flour and curry powder and paste, and cook gently for several minutes so the 'raw' taste of the curry powder is improved. MORE CAN BE USED IF WISHED.

2. Gradually stir in the stock, bring to the boil and cook until thickened, then add the other ingredients, tasting at the end to make sure there is sufficient seasoning and sweetening.

3. Add food to be curried in the case of raw chicken or meat. If putting in hard-boiled eggs, etc., simmer the sauce for about 45 minutes at least, more if possible, then heat the food for the time given.

Uncooked meat curries
Put in 1–1¼ lb. diced raw meat or chicken and simmer for several hours, adding a little more liquid if desired.

Cooked meat curries
Allow the sauce to simmer for about 30 minutes to an hour, then put in 1 lb. diced cooked meat and cook for a further 30 minutes.

Fish curries
Put in 1–1½ lb. diced raw fish and simmer for 20–25 minutes in the cooked sauce, or if using shell fish or cooked fish, heat for about 5 minutes

only in the thickened curry sauce. Allow 2–4 oz. shell fish per person.

Vegetable curries
Cook sauce for about 30–35 minutes, then add 1–1¼ lb. diced vegetables and simmer gently for about 25–30 minutes. A good mixture of flavours would be diced carrots, sprigged cauliflower, sliced runner or whole green beans, and diced onion.

Hot curry

Use the recipe for the mild curry sauce but add—	pinch of cayenne ④ pepper or a few crushed peppercorns
To the flour:	½–1 teaspoon mustard
¼–1 teaspoon chilli powder (depending upon personal taste)	½–1 teaspoon ground turmeric
½–1 teaspoon dried ginger	*To the onions:* 1–2 crushed cloves of garlic

A few cloves may be added to give extra flavour during cooking.
The amounts of curry powder and paste may be increased.

Side dishes to serve with curry

Chutney: A chutney of some kind is generally served.
Chapatis, parathas, poppodums: Indian breads which can be bought from shops selling a good variety of imported foods. Reheat these as instructed on the packet.
Bombay duck: Strong smelling dried fish. Fry in a little fat. Crumble over the curry.
Sliced peppers: Both red and green can be used.
Chopped chillis: Use sparingly. Very hot.
Chopped fresh herbs: Mix with a little sugar.
Pickles: Gherkins, sliced or whole; pickled red cabbage or pickled onions.
Fruit and nuts: Sliced banana or apple, sliced lemon, shredded or desiccated coconut, fresh or salted peanuts.

Lentil curry

8 oz. lentils	1 teaspoon sugar
2 large chopped onions	good pinch salt and pepper
1 small peeled, cored and chopped apple	1 teaspoon jam
2 oz. vegetarian fat or margarine	few drops lemon juice
1 tablespoon curry powder	3–4 oz. boiled rice (see below) ④

Put lentils in bowl, just cover with cold water. Soak for a few hours, then simmer in the cold water in which they were soaked, until just soft. Try to keep them whole. Fry the onions and apple in the fat until soft. Mix in all the other ingredients except the rice. Heat well, then pour over the boiled rice.

To cook rice to serve with a curry

Choose long grain rice. This is often described as Patna rice, but this is not always correct for rice comes from many countries. The advantage of long grain and Patna rice is that it keeps its shape if cooked correctly.

Allow 1 oz. rice per person, or for people with small appetites 3 oz. for 4 people.

Method 1

2 pints water	4 oz. rice
½–1 teaspoon salt	

Bring the water to the boil, add the salt and the rice. Cook steadily until the rice is just tender. This takes from 12–15 minutes; strain.

If time permits: Rinse under running cold water—this is easily done if the rice is spread over a fine sieve.

Spread on to a dish or a tin, cover with kitchen paper or a clean cloth. Reheat in a very low oven 225–250°F.—Gas Mark 0–½ for approximately 15 minutes.

A second method of reheating the rice is to rinse as above, then stand the sieve over a pan of boiling water covering carefully with a cloth or large lid.

If in a hurry: Rinse by pouring boiling water through the rice. Shake dry. The rice can be served like this, but many people prefer to put it into a dry pan covered with a tightly fitting lid for about 2 minutes. Reheat if necessary over a very low heat, or it can be put into a hot oven for a few minutes.

This method of rinsing rice makes certain it is absolutely white and not sticky.

Method 2

Either measure or weigh the rice. If measuring, allow an average tea cup or ½ B.S.I. measuring cup of rice for 4 people. Put this into a saucepan, then add exactly double the amount of water, i.e. 2 tea cups or 1 B.S.I. cup, add approximately ½ teaspoon salt.

If weighing, allow 4 oz. rice and 8 liquid oz. of water.

Bring the water to the boil as quickly as possible. Stir the rice briskly with a fork. Put a tightly fitting lid on the saucepan, lower the heat so that the water simmers steadily, and cook for 15 minutes. At the end of this time the rice should have absorbed all the water, be tender without being over-cooked, and every grain should be separate.

If the liquid does not all evaporate, it means too little heat was used. On the other hand, it is very important to watch the cooking the first time to make certain that too much heat is not used, otherwise the rice will burn.

Rinsing is not necessary with method 2.

7. VEGETABLES

BOOK 2 gave a very full table of all vegetables and the most usual way of serving them. Obviously there are many other ways of cooking and serving vegetables, and this chapter gives some suggestions.

a. Braised vegetables
Onions, celery, leeks are often served 'braised'. The correct method of braising is similar to that given under braised beef. If this is too complicated, the vegetables may first be tossed in a little margarine or butter, covered with a thin brown sauce or tomato-flavoured brown sauce and simmered in a covered pan until tender.

b. Creamed vegetables
Many vegetables are excellent if served in a white or Béchamel sauce—broad beans, carrots, mixed vegetables.

Spinach loses some of the rather strong flavour that many people dislike, if chopped or sieved and added to a small quantity of white sauce. Allow $\frac{1}{4}$ pint sauce to 1 or $1\frac{1}{2}$ lb. cooked sieved spinach.

c. Fried vegetables
Book 2 gives full instructions for frying potatoes and onions. Other vegetables suitable for frying are:

Aubergine or egg plant: Do not peel. Slice thinly, coat in seasoned flour and fry until crisp and brown.

Cauliflower: Sprig, cook lightly, dip in egg and crumbs or coating batter and fry.

Carrots: Slice and fry slowly or parboil, dry and slice.

Cucumber: Do not coat; fry slices of peeled cucumber gently until tender.

Other vegetables which can be fried are tomatoes and mushrooms.

d. Purée of vegetables
Many vegetables are delicious if made into a smooth purée, i.e. mashed like potatoes. Try: a mixture of swede and potato; carrot and potato; swede by itself; cauliflower; green peas.

e. Roast vegetables
Full details for roasting vegetables are given in Book 2. Many vegetables are excellent roasted, particularly potatoes, onions, parsnips, swedes, the white part only of leeks.

Garnishing vegetables
An attractive garnish improves the look of vegetables as any other food. Use contrasting

colours, e.g. chopped parsley, etc. A particularly good garnish for cauliflower is to top the cauliflower with lightly fried breadcrumbs, chopped hard-boiled egg and parsley. The name for this dish is Cauliflower Polonaise.

f. Stuffed vegetables

Vegetables make a complete meal when stuffed. The recipe that follows for stuffed marrow may be taken as one interesting stuffing, but alternatives are given under the other recipes.

Stuffed marrow—No. 1

1 medium-sized marrow, peeled	8 oz. raw minced beef
4 oz. long grain rice	2 level tablespoons chopped parsley
1 tablespoon oil	seasoning
1 small onion, finely chopped	1 egg
2 oz. mushrooms, finely chopped	*To garnish:* a few cooked peas ④

Slit the marrow lengthwise to make a base and a lid, scoop out the seeds. Cook the rice in boiling salted water until tender, drain well. Heat the oil, fry the onion for a few minutes. Add the mushrooms and beef and cook a further 5 minutes. Remove from the heat and add the parsley and rice. Mix well and season to taste. Bind with the beaten egg. Fill the centre of the marrow with the stuffing mixture. Replace the lid and wrap completely in foil. Place in a baking tin and cook for approximately $1–1\frac{1}{4}$

hours in a moderate oven, 375°F.—Gas Mark 4–5. Garnish with peas.

Variation on stuffed marrow method 1: Instead of the cooked rice, use 4 oz. soft breadcrumbs.

Stuffed marrow—No. 2

1 medium-sized marrow, peeled	*Other stuffing ingredients:* ④
Cheese sauce:	2 chopped hard-boiled eggs
2 oz. margarine	4 oz. soft breadcrumbs
2 oz. flour	pinch of mixed herbs
$\frac{3}{4}$ pint milk	
4 oz. grated cheese seasoning	

Prepare the marrow as recipe 1 and then fill with the stuffing, made by adding the other ingredients to the thick cheese sauce.

To stuff peppers (capsicums)

Halve the peppers, remove the core and seeds. Put for five minutes only in boiling salted water, strain. Put the peppers into a well-greased dish, fill with the stuffing. Either of the stuffings given under marrow is suitable for filling four halved peppers. Cover with greased foil and cook for approximately 30 minutes in a moderate oven, 375°F.—Gas Mark 4–5.

To stuff aubergines (egg plants)

Wipe and halve four egg plants, or two very large egg plants. Scoop out the centre pulp.

Chop this finely and mix with the stuffing. Select either the stuffing in marrow No. 1 or No. 2. Put into a well-greased dish, fill with the stuffing. Cover with greased foil and cook for approximately 30 minutes in a moderate oven, 375°F.—Gas Mark 4–5.

Aubergines have a slightly bitter taste. This is lessened if they are sprinkled with salt and left a short time before cooking.

Stuffed tomatoes

For a main dish allow 8 large tomatoes. Cut a slice from each, scoop out the pulp. Chop, and add to either of the prepared stuffings given under stuffed marrow. Press the stuffing firmly into the seasoned tomato cases, then replace the slices of tomato. If any stuffing is left, it can be baked separately to serve with them. Place the tomatoes in a greased dish and cook for approximately 20 minutes in the centre of a very moderate to moderate oven, 350–375°F.— Gas Mark 4, until the tomatoes are soft but unbroken.

Cooking potatoes

Although potatoes are eaten more often than any other vegetable, it is surprising how few varieties of cooked potatoes are served. The recipes in the potato table (page 113) are additional to those given in the previous books.

Preparing Parisienne potatoes

Vegetable cutlets

12 oz. cooked mixed vegetables*	2 oz. breadcrumbs seasoning
White sauce:	*To coat:*
1 oz. butter or vegetable fat	1 beaten egg
1 oz. flour	2 oz. crisp breadcrumbs
¼ pint milk	*To fry:*
3 oz. grated cheese (optional)	little fat or oil
	④

*Diced carrot, turnip, peas, diced beans, diced onion, etc.

Drain the vegetables very thoroughly. Add to the sauce made with the butter or fat, flour and milk. Stir in the rest of the ingredients, divide the mixture into four large or eight smaller portions, form into cutlet shapes. Brush with the beaten egg, coat with the crumbs and fry in the hot fat until crisp and golden brown, or cook on a greased baking sheet in a hot oven, 425–450°F.—Gas Mark 6–7, for approximately 15 minutes until crisp and brown.

Lentil cutlets

8 oz. lentils	1 teaspoon sage
2 oz. vegetarian fat	seasoning
or oil for frying	1 egg
2 chopped onions	*To coat:*
2 large tomatoes	2 oz. breadcrumbs,
1 small apple–peeled,	little beaten egg
cored and chopped	*To fry:*
2 oz. breadcrumbs	fat or oil ④

Soak the lentils overnight in cold water. Cook in the same water until they are soft and the water absorbed. Beat until smooth. Heat the fat and fry the onions, skinned tomatoes and apple until quite soft. Add to the lentils together with the breadcrumbs, sage and seasoning. Bind with the egg and form into cutlet shapes. Roll in breadcrumbs after brushing with a little beaten egg and fry or bake in a hot oven 425–450°F.—Gas Mark 6–7 until crisp and brown—approximately 15 minutes.

Bacon potato cakes

8 oz. sieved or well-	little flour
mashed potatoes	*To fry:*
2 rashers fried bacon	1 oz. fat ④

Blend the potatoes with the finely chopped bacon. If necessary, add a little flour to make a firm consistency. Form into four flat cakes with floured hands. Fry in hot fat until crisp.

Tomato and cauliflower fritters

1 cauliflower	1 egg
For the batter:	*To fry:*
3 large tomatoes	fat or oil
cauliflower stock	*To coat:*
3 oz. flour, preferably	2 oz. grated Cheddar
plain	cheese
seasoning	④–⑥

Cook the cauliflower sprigs in boiling salted water until just tender. Strain and retain the stock. Skin the tomatoes and rub through a sieve or put into an electric blender to give a pulp. Add to it enough cauliflower stock to make $\frac{1}{4}$ pint. Blend the flour, seasoning and egg with the tomato mixture. Heat the fat and test as page 75. Dip the sprigs of cauliflower in the batter and fry for a few minutes until crisp and brown. Drain on absorbent paper and sprinkle with the cheese. Excellent as a light supper dish or with cold meat.

Ways with potatoes

Ingredients refer to 1 lb. potatoes (weight when peeled)

Name of dish	Method	Name of dish	Method
SCALLOPED	Slice potatoes, put in layers in an ovenproof dish with seasoning, 2 oz. of butter, $\frac{1}{2}$ pint milk. Cook very slowly in a cool oven, 250°F. Gas Mark $\frac{1}{2}$ OR cook approximately $1\frac{1}{4}$-$1\frac{1}{2}$ hours in a very moderate oven, 300-350°F. Gas Mark 2-3, OR cook for approximately 1 hour in a moderate to moderately hot oven, 375-400°F. Gas Mark 4-5. The slower these are cooked, however, the nicer they are. Garnish with chopped parsley. Grated cheese may be added to this dish.	LYONNAISE	Half-cook the potatoes, then slice. Chop or slice 8 oz. onions thinly, fry for five minutes in 2 oz. of fat, add the potatoes, continue cooking until tender. Garnish with chopped parsley.
		CROQUETTES	Mash potatoes, adding little milk, butter or margarine. Form into fingers. Coat with 1 oz. seasoned flour, then a beaten egg and 2 oz. crisp breadcrumbs. Fry in deep fat (see page 75). Temperature of fat is very important, so test carefully.
SAUTÉ	Boil potatoes, slice, fry in 2 oz. hot fat until brown on either side, garnish with chopped parsley.	ANNA	Cut potatoes in slices the thickness of a shilling. Put into greased tin, season each layer and brush with melted dripping or butter. Cook for approximately 1 hour below the centre of a moderately hot to hot oven, 400-425°F. Gas Mark 5-6, until the potatoes are tender and the top layer brown. Turn out of the tin and garnish with chopped parsley.
DUCHESSE	Mash the potatoes with 1-2 oz. butter or margarine, add seasoning and 1-2 egg yolks, no milk. Put a $\frac{1}{2}$-1 inch rose pipe into a cloth bag. Half fill the bag with the potatoes, pipe into desired shape on greased ovenproof dish or tin. Brush with egg white to glaze, heat and brown for a short time in the oven.	PARISIENNE	Scoop out balls of raw potato as in the picture (page 111). Roast in hot oil or fat for 30-40 minutes in a moderate to moderately hot oven 375-400°F. Gas Mark 5-6. If preferred, however, they may be fried as a chipped potato.

8. SALADS AND SANDWICHES

BOOK 2 gave suggestions for preparing the more usual ingredients for a salad and ideas for various salads. Salads lend themselves to infinite variety, for example: use fruit for contrasting flavour, texture and colour. This picture shows a sausagemeat salad with diced potato, dessert apple, chopped gherkin and stuffed olives, mixed with mayonnaise. Fruit is particularly good with meat and cheese.

Use grated, finely diced or shredded raw vegetables, such as carrots, turnips, swedes, cabbage, celery, to retain the maximum of vitamins. Try new vegetables: sliced red or green peppers (capsicums), chicory, celeriac.

Flavour the salad or dressing with chopped herbs—parsley, chives, mint, fresh thyme, are particularly good.

Rice in salads

Rice is an excellent ingredient for a sustaining as well as interesting salad. Choose long or medium grain, but never round grain rice. Cook until just tender (page 108) strain and mix with diced vegetables and/or fish, and/or chicken or meat. The rice has a better flavour if tossed in mayonnaise or French dressing while still warm.

Stuffed eggs

Hard-boiled eggs are a more interesting ingredient in a salad when stuffed, e.g.

(a) Halve and blend the yolk with a little butter or mayonnaise, curry powder and chutney.

(b) Halve and blend the yolk with mashed sardine and lemon juice.

(c) Picture page 195—blend the yolk with mayonnaise and prawns.

(d) Blend the yolk with finely chopped or minced ham and mayonnaise.
Pile the filling back again in the white cases and serve on a bed of salad.

Sandwich fillings

The two previous books in this series give suggestions for sandwiches. Here are some additional ideas:

Rolled sandwiches: Choose really fresh bread, butter it lightly and remove the crusts. Put the sandwich filling on top or use well-drained asparagus tips, and roll firmly. Keep covered with a cloth to prevent the sandwiches becoming unrolled.

Ribbon sandwiches: Use equal quantities of buttered white and buttered brown bread. Make sandwiches of one white and one brown slice, top with more sandwich filling and another sandwich of white and brown. Cut into long narrow fingers, so the sandwiches look like striped ribbons.

Sandwich whirls: Cut thin slices of fresh bread and butter—it saves time if the sandwich loaf is cut lengthways. Spread with the sandwich filling, roll as a Swiss roll, then cut into slices.

New sandwich fillings

1. Mix 2 tablespoons cream cheese with 1 tablespoon sultanas (moistened with a little

Rolled sandwiches. One end of each roll has been dipped in chopped parsley

lemon juice). If cream cheese is not available, grate 2 oz. Cheddar cheese, gradually work in 1 tablespoon of evaporated milk, or cream, and seasoning.

2. Mix together 2 oz. cream cheese, 2 oz. chopped dates and 1 dessertspoon chopped nuts. This is particularly good with malt bread.

3. Mix together 2 oz. cream cheese or pounded Gorgonzola cheese with 2 teaspoons finely

chopped or grated onion and 1 good teaspoon of sweet chutney.

4. Mix together 1 oz. margarine, 1 oz. finely grated cheese, 2 tablespoons chopped watercress, few drops lemon juice and seasoning. There is no need to use butter with this filling.

5. Mix together 2 oz. grated cheese, 1 dessertspoon chopped nuts and one sweet apple (finely grated). Add a pinch of sugar and work together until smooth.

6. Bacon sandwiches—cut pieces of bread the size of the rashers of bacon. Do not butter the bread. Grill or fry the bacon and put it on to the bread while still hot. Cover with another slice of bread and when all the sandwiches are ready, put under a bread board with a weight on top for a short time. This makes them into neat shapes and holds the sandwiches together.

7. Mix 2 oz. flaked corned beef with a skinned tomato. Pound into a smooth paste, then add a good pinch curry powder and a few drops Worcestershire sauce.

8. Mix 2 oz. liver sausage or 2 oz. finely minced cooked liver with $\frac{1}{2}$ oz. margarine, 2 teaspoons grated onion and 1 teaspoon chopped parsley.

9. Mix 2 oz. chopped ham with $\frac{1}{2}$ oz. margarine, 1 teaspoon capers, 2 teaspoons finely chopped gherkins or cucumber and seasoning. This makes the ham go further and tastes delicious.

10. Mix 4 oz. cooked hard roe—either herring or cod—with 1 oz. margarine, 1 tablespoon chopped watercress, few drops lemon juice and seasoning. Use no butter on bread.

11. Mix 4 oz. cooked hard roe—herring or cod—with $\frac{1}{2}$ teaspoon curry powder, 1 oz. margarine, 1 teaspoon Worcestershire sauce and $\frac{1}{4}$ teaspoon celery salt.

12. Mix cooked and boned kipper with a few drops of lemon juice, good pinch cayenne pepper, 1 tablespoon finely chopped cucumber or gherkin.

Open sandwiches

These are a feature of Scandinavia—Denmark in particular—and their success depends on:

(a) Using plenty of butter, as shown in picture 1. A variety of breads can be used: white, brown, wholemeal or rye bread (generally available from health food stores), or crispbread.

(b) Arranging the basic ingredient—in picture 2 it is canned Danish luncheon meat—neatly on top.

(c) Using a variety of colourful and interesting toppings—pictures 3 and 4 show cream cheese, a twisted orange slice, parsley and prunes being added.

Other simple open sandwiches in the pictures:

5. Lettuce, salami and raw onion rings.

6. Lettuce, sliced Danish Blue cheese and halved, seeded black grapes.

9. SAVOURIES

ALL the recipes in this section are suitable for a light meal. With the exception of the toasted cheese club sandwich and the poached eggs in cheese sauce, they could be served at the end of a meal, in place of or after a sweet. If serving a savoury after a sweet, the portion is very small—that is why suitable recipes are marked 2–4 or 4–8. The first number refers to the portions for a fairly substantial course, the second to the amount served as a savoury at the end of a meal.

Bengal canapés

½ oz. butter	sweet chutney
½ oz. flour	or finely chopped
¼ pint milk	piccalilli
seasoning	2 tablespoons grated
4 fingers bread	cheese
4 oz. cooked ham	*To garnish:*
1 tablespoon cream	parsley and strips
2 tablespoons	of tomato ②–④

Heat the butter gently, remove from the heat and stir in the flour. Return to the heat and cook gently for a few minutes. Remove from the heat, gradually blend in the milk. Bring to the boil, stirring continuously till smooth. Season well. Toast or fry the bread. Finely chop the ham, heat for several minutes in the white sauce, adding the cream. Spread over toast or fried bread, then add the chutney. Cover with grated cheese and put under a hot grill for a few minutes until crisp and golden brown. Serve hot, garnished with parsley and tomato.

Devils on horseback

8 large juicy cooked prunes	2 slices buttered toast
4 long rashers bacon	paprika (red) pepper ②–④

Stone the prunes. Cut each rasher of bacon into half. Wrap round the prune, securing with a cocktail stick. Cook under the grill until the bacon is crisp and brown. Cut the toast into fingers. Serve grilled bacon and prunes on the toast. Dust with paprika pepper.

Angels on horseback
Wrap small piece of bacon round well-seasoned oyster.

English monkey

1 oz. butter	little made mustard
¼ pint milk	few drops
2 oz. breadcrumbs	Worcestershire sauce
4 oz. grated cheese	4 slices toast
1 egg, beaten	*To garnish:*
seasoning	sliced tomato ④–⑧

Heat the butter in a pan. Add the milk and breadcrumbs. When very hot add the grated cheese and the beaten egg. Season well. Add a little made mustard and a few drops of Worcestershire sauce. Stir together until thick and creamy. Pour on to toast. Garnish with tomato.

Poached eggs in cheese sauce

4 oz. mushrooms (omit for a more economical recipe)	1 oz. flour ③–⑥
	pinch of salt
	shake of pepper
1 oz. butter or margarine	¼ level teaspoon dry mustard
4–6 eggs	½ pint milk
Cheese sauce:	tablespoon grated cheese
1 oz. butter or margarine	4 slices of bread

Prepare and slice the mushrooms, fry in the butter or margarine until soft, put in the bottom of an ovenproof dish and keep hot. Prepare the water for the poached eggs but do not cook these until after making the sauce.

Make the cheese sauce (see page 101).

Remove the pan from the heat.

Poach the eggs and while these are cooking, toast the bread under the grill and put on a plate to keep warm. Place the poached eggs on top of the mushrooms or into a hot dish if the mushrooms are being omitted. Re-heat the sauce and spoon carefully over the eggs, sprinkle with the tablespoon grated cheese and put under the grill until this begins to brown. Cut the toast into triangles and arrange on the dish as in the picture.

Six eggs, as in the picture, would serve 3 adults as a main dish; but 1 egg each would be enough for a lighter meal.

Soft roes on toast

8–12 oz. soft roes, fresh or frozen	2 tablespoons milk
	seasoning
2 oz. butter	4 slices of bread ④–⑧

If frozen, allow roes to thaw. Wash and strain to remove all surplus liquid. Put on to large plate with half butter, the milk and seasoning.

Cover with foil or a second plate and place over a pan of boiling water and cook for approximately 10–15 minutes. Toast and butter the bread. Put the roes on the toast and serve.

Soufflé rarebit

2 eggs	pepper
1 oz. butter	2 large slices toast
3 oz. grated cheese	*To garnish:*
1 teaspoon mustard	sprigs of parsley
salt	④

Separate the egg yolks from the whites. Blend the butter with the cheese, seasonings and egg yolks. Stiffly beat whites and fold into the cheese mixture. Spread on toast and set under grill until golden brown. Cut into fingers.

If preferred, toast or fry the bread, spread with the butter, put on the soufflé topping and set for approximately 20–25 minutes in a very moderate oven, 350°F.—Gas Mark 3–4. Garnish with sprigs of parsley.

Welsh Rarebit, one of the traditional savoury dishes, is in Book 2, pages 68–9.

Toasted cheese club sandwich

3 slices white or brown bread	tomato
1–2 oz. Cheddar cheese, thinly sliced	1–2 rashers of grilled bacon
made mustard	lettuce
a few thin slices of	salad cream or mayonnaise ①–②

Toast the bread on both sides. Cover one slice with the cheese and a little mustard, and the thinly sliced tomato. Lay the second slice of toast on top, and then the grilled bacon. Top with a lettuce leaf and a little salad cream or mayonnaise and the third slice of toast. Cut across, and serve at once.

Many toasted sandwiches can be made, e.g.

(a) Sliced ham and sliced cheese.

(b) Mashed sardines and chopped hard-boiled egg.

(c) Flaked canned salmon and chopped gherkin.

(d) Fried bacon and fried egg.

cooked the cheese straws can be threaded through these.

3. Brush with very little egg white. Bake for approximately 7 minutes on lightly greased tins in a hot oven, 425–450°F.—Gas Mark 6–7. Allow to cool slightly on the tins.

Cheese dreams

8 slices bread and butter	2–3 oz. grated cheese fat for frying
8 slices cheese or	④–⑧

Make sandwiches of the bread and butter and cheese, cut into neat fingers and fry in the hot fat until crisp and golden brown.

Fluffy cheese with toast

4 oz. grated Cheddar cheese	4 lightly boiled eggs
4 tablespoons milk	4 slices buttered toast
2 eggs	④

Stir the cheese and milk together in a small pan over a very low heat. When the cheese has melted add the egg yolks and continue cooking slowly until mixture thickens, stirring continuously.

Whip the egg whites stiffly and fold into the cheese mixture. Shell the boiled eggs, place on the toast, put into serving dishes, pour over the fluffy cheese mixture (see picture). Brown lightly under the grill if desired. Serve at once.

Cheese straws

4 oz. plain flour	2½ oz. butter
salt	2 oz. grated cheese
cayenne pepper	1 egg yolk
little dry mustard	egg white

Book 2 gave a cheese-flavoured pastry which can be used for cheese straws, but the following richer pastry produces a much more crisp and delicious cheese straw. These are often served at the end of the meal. Handle carefully. They can be stored in an airtight tin for a long time.

1. Sieve the flour and seasoning together, rub in the butter. Add the cheese and bind with the egg yolk; if necessary add a little water as well.

2. Roll out firmly and cut into thin fingers. Use a little of the pastry to make circles so when

10. OMELETTES

BOOK 2 gave detailed instructions on making a plain omelette and a number of suggested fillings, together with information on looking after and 'seasoning' an omelette pan.

Since every type of omelette is extremely useful at various meals, additional plain omelette recipes are included together with step-by-step directions for the more complicated soufflé omelette.

Plain omelette

3 eggs	water
pinch salt	1 oz. butter
shake of pepper	②–③

If serving this for a main meal, it is sufficient for 2 small portions. For a more generous portion, allow 2 eggs per person. If serving the omelette as an hors d'oeuvre 1 egg per person is sufficient.

Beat the eggs with the seasoning and if using water (this is a matter of personal taste) allow 1 tablespoon to the 3 eggs. Heat the butter in the omelette pan, pour in the eggs and leave for ½ minute until set at the bottom. Hold the handle of the pan in one hand and tilt it slightly. Move the mixture away from the edge of the

pan with either a palette knife or fork. In this way the liquid egg runs to the bottom of the pan, and the omelette cooks quickly. Cook for 2–3 minutes, add the filling, then fold or roll away from the handle. Hold the warm plate or dish in one hand and the omelette pan in the other, then tip the folded omelette on to the plate or dish and serve at once.

In addition to the fillings given in Book 2, these are very interesting ways of serving an omelette:

Omelette aux fines herbes
Mix a pinch dried or teaspoon chopped fresh herbs with the beaten eggs before cooking.
Bacon omelette
Dice 2–3 rashers of bacon (this is an extremely good way of using cheap streaky or bacon pieces), fry until crisp. Add 1 oz. butter and heat, then pour in the eggs and cook in the usual way.
Crisp crust omelette
Use 2 oz. instead of 1 oz. butter. Heat the butter and fry about 1 oz. diced bread until crisp. Pour in the eggs and cook in the usual way.

Soufflé omelette

This type of omelette is very light and fluffy, as the egg whites are whisked stiffly and incorporated into the mixture. A soufflé omelette

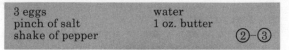

Plain soufflé omelette

3 eggs	water
pinch of salt	1 oz. butter
shake of pepper	②—③

1. Put a plate to warm and have 2 bowls, side by side.
2. Crack the first egg, put the yolk into one bowl and the white into the other.
Repeat this with the second and third eggs, breaking the yolks first into a cup before transferring them into the bowl to make certain they are perfectly fresh.
3. Add the salt and pepper to the egg yolks, then add ½ egg shell of water to each egg, i.e. a total of approximately 1½ tablespoons of water.
4. Beat the yolks with a fork; whisk the egg whites until very stiff and white, add the egg whites to the beaten egg yolks, folding them in carefully with a metal spoon.
5. Heat the butter in an omelette pan, and when hot pour in the eggs.
6. Cook for approximately half a minute until the bottom part of the egg is set, then tilt the pan and move the mixture gently away from the edge and continue like this for 1 minute.
7. While the omelette is cooking, switch on or light the grill. Because the soufflé omelette is so thick, it is almost impossible to get this cooked right through by applying heat under-

Soufflé omelette

may be served plain; it may have a savoury filling or it may have sugar added and a sweet filling put in. This is the most usual way of serving this type of omelette.

neath alone, so transfer the omelette pan under the grill and cook steadily for 2–3 minutes with the heat turned low.

8. When the egg is set on top, add the filling, fold away from the handle and turn out.

Fillings for savoury soufflé omelette
These will be found on page 126.

Sweet soufflé omelette

3 eggs	1 oz. butter
2–3 teaspoons sugar	1 tablespoon icing
1½ tablespoons milk	sugar
or cream	②–③

This is made in the same way as a plain soufflé omelette, except that the egg yolks should be beaten with sugar and milk instead of salt and pepper and water.

When serving, dust lightly on top with a tablespoon of sieved icing sugar.

Fillings for a sweet soufflé omelette

1. *Jam or jelly.* Heat 2–3 tablespoons jam or redcurrant jelly, put into the omelette just before serving.
2. *Fruit.* Cook approximately 4–6 oz. fruit with sugar to taste and a little water until the fruit is soft. Put into the omelette just before serving.
3. *Ice cream.* Put in 2–3 spoonfuls ice cream, fold and serve immediately.

Oven baked omelette

1 oz. butter	1 teaspoon chopped
6 eggs	parsley or chives
2 oz. cheese	seasoning
2 skinned tomatoes	④–⑥

This omelette is based on the Spanish Tortilla. Heat the butter for a few minutes. Beat the eggs, add the grated cheese, thinly sliced tomatoes, parsley and seasoning. Pour into an ovenproof dish and cook for 10–15 minutes in the centre of a hot oven, 425–450°F.—Gas Mark 6–7, until the egg mixture sets.

11. SOUFFLÉS

A SOUFFLÉ is a mixture of sauce, eggs and flavouring. The light texture is given by adding the stiffly beaten egg whites to the prepared mixture.

A soufflé is often considered a rather advanced cooking dish, but it is quite simple if the directions are followed carefully.

The recipes that follow are for hot soufflés—savoury or sweet.

Recipes for cold soufflés are in the gelatine section, pages 167–9.

Basic savoury soufflé

¼ *pint thick white sauce made with:*	3–4 eggs (4 eggs gives a lighter soufflé, or if
1 oz. margarine	you need a spare egg
1 oz. flour (½ oz. for a rather less firm textured soufflé)	yolk in any dish, use the yolks of 3 eggs and the whites of 4)
¼ pint milk	flavouring (see below)
pinch of salt	
shake of pepper	②–③

A savoury soufflé may be served as a main course of a meal, so the quantities given above would be 2–3 really good portions. A cheese soufflé is often served instead of a sweet at the end of a meal, so the amounts given would be enough for 4–6 smaller portions.

Step by step pictures showing the making of a mushroom soufflé are given on page 127.

1. Make the white sauce as page 101.
2. Separate the egg yolks from the egg whites.
3. Remove the saucepan containing the white sauce from the heat, then gradually beat in the egg yolks with a wooden spoon.
4. Add the flavouring (see page 126).
5. Whisk the egg whites until very stiff, fold into the sauce and egg yolk mixture with a metal spoon.
6. Put into a greased 6-inch soufflé dish—a round casserole can be used instead, but the pictures on pages 127–8 show the correct type of soufflé dish to use. This may be obtained in china or ovenproof ware. Stand the soufflé dish on a baking sheet for quick and easy removal from the oven.
7. Smooth the mixture flat with a knife, then put the dish, etc. into the centre of a moderately hot oven (375°F.—Gas Mark 5) and bake for 25 minutes until well risen and golden brown.

N.B. It is important to have the rest of the meal all prepared and the table laid before you bring a soufflé out of the oven, for the correct soufflé mixture containing egg yolks, etc. as given above, will sink when once it comes from the oven.

Flavourings for a savoury soufflé

Do not exceed the amount of flavouring for the soufflé otherwise the mixture becomes too heavy and will not rise properly.

1. *Cheese* (see title page picture). Add 4 oz. finely grated Cheddar cheese to the mixture.
2. *Ham*. Add 2–3 oz. finely chopped cooked ham to the mixture.
3. *Fish*. Add 4 oz. cooked flaked white fish or smoked haddock to the mixture. If using smoked haddock, be sparing with the salt.
4. *Chicken*. Add 3–4 oz. finely chopped cooked chicken to the mixture. Chicken stock may be used in place of milk.
5. *Spinach*. Use 4 tablespoons milk and $\frac{1}{4}$ pint of cooked creamed spinach in place of all milk.
6. *Mushroom*. Chop 2–3 oz. mushrooms finely, fry in $\frac{1}{2}$ oz. margarine or butter until just tender, then add to the thick sauce (see step-by-step pictures opposite).

Basic sweet soufflé

1 level tablespoon cornflour	if you need a spare egg yolk in any dish,
$\frac{1}{4}$ pint milk	use the yolks of
$\frac{1}{2}$–1 oz. butter or margarine	3 eggs and the whites of 4)
2 oz. sugar	flavouring (see below)
3–4 eggs (4 eggs give a lighter soufflé, or	1 tablespoon icing sugar ④

1. Blend the cornflour with the milk until smooth, put into a saucepan and bring the mixture to the boil over a moderate heat, stirring all the time, until thick.
2. Separate the egg yolks from the egg whites.
3. Remove the saucepan containing the sauce from the heat and stir in the butter and sugar, then gradually beat in the egg yolks with a wooden spoon.
4. Add the flavouring (see page 128, picture 1).
5. Whisk the egg whites until really stiff and fold into the sauce and egg yolk mixture with a metal spoon, picture 2.
6. Put into a soufflé dish, stand on a baking sheet and bake as savoury soufflé, page 125.
7. Dust the top of the soufflé with a tablespoon of sieved icing sugar before putting on to the table; make sure the icing sugar is all ready before the soufflé is brought from the oven (see remarks on page 125).

Flavourings for a sweet soufflé

Do not exceed the amount of flavouring, otherwise the mixture becomes too heavy and will not rise properly.

1. *Chocolate*. Either blend 1 oz. sieved cocoa or 2 oz. chocolate powder with the sauce. Since chocolate is sweetened, use a little less sugar. A better flavour is given if $\frac{1}{4}$ teaspoon vanilla essence is also added.

Making a mushroom souff.

2. *Coffee*. Either add 1 level dessertspoon instant coffee powder or 1 tablespoon bottled coffee essence to the milk (picture below) or use ¼ pint strong black coffee in place of milk.

3. *Pineapple*. Open a small can of pineapple, drain the syrup, use ¼ pint of this in place of milk. Chop the fruit finely and add to the sauce when thickened. Because this filling is rather sweet, 1 oz. sugar only need be used.

4. *Lemon or orange*. Add the grated rind of 1–2 lemons or oranges to the cornflour, squeeze the juice and if necessary add enough water to give ¼ pint. Use in place of milk.

What went wrong

1. If the soufflé did not rise as much as planned?
(a) The dish was not sufficiently filled. Choose a soufflé dish where the uncooked mixture comes just to the top.
(b) The weight of flavouring was too great for the amount of eggs used.
(c) The soufflé may not have been adequately cooked. Place just above the centre of the oven so it rises steadily. If it browns too quickly it looks cooked, but is still soft in the centre.

2. If the soufflé dropped very badly before reaching the table?
(a) It may be slightly under-cooked (see above).
(b) You were too slow in carrying it from the kitchen to the table or it was kept waiting.
Some modern soufflé recipes omit the egg yolks. If you use the whites only the soufflé does not drop, but naturally it does not contain as much protein food or flavour.

3. If the soufflé was rather tough and leathery?
It was cooked too slowly.

1   2   *Making a coffee soufflé*   **3**

12. BATTERS

PANCAKES are a general favourite, whether served as a sweet or a savoury. Book 2 gave detailed information on making and cooking pancakes and looking after the pan.

Basic pancake batter

4 oz. flour, plain or self-raising pinch salt	1 egg (a second egg gives a richer batter) ½ pint milk or milk and water

The mixture is beaten into a smooth batter, then small quantities are fried in a very little hot oil or fat until crisp and brown on either side.

The pictures show two interesting ways of serving pancakes. Picture 1—layer pancakes, in which cooked fish, cooked meat, cooked vegetables are heated in a cheese sauce then put between cooked pancakes.

Picture 2 shows pancakes filled with a mixture of fried tomato and fried mushrooms and topped with fried mushrooms.

For more suggestions, see Book 2.

The principle of making a batter is also used in fruit fritters, popovers, Scotch pancakes or drop scones and French or saucer pancakes, all given in this chapter.

129

Fruit Fritters

4 oz. self-raising flour (or plain flour and 1 level teaspoon baking powder)	1 oz. melted butter (optional) Fruit (see below)
pinch salt	*To coat fruit:*
1 oz. sugar	½ oz. flour
1 egg	*For frying:*
¼ pint milk or milk and water	oil or fat* *To coat:* 1 oz. castor sugar (4)

*lard, pure cooking fat.

1. Sieve the dry ingredients together, add the egg.
2. Gradually beat in the milk.
3. Lastly add the butter. This is not essential but it does give a more crisp batter (oil could be used instead).
4. Heat the oil or fat—use either shallow or deep fat—instructions for testing the correct heat are on pages 75-6.
5. Dip the fruit in the flour—this makes sure the batter clings to the fruit—then in the batter—the easiest way to do this is to insert a fine skewer in each piece of fruit.
6. Lower the fruit into the fat and fry steadily—too rapid cooking browns the outside of the batter but does not heat or cook the fruit.
7. Lift from the oil or fat and drain on crumpled tissue or kitchen paper.
8. Sprinkle with the sugar and serve at once.

Fruit to use for fritters

Apple: Allow 4 medium or 2 very large cooking apples of good quality; peel, core and cut into thin slices.
Banana: Use very small whole bananas or halve large bananas; allow 6 small bananas for 4 people.
Pineapple: Drain canned pineapple rings thoroughly; allow 1–2 rings per person.

Popovers

4 oz. flour	and water
pinch of salt	approximately ½ oz.
1 egg	fat
¼ pint milk or milk	④

Make the pancake batter; it will be considerably thicker than for an ordinary pancake. Allow it to stand in a cold place. Grease 8 or 9 rather deep patty tins. Put towards the top of a hot oven, 425°F.—Gas Mark 6, and heat for 5 minutes. Bring the very hot tins out of the oven. Put a spoonful of the batter into each hot tin and return to the hot oven and cook for approximately 12–15 minutes until well risen and brown. Turn out of the tins as quickly as possible and serve.
Here are ways of serving popovers:

Sweet

Jam popovers: Heat 2 good tablespoons of jam in a saucepan. Put the popovers on to a hot dish and fill the centres with jam.
Fruit popovers: Heat fruit in a saucepan or use a small amount of canned fruit. Put the popovers on to a hot dish and fill with the fruit. Serve at once.
Honey and raisin popovers: Put the hot popovers on to a dish and fill the centres with a little honey and seedless raisins.

Savoury

Cheese popovers: Add a good teaspoon of grated cheese to the top of each cooked popover, return to the oven for 2–3 minutes to melt the cheese. Serve with baked or raw tomatoes.
Bean popovers: While the popovers are cooking in the oven, open a small or medium-sized can of baked beans in tomato sauce. Heat these gently. Bring the popovers out of the oven and fill the centre of each popover with the hot baked beans. Serve with a green salad.
Fish or meat heated in a sauce could be used as a filling.

Saucer pancakes

2 oz. butter or margarine	squeeze of lemon juice
2 oz. sugar	1 oz. fat for greasing tins
2 eggs	
2 oz. rice flour or plain self-raising flour	*To coat:* little sugar
12 tablespoons milk	*To fill:* jam ④-⑥

Cream the butter and sugar until soft and light. Separate the eggs, beat in the yolks, fold in the flour, milk and lemon juice. The mixture may curdle, but in this particular recipe it is quite unimportant. Grease approximately 12 ovenproof flat tins or saucers. Heat for 5 minutes in a hot oven (425–450°F.—Gas Mark 6–7). Fold the stiffly beaten egg whites into the batter mixture, divide between the hot tins and bake for approximately 10–15 minutes towards the top of the oven. Turn out on to sugared paper, then sandwich together with hot jam.

Drop scones or Scotch pancakes

4 oz. flour (with plain flour use either 2 teaspoons baking powder or ½ small teaspoon bicarbonate of soda and 1 small teaspoon cream of tartar)	pinch of salt 1 oz. sugar 1 egg ¼ pint milk 1 oz. melted margarine (not essential) ⑫–⑱

Sieve together dry ingredients. Beat in the egg, then the milk. Lastly, stir in the melted margarine. This is not essential but helps to keep the scones moist. Grease and warm the girdle, electric hot-plate or frying pan. It is best to turn the frying pan upside down and use the base—the part that usually goes over the heat. It must be very clean. To test for correct heat, drop a teaspoon of the mixture on this and if it goes golden brown within 1 minute the plate is ready. Drop spoonfuls of the batter on to the plate. Cook for about 2 minutes, then turn and cook for a further 2 minutes. To test whether cooked, press firmly with the back of a knife, and if no batter comes from the sides and the scones feel firm, cool on a wire sieve. The pancakes keep more moist if wrapped in a clean teacloth on the sieve. They can be served with butter, jam, or are delicious as a sweet, if served with apple purée.

Baking powder doughnuts
Follow recipe for drop scones, but use 4 tablespoons milk only. Drop spoonfuls of batter into hot fat and fry for 4 minutes on either side until crisp and golden brown. Drain well, split and fill with jam, then roll in castor sugar.

13. PASTRY

BOOK 2 gave detailed instructions for short crust pastry and economical sweet and cheese crust based on this, also suet crust pastry and rough puff pastry.

This chapter completes the information on pastry-making with details of flaky and puff pastry, which are both similar to rough puff in their method of handling and rolling (Book 2, pages 188–9). A quick short crust pastry using the easy-to-handle modern fat or margarine is given on page 139; rich flan pastry is on page 140; choux pastry, with many ways of using it, is on pages 147–9.

Hot water crust pastry appears at the end of the meat section, on page 99.

Flaky pastry

8 oz. plain flour	water to mix
pinch salt	squeeze lemon juice
5–6 oz. fat*	(optional)

*Fats to use: all butter; all margarine; a mixture of margarine or butter and cooking fat or lard.

Sieve flour with salt (picture 1 overleaf). Divide the fat into 3 portions. Rub one portion into the flour in usual way and mix to rolling consistency with cold water, adding a little lemon juice if wished. Roll out to oblong shape. Now take the second portion of fat, divide it into small pieces and lay them on the surface of two-thirds of the dough (picture 2). Leave the remaining third without fat. Take its two corners and fold back over second third so that the dough looks like an envelope with its flap open (picture 3). Fold over top end of pastry, so closing the 'envelope'. Turn pastry at right angles, seal open ends of pastry and 'rib' it, to give a corrugated effect (picture 4). This equalises the pressure of air, and makes certain that the pastry will rise evenly. Repeat the process again, using the remaining fat and turning pastry in the same way. Roll out the pastry once more, but should it begin to feel very soft and sticky put it into a cold place for 30 minutes to become firm before rolling out. Fold pastry as before, turn it, seal edges and 'rib' it once more. Altogether the pastry should have three foldings and three rollings. It is then ready to stand in a cold place for a little while before baking.

Flaky pastry needs a very hot oven to make it rise. Individual recipes give full details.

Some uses for flaky pastry

Flaky pastry may be used in place of puff pastry or rough puff pastry (Book 2). It is particularly suitable for steak and kidney pie, sausage rolls (Book 2) and for mince pies (page 137).

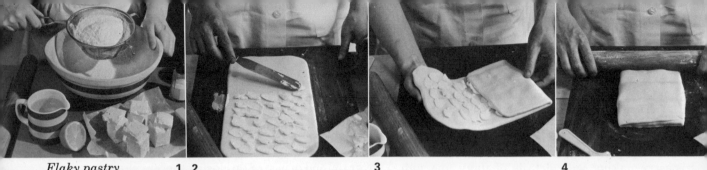

Flaky pastry 1 2 3 4

Puff pastry

8 oz. plain flour	few drops lemon juice
good pinch salt	7–8 oz. fat*
cold water to mix	

*Use: all butter, half butter, half margarine, or mixture as flaky pastry.

Sieve flour and salt together. Mix to rolling consistency with cold water and lemon juice, and roll to an oblong shape. Make fat into a neat block and place in the centre of the pastry and over it fold first the bottom section of pastry and then the top section, so that the fat is quite covered. Turn the dough at right angles, seal the edges, 'rib' carefully (see flaky pastry, page 133) and roll out. Fold the dough into an envelope, turn it, seal the edges, 'rib' and roll again. Repeat this process 5 times, making in all 7 rollings and 7 foldings. To prevent the pastry becoming sticky and soft it must be put to rest in a cold place once or twice between rollings. Always put it to rest before rolling it

for the last time, and before baking.
Puff pastry must be baked in a very hot oven to make it rise and prevent any of the fat from running out—see the individual recipes.

Some uses for puff pastry

Puff pastry can be used for meat or fruit pies, mince pies, etc., but it is particularly successful in the following recipes.
Where a recipe says 8 oz. puff pastry it means pastry made with 8 oz. flour, etc., so 1 lb. frozen puff pastry must be substituted.

Vol-au-vent or Bouchée cases

8 oz. puff pastry will produce:
1 really large vol-au-vent case enough for
6 portions when filled OR
6–8 large individual cases OR
12 medium sized cases OR
24 tiny cocktail sized bouchées

Method 1

Roll out the pastry until just under $\frac{1}{2}$ inch thick. Cut into rounds. From half the rounds make a circle by cutting out the centre. Place the circle on top of complete round. Seal edges and put on to *damp* baking trays. Glaze with beaten egg.

Method 2

Roll out the pastry until a good $\frac{3}{4}$–1 inch thick. Cut into rounds or one required shape. Put on to a *damp* baking tray. With a smaller cutter press half way through the pastry. Glaze with beaten egg.

Bake in a very hot oven 450–475°F., Gas Mark 8–9 for 15–25 minutes depending on size, until quite brown. Tiny cases for cocktail parties need about 10 minutes; with large cases lower the heat after 10–15 minutes to moderate.

Lift the cases off the tins and with the help of a sharp pointed knife carefully take out the centre ring of pastry. You will find this has shrunk during cooking and it is not difficult.

Put the outer cases back in the oven for a few minutes to dry out, reducing heat to moderate.

Savoury fillings for vol-au-vent cases.

(a) Minced or chopped chicken in a well-seasoned thick white sauce

(b) Cooked mushrooms in thick white sauce.

(c) Shell fish in a white sauce, mayonnaise or mixed with lightly scrambled eggs.

(d) Thick cheese sauce.

(e) Cream cheese and chopped cucumber.

(f) Thick meat or vegetable creamy mixture.

(g) Steak and kidney.

If serving cold, allow pastry to cool before adding filling.

If serving hot, put hot filling into hot pastry at the last minute.

Sweet fillings for vol-au-vent cases

(a) Thick fruit purée and whipped cream.

(b) Vanilla cream filling topped with jam.

(c) Jam or jelly with cream or packet topping.

Jam puffs

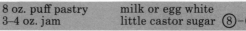

8 oz. puff pastry	milk or egg white	
3–4 oz. jam	little castor sugar	⑧-⑩

Vol-au-vent cases filled with jam

135

Roll out the puff pastry until very thin, cut into squares. Put a small amount of jam in the centre of each square, brush the edges with water then fold to make a triangle. Seal the edges firmly. Brush with a little milk or egg white and sprinkle with sugar.

Bake for 10–15 minutes just above the centre of a very hot oven (475°F.—Gas Mark 8–9) until crisp.

Mille-feuilles or vanilla slices

8 oz. puff pastry will make:
1 large shape OR
8–12 individual slices
Roll out the puff pastry until the thickness of a shilling.

For a large shape cut into 2 or 3 equal sized rounds, squares or oblong shapes. For individual slices cut into 16–24 fingers or 8–12 *slightly* thicker fingers that may be split and filled.
Bake as vol-au-vent cases.
When cold, cut the sides to neaten edges if wished.
Fill with whipped or mock cream, crème chantilly, vanilla cream filling (page 170), and fruit or jam.
Top with fruit and cream or sieved icing sugar or glacé icing made with 4–6 oz. icing sugar, etc.

Cream horns

8 oz. puff pastry*	*To fill:*
little milk	little jam, ¼ pint
egg white (optional)	whipped or mock
little castor sugar	cream
*or use rough puff as	*To decorate:*
in picture	1 oz. sieved icing
	sugar (12)–(16)

Roll out the pastry to the thickness of a shilling and cut into long strips 1 inch wide. By cutting these strips 'on the cross' you will achieve a better shaped cornet. Brush lightly with milk at the joins and roll carefully round the horn cases, being careful not to stretch the pastry. Brush with a little more milk, or use egg white, and dust with castor sugar. Bake for 10–15 minutes near the top of a very hot oven (475°F.

—Gas Mark 8–9). Cool slightly, then gently withdraw the cases. When quite cold, fill with jam and cream. Dust with icing sugar.

Mincemeat

Do not cut down on the quantities of sugar, fat or spirit if you wish this to keep well. Make quite certain the fruit is dry. Where fruit has been washed, let it dry for at least 24 hours before making the mincemeat.

4 oz. shredded suet	½ teaspoon grated
4 oz. grated apple	nutmeg
1 lb. mixed dried fruit	4 oz. mixed peel
1 teaspoon mixed	4 oz. blanched and
spice	well dried almonds
½ teaspoon cinnamon	finely grated rind
4 oz. sugar	and juice of 1 lemon
(preferably	4 tablespoons brandy,
Demerara)	whisky or rum

Mix all the ingredients together. Put into dry jam jars and cover thoroughly. Leave in a cool dry place. (Mincemeat can last for months if it is correctly made.)
This makes nearly 2½ lb. of mincemeat and 1 lb. fills approximately 24 mince pies.

Mince pies

8 oz. short, flaky or puff pastry	Approximately 6–8 oz. mincemeat ⑫

Roll out the pastry. Use a cutter a little larger than the size of the patty tins and press the rounds of pastry into each tin. Place a spoonful of mincemeat on each round. Do not be too generous or the filling will boil out and make the tarts sticky. Cut out 12 rounds for the lids, making these a little smaller than the cases. Press top and bottom edges together. Make a slit on the lids with kitchen scissors or a sharp knife. Bake for 20–25 minutes above centre of a hot oven, 425–450°F.—Gas Mark 6–7 reducing the heat after 15 minutes, if necessary.

Lemon meringue pie

6 oz. short crust, sweet short crust or flaky pastry	1–2 oz. butter or margarine
1½ level tablespoons cornflour	3–4 oz. sugar
	2 large eggs
or custard powder	grated rind of
water	2 lemons
juice of 2 lemons	*Meringue:*
	2–4 oz. sugar ⑥

Take a 7–8 inch *deep* flan ring or sandwich tin, or a 1–1½ pint pie-dish and line it with the pastry. Blend the cornflour or custard powder with the cold water and lemon juice to give ½ pint. Put into a saucepan and cook gently until thickened. Add the butter or margarine, sugar, egg yolks and the very finely grated 'zest' of the lemon rind. Cook very gently for a few minutes, but do not boil.

Pour into the pastry case. Whisk the egg whites stiffly, fold in all the sugar, page 189.

If serving the pie hot, bake for approximately 20 minutes in the centre of a very moderate oven, 325–350°F.—Gas Mark 3–4.

If serving cold, bake for approximately 1 hour in a very slow oven, 250–275°F.—Gas Mark ½–1 so the meringue remains crisp.

An even better result is obtained when wishing to serve cold if 4 oz. sugar is used in the meringue.

Orange meringue pie: Use 2 oranges in place of the lemons.

Dutch apple squares

8 oz. short crust pastry	1 oz. brown sugar
Apple filling:	1 level teaspoon cinnamon
1½ lb. cooking apples	*To decorate:*
2 tablespoons black treacle	little icing sugar ⑫

Make and roll out the pastry into two oblong shapes to fit a small Swiss Roll tin. Line the tin with greaseproof paper. Put in one oblong of pastry. Peel, core and slice the apples. Mix with black treacle, sugar and cinnamon and spread over the pastry. Moisten the edges of the pastry with water and top with the second piece of pastry. Press down gently along the edges to seal. Bake in the centre of a hot oven, 425–450°F.—Gas Mark 6–7 for 15 minutes, and

then at very moderate, 350°F.—Gas Mark 3–4 for approximately 30 minutes until the pie is evenly brown and the apple is tender. Allow to cool slightly. Lift the pie out of the tin by gently raising the greaseproof paper. Sieve the icing sugar over the top. Cut into squares, serve with cream. (See picture above.)

Eccles cakes

8 oz. puff, flaky or rough puff pastry	grated rind and juice of 1 lemon
Filling:	good pinch mixed spice
2 oz. margarine	*To glaze:*
2 oz. sugar	little milk, castor sugar
2 oz. sultanas	
2 oz. currants	
2 oz. chopped candied peel	⑧–⑩

Roll the pastry out until it is about the thickness of a shilling. Cut into large round shapes.

Cream the margarine and sugar together, then work in all the ingredients. Put a spoonful of this mixture on one half of the pastry. Fold over, then press the edges very firmly together. If necessary, brush with a little milk to seal. Shape with a rolling pin and fingers until round. Make 2 or 3 splits on the top of each cake. Brush lightly with milk and castor sugar. Bake in the centre of a hot oven, 425–450°F.— Gas Mark 6–7 for about 20 minutes. After 15 minutes the heat can be reduced if the cakes are becoming too brown.

Banbury cakes ⑧-⑩
Add 2 oz. cake or macaroon biscuit crumbs to Eccles cake filling. Make as Eccles cakes but in an oval shape, *not* a round.

Eccles cakes

Quick short crust pastry

3½–4 oz. fat* 3 tablespoons water	8 oz. flour—plain or self-raising pinch salt

* Use 3½ oz. modern fat (shortening) or 4 oz. quick-creaming margarine, often called luxury margarine.

Because the modern cooking fats and margarines soften so rapidly, you can use this quick method to make pastry. In a mixing bowl place cooking fat or margarine in one piece, water and 2 rounded tablespoons of the sieved flour and salt. Whisk together with a fork for about half a minute until well mixed and fluffy. Add remaining flour and stir to form into a firm dough. Knead very lightly on a flour dusted board, moulding to a smooth ball. Roll out and use in the same way as short crust pastry.

Rich flan pastry

5 oz. butter*	pinch salt
2 oz. sugar	egg yolk water
8 oz. flour	to bind

*Table, luxury or superfine margarine.

Cream together fat and sugar until light in colour. Sieve flour and salt together and add to creamed fat, mixing with a knife. Gradually add enough water or egg and water to make a dough with a firm rolling consistency. Use fingertips to gather the pastry together and knead lightly. Roll out lightly and carefully, since this pastry is very brittle.

Fruit flan

5–6 oz. short crust,	little water and sugar
sweet short crust or	or frozen fruit
rich flan pastry	Glaze as selected
1 large can fruit	(pages 143–4)
or ¾–1 lb. fruit with a	

While short crust or sweet short crust pastry can be used, richer flan pastry is better as it remains crisp when cold.

Quantities to allow

The ingredients in the coloured panel are for a 7–8 inch flan. The following assume it is a fairly deep flan case, and the pastry is moderately thick.

For a 6–7 inch flan allow 4–5 oz. pastry.
For a 7–8 inch flan allow 5–6 oz. pastry.
For an 8–9 inch flan allow 6–7 oz. pastry.
For a 9–10 inch flan allow 7–8 oz. pastry.

To make and fill a flan

Make the pastry, line the flan case (see below) and bake 'blind', see page 240. If using short or sweet short crust pastry a hot oven, 425–450°F. —Gas Mark 6–7, is correct.

If using rich flan pastry it is advisable to use a moderately hot oven, 400°F.—Gas Mark 5–6. The best position for a flan case is just above the centre of the oven.

While the pastry is cooking, prepare the fruit:

1. *Canned fruit*—drain the fruit over a fine sieve so that it is quite dry and no syrup is wasted. To make sure it is very dry, the fruit could be put on kitchen paper before actually going into the flan.

2. *Cooked fruit*—make a syrup of approximately ½ pint water and 2–3 oz. sugar. Bring to the boil and then put in the prepared fruit. Simmer very gently until just soft but not broken. Lift out and drain as for canned fruit. Cool.

3. *Frozen fruit*—allow to defrost but not to become over-defrosted. Drain as canned fruit but when making the glaze allow a little less

Quiche Lorrai

liquid since there will be further defrosting while the fruit actually stands in the pastry case.

4. *Fruit that does not need cooking*, such as strawberries, cherries, etc. In order to sweeten the fruit, put it in the glaze (see below) for a few minutes. Lift out, drain and proceed as for other fruit.

Arrange the well drained cold fruit in the cold pastry case.

Make the glaze and allow this to cool but not become too thick, then spoon or brush over the fruit.

To line a flan case

Roll out the pastry to an approximate size—measure this by laying the ring or tin over the pastry and allow an extra 1–1½ inches around the edge.

Grease a sandwich tin lightly. A flan ring, unless new, need not be greased. If using a flan ring, stand this on an upturned baking tin to facilitate removal when baked. Support the pastry over the rolling pin and lower into the sandwich tin or flan ring. Press down firmly to the base and against the sides. Either cut away the surplus pastry, or roll over the top of the ring and the pastry drops away easily. The case is then ready. Fill and bake, or bake 'blind'. (See page 240 and picture above.)

Small tarts or flans

These are made and filled in the same way as large ones. Bake the individual pastry cases 'blind' for 10–12 minutes only, cool then fill with fruit and glaze.

The picture on page 142 shows cooked apples and cooked pears blended with preserved ginger and topped with cornflour glaze (page 144).

Glazes for fruit flans

Glazes are used to keep the fruit moist and give an attractive appearance.

The quantities given are sufficient for a 7–8 inch flan. If a thicker layer is required, then use a greater quantity of ingredients.

individual apple, pear and ginger flans

Glaze with arrowroot or cornflour

$\frac{1}{4}$ pint liquid*	arrowroot
1 level teaspoon	2–3 drops vegetable
cornflour or	colouring (optional)

*The liquid can either be the syrup from cooked fruit or canned fruit or water flavoured with a little lemon juice and sweetened to taste.

Blend the ingredients together until smooth. Put into a saucepan and boil until thickened and clear—approximately 4–5 minutes.
Add 2–3 drops vegetable colouring if the mixture looks very pale.

Glaze with flavoured jelly mixture or gelatine

$\frac{1}{4}$ flavoured jelly tablet or 1 level teaspoon powdered gelatine	$\frac{1}{4}$ pint liquid few drops vegetable colouring

Dissolve the jelly tablet or gelatine in the very hot liquid. Allow to cool and begin to stiffen slightly. Add a few drops of colouring if necessary.

French apricot flan ⑥-⑧

The pictures show another interesting way of making a flan.
Picture 1: Make and roll out 8 oz. rich flan pastry.
Picture 2: Form most of this into a neat oblong shape, but cut out the remainder to give two bands to fit at either side. Bake as a flan, page 140.
Picture 3: Top with either $\frac{1}{2}$–$\frac{3}{4}$ pint thick cold custard or vanilla cream filling—use double the quantity in the recipe, page 170.
Picture 4: Finally top with a medium-sized can of well drained apricot halves—these may be covered with a glaze as above if wished.

1   **2**   **3**   **4**

Custard tart or flan

5–6 oz. short or sweet short crust pastry	1 oz. sugar
	½ pint milk
Filling:	a little grated
2 egg yolks or whole eggs	nutmeg or a few drops of vanilla essence ④–⑥

Roll out the pastry and line a sandwich tin, pie-plate or 7–8 inch flan ring.

A custard tart is difficult to bake since the custard needs a more moderate heat than the pastry, and sometimes the pastry rises and the custard sinks. There are two methods of dealing with this.

1. Bake the pastry 'blind' (page 240) for 10 minutes in a hot oven, then add the warm custard. Lower the heat to very moderate, 325–350°F.—Gas Mark 3 and bake for approximately 30 minutes until the custard is set. Top with a little grated nutmeg.

2. Brush the pastry case with egg white then pour in the cold custard. Bake for 10 minutes in a hot oven, see above, then for 35–40 minutes in a very moderate oven. Top with a little grated nutmeg.

To make the custard

Beat the egg yolks or eggs and sugar. Pour over the milk, strain if necessary.

If preferred, the nutmeg may be omitted and the custard flavoured with vanilla essence.

Biscuit crumb crust

It is possible to line a flan ring or baking dish with a crust made of biscuit or cornflake crumbs, etc.

The following recipe gives one good biscuit crumb crust which can be varied by adding flavouring, grated lemon rind, spice, etc., or using other biscuits. It is not essential to bake this mixture—it can be formed into the required shape and put into a cool place to set. Baking gives a more crisp crust and one that is easier to cut.

Peach and lemon squares

Crumb crust:	*For the filling:*
3 oz. butter	large can peach slices
6 oz. digestive biscuits	1 lemon
2 oz. castor sugar	*To decorate:*
good pinch cinnamon	1 sliced fresh lemon
	or 12 crystallised lemon slices ⑫

1. Cream or melt the butter—if using this method allow to cool. Crush biscuits to fine crumbs between 2 sheets of greaseproof paper. Stir into the butter with the sugar and cinnamon. Press just over half into a 12 inch by 8 inch greased tin.

2. Drain the juice from the canned peaches, reserve 12 slices for decoration, and chop the remainder. Finely grate the lemon rind. Re-

move the pith and chop the flesh. Mix the chopped lemon and rind into the chopped peaches, and spread this mixture over the crumb crust base. Sprinkle with the remaining crumb crust mixture. Press down lightly with the tips of the fingers.

3. Bake for 35–40 minutes in the centre of a very moderate oven, 350°F.—Gas Mark 3–4, then chill in the tin.

Cut into 12 squares and decorate with a peach and ½ a lemon slice or a crystallised lemon slice. Serve cold with ice cream and the juice from the peaches.

Variations

Use apricots instead of peaches or cooked, well drained apple slices.

Savoury flans

A savoury flan case can be filled in a number of ways. Use short crust or economical cheese crust pastry, Book 2. Make and bake the flan 'blind'.

Here are suggested fillings:

(a) Cooked vegetables in a thick cheese sauce, garnished with hard-boiled eggs and chopped parsley.

(b) Grated raw carrot in a thick cheese sauce, garnished with chopped parsley.

(c) Minced or diced cooked meat in a brown sauce, garnished with sliced tomatoes.

(d) Flaked cooked fish in a white anchovy or cheese sauce, garnished with lemon and prawns. One of the most famous of savoury flans is a Quiche Lorraine, which is a mixture of bacon, eggs, etc.

Quiche Lorraine

6 oz. short crust pastry	seasoning
Filling:	just under ½ pint milk
2–3 rashers bacon	2–3 oz. grated
2 egg yolks or whole eggs	Cheddar or Gruyère cheese
	④–⑥

Roll out the pastry and line a *deep* 7–8 inch flan ring. Chop and fry the bacon until crisp, put at the bottom of the pastry case. Beat the egg yolks or eggs with the seasoning, add the milk, strain if necessary, then add the grated cheese. Spoon or pour over the bacon. Bake for 10 minutes in the centre of a hot oven, 425–450°F.—Gas Mark 6–7. Lower the heat to moderate, 375°F.—Gas Mark 4–5 and cook for a further 30 minutes until the filling is set. Serve hot or cold.

Variations

Flaky pastry is sometimes used.

A little cream may replace some of the milk.

Choux pastry

1 oz. margarine, butter or cooking fat	3 oz. flour (plain or self-raising) approximately
¼ pint water	
1 teaspoon sugar for sweet cases	2 whole eggs and 1 egg yolk
or good pinch salt for savoury cases	

This quantity will make approximately 8 large buns; 12–14 medium-sized buns; 20 tiny profiteroles; 8–10 good-sized éclairs or approximately 20 very tiny cocktail-sized éclairs.

Heat fat in water in a saucepan until melted, add sugar *or* salt (picture 1). Remove from heat, stir in flour and continue stirring over low heat until a really *dry* mixture (picture 2). Take off heat, add first egg—beat in very thoroughly until smooth mixture, add second egg (picture 3), beat in again, then add as much egg yolk as is needed to give a sticky consistency. The pastry can then be made into a variety of shapes—see individual recipes.

Bun shapes

Either put spoonfuls of the mixture on to well greased and floured baking trays, or pipe rounds of the mixture on to the trays using a

1   **2**   **3**

½–1 inch plain pipe in a cloth or nylon bag.

If you can cover the baking trays with a light, deep tin, you encourage the pastry to rise and swell into a more attractive shape.

If you are covering the pastry, you must allow an extra 5–10 minutes cooking time.

Bake in the centre of a moderately hot to hot oven, 425–450°F.—Gas Mark 6–7, for about 25 minutes for small buns, up to 40 minutes for larger ones. Reduce heat to moderate, 350–375°F.—Gas Mark 3–4, after 15 minutes.

When cooked, cool away from a draught. Split open and remove any small amount of un-cooked mixture in the centre, return to oven for a few minutes to dry out, cool again and fill. If baking day before required, re-crisp for a short time before filling.

For sweet buns

Split buns—fill with lightly whipped cream (sweeten if wished).

Ice cream buns

Fill bun shapes with coffee or vanilla ice cream, serve with chocolate sauce.

Fruit buns

Blend equal quantities of thick fruit purée and whipped cream. Put into the buns and serve with extra pouring cream.

Profiteroles

These are exactly the same as bun shapes. Use only a very small teaspoonful of the mixture and bake for 10 minutes in a hot oven, then 5 minutes in a moderate heat.

There is no need to cover them with a tin.

Fill with whipped cream, pile into a dish and serve with chocolate sauce.

To make an easy sauce: melt 4 oz. plain choco-late, ½ oz. butter, 1–2 tablespoons water in a basin over hot water.

Éclairs

Either put 2-inch lengths of the mixture on to the greased and floured tin, pipe the mixture on to the tin with a ½-inch plain pipe (picture 1 opposite), or put the mixture into straight, well greased and floured finger-shape tins.

Bake as bun shapes, allowing 10 minutes in a hot oven, and 10 minutes in the moderate heat. Do not cover (picture 2). For a cocktail-sized éclair, bake as for profiteroles.

Chocolate éclairs

Split (picture 3); fill with whipped cream (picture 4); coat with melted chocolate *or* a chocolate icing (picture 6).

To make sufficient icing for 12 éclairs: blend 4 oz. sieved icing sugar, 2 oz. chocolate powder or 1 oz. cocoa or 3 oz. melted chocolate with a dessertspoon of warm water and 2 or 3 drops of oil (picture 5).

Savoury fillings

These are suitable for buns, profiteroles or éclair shapes.

Cheese

Blend 4–6 oz. cream cheese with a little milk to give a softer filling, add chopped chives, a little chopped gherkin, a little diced cucumber. Put into the pastry cases, decorate with a rosette of the cream cheese filling, paprika pepper and chopped parsley.

Egg and sardine

Flake 1 can of well drained sardines. Mix with 2–3 chopped hard-boiled eggs, seasoning, a squeeze of lemon juice and a little chopped parsley. Put into the buns and garnish with parsley.

Fish, chicken or ham

Chopped fish, chicken or ham can be put into a thick white sauce flavoured with lemon juice or sherry.

Vegetable and cheese

Make a thick cheese sauce with 1 oz. margarine, 1 oz. flour, ¼ pint milk, 3 oz. grated cheese, seasoning. Cook until thick, add finely diced or grated carrot and peas *or* chopped cooked mushrooms, *or* mixed vegetables.

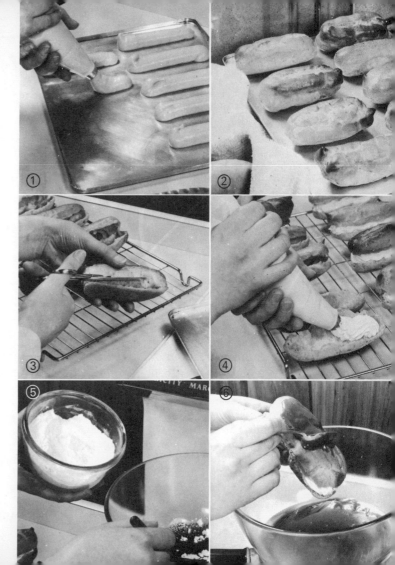

149

14. HOT SWEETS

THERE is a great variety of dishes which may be served as a hot sweet:

(a) The simplest is cooked fruit.
(b) Pancakes, fritters, in Book 2 and in this book pages 129–31.
(c) Sweet omelettes, pages 122–4.
(d) Pies, tarts, flans, in Book 2 and in this book, pages 140–6.
(e) Steamed puddings—there is a wide variety in Book 2, but a very good rich basic steamed pudding is given below.

Rich basic suet pudding

2 oz. plain or self-raising flour	4–5 oz. sugar, preferably brown
6 oz. soft breadcrumbs	2 eggs
4 oz. shredded suet	milk to mix ④–⑥

Mix all the ingredients together, adding sufficient milk to make a sticky consistency. Put into a greased basin and steam for approximately 2 hours. The plain pudding may be served with jam sauce, page 152, or adapted:

Fruit pudding: Add 8 oz. mixed dried fruit, steam for 2½ hours.

Economical Christmas pudding, pictured on page 158, richer recipe Book 2.

Add 1 lb. mixed dried fruit, 2 oz. chopped candied peel, 2 oz. chopped blanched almonds.

Mix with milk or brown ale. Steam for five hours or cook for one hour only at 15 lb. pressure in a pressure cooker. Serve with brandy butter or hard sauce, see below.

Lemon pudding: Add the grated rind of 2 lemons and mix with lemon juice as well as milk.

The rich basic suet pudding may be steamed in a basin, over jam, syrup, well-drained dried prunes, apricots, or canned fruit. It is a particularly light suet pudding, owing to the high proportion of breadcrumbs.

Brandy butter

4 oz. unsalted butter	brandy *or* rum
6 oz. icing sugar	cherries
4–8 dessertspoons	angelica ⑥–⑧

Cream the butter until white. Gradually add the sugar and the brandy. Leave for some little time in a cold place to get really hard. Pipe or pile into pyramid shape and decorate with cherries and angelica.

Puddings based on an egg custard

Book 2 gave directions for making egg custards and simple sweets based on them.

The following recipes, although quite different in taste and appearance from an egg custard, are also based on this, and it is therefore just as important that the mixture is cooked slowly to avoid curdling (pictures page 155).

Apple amber

For the apple base:	2–3 oz. puff *or* flaky
1½ lb. apples	pastry
3–4 tablespoons water	*For the meringue:*
2–3 oz. sugar	2 egg whites
2 egg yolks	2–4 oz. castor sugar
To line the rim of the	
dish:	④–⑥

This sweet has a fruit purée thickened with egg yolks; it therefore needs as careful baking as an egg custard.

Peel the apples, and cook with the water and sugar until a smooth pulp, sieve if wished, then mix with the well beaten egg yolks. It is traditional to line the rim of the dish with pastry, but this could be omitted if desired. If using pastry, bake for approximately 10 minutes in a hot oven (425°F.—Gas Mark 6–7) so this rises well, then put in the apple mixture. If using the apple mixture without the pastry it is unnecessary to allow 10 minutes in a hot oven. Bake the apple mixture for 40 minutes in the centre of a very moderate oven (325–350°F.—Gas Mark 3), do not allow it to become too hot. Whisk the egg whites until very stiff, add the sugar (see meringues pages 189-90) and pile on to the apple mixture.

To serve hot: Allow the smaller amount of sugar and set for 20 minutes in a very moderate oven.

To serve cold: Use the larger amount of sugar and set for 1 hour in a very slow oven (250–275°F.—Gas Mark ½–1).

Variations

Use rhubarb, plums or other fruit.

Add 2 oz. fine cake crumbs to the apple mixture as well as egg yolks.

Lemon soufflé pudding

2–3 oz. margarine	plus 4 tablespoons
3 oz. sugar	milk)
grated rind and juice	*To decorate:*
of 2 large lemons	few glacé cherries
2 oz. self-raising flour	(optional)
(or plain flour and	piece of angelica
½ level teaspoon	(optional)
baking powder)	little sieved icing
2 large eggs	sugar (optional)
12 tablespoons (¼ pint	⑥

Cream margarine and sugar until soft and light. Add lemon rind, juice, flour, egg yolks and the milk. The mixture curdles but in this particular recipe that does not matter. Lastly FOLD in the stiffly beaten egg whites. Pour into a greased pie-dish or soufflé dish and stand this in another containing cold water, i.e. a bain-marie. Bake for approximately 45 minutes in the centre of a very moderate oven, 350°F.—Gas Mark 3–4.

This pudding is nicer hot—although it can be served cold. Top with glacé cherries and angelica or dust with icing sugar if wished. The pudding separates in cooking—the top layer is like a soufflé or very light sponge—the bottom layer is a curd sauce.

Variation

Sieve ½ oz. cocoa with the flour. Omit the lemon juice and rind and use ½ pint milk.

Brisbane meringue

1 medium-sized can apricot halves	1 oz. chopped walnuts *For the meringue:*
1 tablespoon clear honey	2 egg whites 2 oz. castor sugar ④–⑥

Drain the apricot halves. (The juice will not be needed so use for a milk shake, Book 2, pages 44-5). Mix the honey with the walnuts and arrange the apricots, hollow parts upwards, in a shallow ovenproof dish. Spoon a little honey and nut mixture into the hollow of each apricot half. Whisk the egg whites until very stiff. Then add the sugar, page 189. Pile on to the fruit. Cook in the centre of a moderate oven, 375°F.—Gas Mark 4-5, for 15–20 minutes or until the meringue is golden. Serve hot. See picture, page 190.

Beignets soufflés

Choux pastry, using 3 oz. flour, etc. (page 147)	*For deep frying:* oil or fat *To coat:*
few drops vanilla essence	castor sugar *To serve:*
2 teaspoons sugar	jam sauce ④–⑥

1. Make the choux pastry as recipe page 147.
2. Add the vanilla essence and sugar after the eggs, beat these in thoroughly.
3. Heat the oil or fat—instructions for testing for the correct heat are on pages 75–6.
4. Drop small spoonfuls of the mixture into the hot oil.
5. Fry for approximately 3 minutes until well puffed and golden brown.
6. Lift from the oil and drain on crumpled tissue or kitchen paper.
7. Sprinkle with sugar and serve at once.

Jam sauce

2 level teaspoons arrowroot or cornflour ¼ pint water	3 tablespoons jam 1 teaspoon lemon juice

Blend the arrowroot or cornflour with the water. Put into a saucepan with the jam and lemon juice. Bring to the boil, stirring well to keep the mixture smooth. Cook until clear.

15. COLD SWEETS

BOOKS 1 and 2 give a wide selection of sweets, including fruit salad and ideas for using fruit. The table (pages 159–64), gives detailed information on fruits easily obtainable in this country and the best methods of using them. The second table lists less usual fruits which are seen from time to time.

Pink foam apples

Topping:	2 large sweet apples
1 small can evaporated milk	1 tablespoon lemon juice
2 tablespoons rose hip syrup	2 tablespoons seedless raisins
	2 tablespoons rose hip syrup ④

Topping: whisk evaporated milk to the consistency of thick cream. Stir in the rose hip syrup. Peel and core apples and slice very thinly. Toss in lemon juice. Arrange in four individual dishes and top with raisins. Spoon over rose hip syrup and allow to stand for a few minutes. Spoon over the topping. Serve with sponge fingers or thin wafers.

Variation

Use dessert pears instead of apples.
Use cream instead of evaporated milk.

No-bake blackberry Betty

$\frac{1}{2}$ lb. cooking apples	(approximately
$\frac{1}{2}$ lb. blackberries	1 pint)
2 oz. sugar	2 oz. soft brown or
Crumb mixture:	Demerara sugar
2 oz. butter	*To decorate:*
6 oz. fresh white breadcrumbs	a few uncooked, ripe blackberries ⑥

Peel and slice the apples. Gently stew the apples, blackberries and sugar together with 1 tablespoon water until the fruit is tender. Melt the butter in a saucepan. Remove from the heat and mix in the crumbs and sugar. Fill glasses or a glass dish with alternate layers of fruit and crumb mixture, finishing with a layer

of crumb mixture. Leave to stand for a few hours, preferably overnight. Decorate with raw blackberries, serve by itself or with cream, ice cream or custard.

Caramel custard

The caramel:	The custard:	④
3 oz. loaf or granulated sugar	1 pint milk	
4 tablespoons water	3 eggs or 4 egg yolks	
	1 dessertspoon sugar	

1. *First make the caramel:* Put the sugar and half the water into a small strong saucepan. Stir over a low heat until you can no longer feel the grittiness of the sugar on the bottom of the pan; it is then dissolved. Boil steadily, without stirring, until it turns dark brown. Watch carefully during this process for it soon turns black and burns. Take the pan off the heat, then add the rest of the water. When you do this the caramel will become a sticky ball, but return to the heat, stir gently, and it will soon become liquid again. If using a metal mould, you can safely pour in the caramel sauce while very hot. With a china or glass mould or basin allow the caramel to cool slightly. Wait until the caramel sauce is cold before adding the custard.

2. *To make the custard:* Pour hot, NOT BOILING, milk on to the eggs which have been beaten with the sugar. Strain over the caramel. Straining is not essential but it ensures that there are no small pieces of egg floating on top.

3. Half fill a dish slightly larger than the basin or mould with cold water. Stand the mould in this and bake for about $2\frac{1}{2}$ hours in the centre of a cool oven (275–300°F.—Gas Mark 1–2) until firm, or steam over hot water. Cool the caramel custard and when nearly cold, turn out on to a dish. Do not wait until it is quite cold, otherwise some of the caramel will stick to the

mould. A very light greasing of the mould makes sure none of the caramel is wasted when turning out the sweet, or if wished the mould can be warmed slightly after turning out the sweet, so any caramel round the sides will become liquid and run easily.

Curdled and 2. perfectly cooked caramel custard

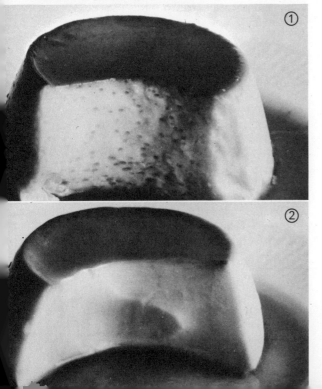

Rich trifle

Book 2, page 221, gave suggestions for various trifles. A really delicious rich fruit trifle is made by moistening the sponge cakes, which should be split and filled with jam, with plenty of sherry or sweet white wine, then adding chopped blanched almonds, ratafia biscuits, before topping with custard, cream, cherries, nuts and angelica. Children often prefer the sponge cakes moistened with syrup and topped with canned fruit or even canned fruit and jelly, before a covering of custard, etc.

Summer pudding

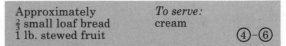

Approximately ⅔ small loaf bread 1 lb. stewed fruit	*To serve:* cream

④–⑥

The fruit can be a mixture of stewed raspberries and redcurrants, blackcurrants, early juicy plums. Sweeten well in cooking, but do not add too much water.

The basic ingredients for this pudding give no idea of how attractive it can look when completed. Cut rather thin slices of bread. Line the sides and bottom of a basin with these slices. Put in the sweetened stewed fruit. Cover with a thin layer of bread and put paper, or a saucer and weight on top. Leave overnight or for some hours. Turn out and serve with cream.

Chocolate mousse

2 oz. plain chocolate	2 eggs

Picture 1: Break chocolate into pieces and gently melt in a basin over a pan of hot water. DO NOT ALLOW TO BECOME TOO HOT.

Picture 2: Separate the egg whites from the yolks and beat the yolks into the melted chocolate, removing basin from heat first.

Picture 3: Whisk the egg whites until very stiff.

Picture 4: Carefully fold the egg whites into the melted chocolate. Use a tablespoon or a plastic spatula to retain lightness. Pour into serving dishes and allow to set. Chocolate mousse is better eaten the same day that it is made. Allow at least 1½ hours for setting if refrigerator is used.

Picture 5: Put into glasses.

Picture 6: This shows a few ideas for serving and decorating chocolate mousse: topped with cream and a cherry; with cream, grated chocolate and nuts; with mandarin orange sections and cream; with cream, walnuts and chocolate 'buttons'; plain, in a shallow bowl; with pineapple pieces, cherry and cream.

Chocolate orange mousse

Add the grated zest (yellow outer part of the skin) of an orange to the grated chocolate.

Fruit

Details of availability apply to Great Britain

Fruit	Obtainable	How prepared
APPLES	Throughout the year. Good cooking apples may be scarce June-September Dessert apples: Cox's Orange, Beauty of Bath, Worcester Pearmain, Ellison Orange, Delicious (from Australia) Cooking apples: Bramley Seedling, Red Newton Wonder, Green King Edward.	Raw: wash or wipe if not peeling Cook: peel (unless baking) and core. Slice if wished. Bake, stew, use in puddings.
APRICOTS	January-March (from South Africa) late May-June (from Spain) Dried apricots throughout the year	Rarely ripe enough to eat raw Cook: whole or halved. Use in pies, puddings, etc.
AVOCADO PEARS	Throughout most of the year Do not expect these to taste like ordinary pears; they are quite different. Slightly acid in taste. Greenish or purplish colour	Raw: halve, remove stone. Serve with oil, vinegar and seasoning as a first course, or fill with shell fish mixed with mayonnaise. Rarely cooked
BANANAS	Throughout the year Jamaican bananas the most usual Canary are small, best-flavoured	Raw: peel. They are less indigestible when skin is turning brown. Cook: in puddings. Coat with batter for fritters
BILBERRIES	Occasionally available in shops, or in canned or frozen form. They grow wild in some parts of the country	Cook as blackcurrants

Apricot

Avocado pear

Bilberries

Fruit (cont.)

Fruit	Obtainable	How prepared
BLACKBERRIES	Early to late autumn	Raw: wash well, serve raw only if very ripe Cook: in pies, puddings; stewed
BLACKCURRANTS	June-August Eat raw whenever possible, since they have a high vitamin C content	Raw: remove stalks, wash Cook: in pies, puddings, stewed. Simmer slowly to soften hard skins
CHERRIES	May (from Italy) late June-August (English cherries)	Raw: mostly eaten raw. Wash Cook: stew, put into pies and puddings. Morello cherries used for cooking
CLEMENTINE	Late Autumn to early Spring A type of tangerine	As tangerines
CRANBERRIES	From North America. Often obtainable frozen	Too bitter to be eaten raw Cook: stew to make a sauce to serve with turkey. Add a few to apples for apple tart. Use in cold sweets
DAMSONS	August-October	Too bitter to eat raw Cook: stew. Put into pies and puddings
DATES (dried)	Throughout most of the year	Raw: as dessert Cook: add to other fruits in cakes, puddings, etc.

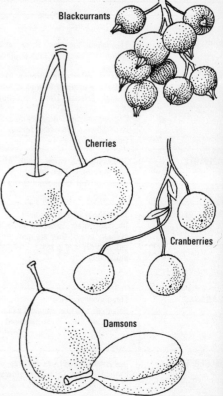

Blackcurrants

Cherries

Cranberries

Damsons

Cherry fl.

Fruit (cont.)

Fruit	Obtainable	How prepared
FIGS	Throughout the year (dried) Fresh figs are rarely obtainable —generally imported	Raw: as dessert Cook: add to other fruits in cakes, puddings, etc. Stew
GOOSEBERRIES	June-July	Raw: only very ripe fruit, or large dessert gooseberries called 'Levellers' are eaten raw Cook: remove stalks, stew, use in puddings, pies, etc.
GRAPEFRUIT	Throughout most of the year	Raw: mostly eaten raw, for breakfast or at beginning of a meal Cook: can be put under grill or in oven and served hot
GRAPES	Throughout the year	Raw: wash or wipe, serve as dessert. Add to fruit salad Cook: not often cooked, but sometimes served with fish
GREENGAGES	July-August	Raw: wipe well or wash Cook: wash, do not halve. Stew or use in puddings or pies
LEMONS	Throughout the year	Too bitter to eat raw Cook: as flavouring in puddings and sweets; as garnish or flavouring for fish dishes

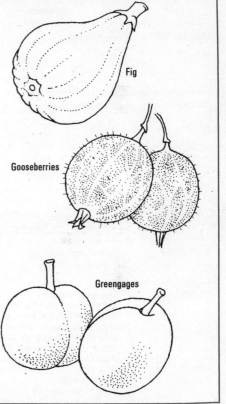

Fig

Gooseberries

Greengages

hristmas pudding

Fruit (cont.)

Fruit	Obtainable	How prepared
LOGANBERRIES	June-August	Raw: can be washed and eaten raw, but rather bitter
		Cook: like raspberries in puddings and sweets
MANDARIN	A type of tangerine	As tangerines
MELON	Throughout the year	Raw: as dessert or at beginning of a meal, serve in slices. Add to fruit salad Rarely cooked
MULBERRIES	Late summer, Very rare nowadays	Raw: handle carefully as the fruit is very soft and stains badly. Serve as dessert Cook: as raspberries
NECTARINES	July-August	Raw: eat as peaches Cook: as peaches
ORANGES	Throughout the year Jaffa oranges—extra fine flavour, few pips; Spanish—thin skins, plentiful pips; Blood oranges have red tinted pulp; Navel oranges are seedless; Seville or Bitter oranges used for marmalade	Raw: eat often, since they have a high vitamin C content Cook: to flavour puddings, sweets and cakes
PEACHES	July-September Imported peaches can be bought at other times. Canned available throughout the year	Raw: wipe or peel Cook: in pies, flans; baked or poached

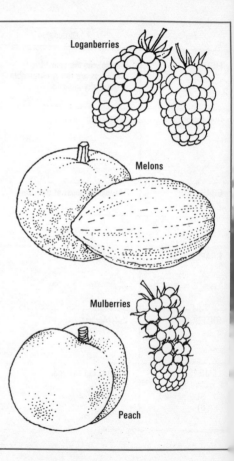

Loganberries

Melons

Mulberries

Peach

Fruit (cont.)

Fruit	Obtainable	How prepared	
PEARS	Throughout the year Comice pears are the finest. Williams and Conference pears are widely marketed	Raw: wipe or wash if not peeling Cook: peel or core. Use in puddings. Serve with chocolate sauce	Pears
PINEAPPLE	Fresh or canned throughout the year	Raw: cut fresh pineapple into thick slices, remove skin with a sharp knife Cook: canned pineapple is better cooked, particularly if added to jellies, since fresh pineapple stops jelly setting	
PLUMS	August-October (home-grown) January-April (imported) Dessert plums: the big Czar plums and Victoria plums For cooking: Early Rivers are small, cheap, have good flavour. They make excellent jam	Raw: wash, wipe or peel Cook: use in pies, puddings, or stew	Pineapple
PRUNES (dried)	Throughout the year	Rarely eaten raw Cook: soak for several hours in cold water. Stew, or use in puddings, add to cakes, etc. Can be served wrapped in bacon as a savoury	Plums
RAISINS, CURRANTS and SULTANAS (dried)	Throughout the year	Raw: not often served as dessert Cook: used in cakes, puddings, mincemeat	

Fruit (cont.)

Fruit	Obtainable	How prepared
RASPBERRIES	June-August	Raw: wash and allow to dry Cook: can be used in pies, puddings and sweets, though at their best raw
REDCURRANTS	June-August	Raw: wash, remove stalks, sprinkle with sugar and leave for several hours before serving Cook: usually mixed with other fruits in pies and tarts, or made into jelly
RHUBARB	Early spring, later summer and autumn	Never eaten raw Cook: wash, cut into neat pieces, use in pies or puddings or stewed
ROSE HIPS	In syrup throughout the year	Never eaten raw Cook: not used by themselves, but the syrup can be used to flavour puddings. High vitamin C content
SATSUMAS	A type of tangerine	As tangerines
STRAWBERRIES	May-July Imported strawberries can be bought at other times	Raw: wash in cold water and leave to dry Cook: in tarts, flans, etc.
TANGERINES	Most plentiful from late autumn till spring	Raw: as oranges Cook: as oranges
WHITE CURRANTS	June-August	Raw: as redcurrants

Redcurrants

Rhubarb

Rose hips

Tangerine

Some unusual fruits

Fruit	Description	How prepared
CUSTARD APPLES	These bear no resemblance to ordinary apples. The fruit is grey-green and 3-5 inches in diameter. The edible part is the fleshy, custard-flavoured pulp	Eaten raw
CAPE GOOSEBERRIES	Orange-coloured fruits often sold for decoration by florists	Skinned and eaten raw, when ripe
CHINESE GOOSEBERRIES	A fleshy fruit, not unlike a lychee (see below)	
GUAVAS	Occasionally obtainable canned, as well as fresh	Halve and scoop out the pulp. Eat raw
LIMES	Rarely seen in this country	Use in place of lemons
LYCHEES	Can be obtained canned and, occasionally, raw	Remove the husk or skin and eat raw, or poach in a sugar syrup
MANGOES	Usually obtained in the form of ready-made chutney	Eat fresh when very soft and looking almost bad

Custard apple

Cape gooseberry

Guava

Lychee

Mango

Some unusual fruits (cont.)

Fruit	Description	How prepared
MEDLARS	This rather tart fruit is usually bought in the form of jam or jelly	Eat only when thoroughly ripe and soft
ORTINIQUES	A cross between an orange and a tangerine	Eat as oranges
PASSION FRUIT or GRANADILLA	Occasionally obtained canned, as well as fresh	Halve and scoop out the pulp. Eat raw
PAW-PAW or PAPAYA	A fruit not unlike a small melon in taste and appearance. Sometimes available canned	Eat as melon
POMEGRANATES		Remove the skin and suck the pulp from the pips Not suitable for cooking
QUINCES	A very hard fruit which cannot be eaten raw but is excellent for cooking with apples or in jams and jellies	Cook: add a little to apples or use for jam or jelly
UGLI	A cross between an orange and a grapefruit	Serve as grapefruit

Medlar

Paw-Paw (Papaya)

Pomegranate

Quince

16. USING GELATINE

GELATINE is the substance used to make liquids or semi-liquid mixtures set. The fruit flavoured jellies obtainable in packets have a flavouring added, and are generally in tablet form. Gelatine bought unflavoured is normally in powder form, although leaf gelatine can be obtained in some shops.

The quantity of gelatine used varies a little according to the make, but the following are average proportions:

1. *To set 1 pint of clear liquid*
Use a good $\frac{1}{2}$ oz. = 1 tablespoon = 1 envelope.

2. *To set a semi-thickened liquid*
Use half this quantity.

There are several ways of mixing gelatine. With some gelatine, it is best to soften it in a little cold liquid (taken from the total amount) and then stir it into the very hot liquid. Other gelatine can be dissolved immediately in the hot liquid, so follow the printed directions.

Rules for using gelatine

(a) Do not boil gelatine unless instructed.

(b) Do not exceed the amount of gelatine or use less than stated.

(c) In any recipe it is very important that the gelatine is thoroughly dissolved before adding to the rest of the ingredients.

(d) When setting fruit in layers in a jelly, the liquid jelly not being used must be kept warm to prevent it setting. If it *does* set, however, stand the container in a pan of warm water.

(e) When adding egg whites, whipped cream, etc., to a jelly mixture this must be partially set. If not, the whites will not remain light. If it is too set, the whites will not blend in smoothly.

Honeycomb mould

$\frac{1}{4}$ pint lemon juice	1 large egg
$\frac{3}{4}$ pint water	$\frac{1}{2}$ oz. powdered
2 oz. sugar	gelatine ④

Put the lemon juice, water, sugar and egg yolk into a saucepan and heat well for about 5 minutes until very slightly thickened. Remove from heat and cool slightly. Soften the powdered gelatine in 2 tablespoons of cold water and pour on the lemon mixture. When this is quite cold, FOLD in the stiffly beaten egg white. Pour into a rinsed mould to set.

Simple soufflé

1 fruit flavoured jelly	$\frac{1}{4}$ pint thick (double)
just under $\frac{3}{4}$ pint	cream
water	*To decorate:*
1 egg	4 glacé cherries
1 oz. sugar	angelica or walnuts ④

1. Dissolve the jelly in the hot water; cool but do not allow to set.
2. Whisk the egg yolk and sugar in a large basin until thickened, then whisk in the jelly. Allow the mixture to become quite cold and begin to thicken—it should have the consistency of a thick syrup.
3. Whisk the cream until it *just* holds its shape. Whisk the egg white until very stiff. Fold first the cream and then the egg white into the jelly.
4. Put into a serving dish or individual dishes until quite firm and set. Decorate with a few glacé cherries and angelica, or with chopped nuts.

Cold soufflé—rich

3 eggs	¼ pint plus 4 table-
3 oz. sugar	spoons cream or
¼–½ teaspoon vanilla	evaporated milk*
essence	*To decorate:*
1 level dessertspoon	chopped nuts,
powder gelatine	whipped cream
3 tablespoons water	④–⑥

*If using evaporated milk, boil this the night before for 15 minutes, then open tin, turn out milk and leave in cool place, then whisk until light and thickened.

1. Prepare a 4–5 inch soufflé dish by putting a deep band of buttered paper round it, standing up above the dish. Tie tightly.
2. Put the egg yolks, sugar, vanilla essence into a basin over a pan of boiling water and whisk until very thick. Whisk until cold.
3. Either dissolve the gelatine in the hot water or soften in cold water and dissolve over a pan of hot water. Add to the egg yolk mixture and allow to cool and *thicken slightly*.
4. Then fold in the lightly whipped cream or evaporated milk and finally, the stiffly beaten egg whites. Pour or spoon into the soufflé dish so that the mixture is supported by the band of paper. Leave until firm, remove the band of paper and decorate.

Variations

Lemon soufflé: Add the grated rind of a lemon to the egg yolks. Dissolve the gelatine in lemon juice instead of water.
Chocolate soufflé: Add 1–2 oz. plain chocolate or chocolate powder to the egg yolks.
Coffee soufflé: Dissolve the gelatine in 1 table-spoon of coffee essence and 2 tablespoons water, or in 3 tablespoons VERY STRONG coffee.

Economical soufflé

3 eggs	1½ dessertspoons ⑥–⑧
½ pint milk	powder gelatine
3 oz. sugar	3 tablespoons water
¼–½ teaspoon vanilla	12 tablespoons cream
essence	or evaporated milk

Put the egg yolks, milk, sugar and vanilla essence into a basin over hot water and cook until the custard coats the back of a wooden spoon.

Allow to cool, stirring from time to time. Continue as previous recipe, adding flavourings as wished.

Savoury uses of gelatine

Gelatine is used for setting the ingredients in a savoury as well as a sweet jelly, e.g. a little may be added to the stock in a brawn for a firmer result.

Often aspic jelly, i.e. savoury flavoured gelatine is given in a recipe. It is a long process to prepare home made aspic and therefore it is generally purchased in a packet and the contents dissolved in water.

Aspic mould

1 pint packet aspic flavoured jelly	2 tablespoons cooked peas
1 pint water	3–4 sliced carrots
To fill:	3–4 oz. diced ham or
2 hard-boiled eggs	other cooked meat or flaked fish ④–⑥

1. Dissolve the aspic jelly in the hot water as directed on the packet. Pour some of it into a mould either rinsed in cold water or brushed with oil, to facilitate turning out. Allow this layer to set until firm, and keep the rest of the jelly a liquid.

2. Plan a design of sliced hard-boiled egg, a few peas and 1 or 2 slices of carrot. Dip the pieces of egg and vegetables in a little aspic, or place on to the set aspic and·brush with liquid jelly.

3. Leave until the vegetables are set in position —spoon another layer of cold, but still liquid jelly over them; allow to set. Continue filling the mould as above allowing each layer to set in position before adding the next. The meat or fish is added to the vegetables after the first layer. Dip the mould in warm water for a few seconds before turning out.

Serve this with green salad.

Aspic canapés

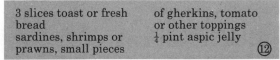

3 slices toast or fresh bread	of gherkins, tomato or other toppings
sardines, shrimps or prawns, small pieces	¼ pint aspic jelly ⑫

Cut the toast or bread into neat fingers. Arrange a topping on each, brush with half set aspic jelly. Do this on a wire cooling tray over a flat plate or dish, so that any aspic that drops off the canapes may be picked up and used again. Use either a palette knife, dipped in hot water, or a pastry brush.

The aspic keeps the sardines, etc. moist.

169

17. CREAMS AND ICE CREAM

Mock cream

1 tablespoon cornflour	1–2 oz. butter
¼ pint milk	1 oz. castor sugar

Blend cornflour to a smooth mixture with the milk, put into a saucepan and bring slowly to the boil, stirring all the time. Cook until thick. Allow to become quite cool. Cream the butter and sugar until very soft. ON NO ACCOUNT WARM THE BUTTER. Gradually beat in spoonfuls of the cornflour mixture. The more you beat this the better the cream becomes.

Crème chantilly

¼ pint cream	essence
few drops vanilla	1–2 teaspoons sugar ④

Whip the cream until it is just stiff enough to stand in peaks—do not continue to whip after this. Fold in the vanilla essence and sugar, and whisk once or twice more if you want it sufficiently stiff to pipe.

Vanilla cream filling

1 oz. plain flour or	2 teaspoons sugar
½ oz. cornflour	1–2 egg yolks
¼ pint milk	4 tablespoons
few drops vanilla	whipped cream
essence	④–⑥

Mix the flour or cornflour to a smooth paste with the milk. Heat carefully with the vanilla essence and sugar, stirring until the mixture comes to the boil and thickens. Cook for 1 minute, add the egg yolk or yolks and cook for a further few minutes without boiling. Cool again, stirring from time to time, then fold in the whipped cream.

For a richer version, blend with ¼ pint whipped cream.

Evaporated milk

In addition to the mock cream and vanilla cream filling, evaporated milk is an excellent substitute for cream. The method of whipping is given below.

To make ice cream

The temperature indicator must be set for the coldest position 30 minutes before the mixture is put into the refrigerator. This ensures that the ice cream does not separate and become full of tiny splinters of ice. It is important to use an adequately rich mixture. With most recipes better results are obtained if the mixture is beaten when half frozen, then put back into the freezer. Return refrigerator temperature to normal setting when ice cream is firmly set.

Ice cream with evaporated milk ④–⑤

Boil a large can of evaporated milk in water for 15 minutes, then cool. Whisk until light and fluffy, adding 2 oz. sugar and flavouring. Pour into freezing trays and freeze until firm, take out, whip briskly then refreeze.

Rich ice cream

½ pint whipped cream	2 oz. sugar
2 whisked egg whites	flavouring ③–④

Mix all the ingredients together. Pour into freezing tray and freeze until firm, take out, whip briskly, then refreeze.

Ice cream with custard base

½ pint sweetened custard sauce, made either with custard powder, Book 2 page	52 or egg custard, Book 2 page 62 ¼ pint thick cream flavouring

Make the custard in the usual way. Allow the custard to become quite cold, stirring from time to time to prevent a skin forming. Whip the cream until it holds its shape. Fold into the custard, pour into the freezing tray, freeze until firm, take out. Remove the ice cream from the tray, whip briskly in a bowl. Return to the tray and re-freeze.

Flavourings for ice cream

Vanilla: Use 1 level teaspoon of vanilla essence, or put a broken vanilla pod into the custard mixture while cooking.

Almond: Add ½ teaspoon almond essence and 2 tablespoons chopped blanched almonds.

Coffee: Dilute 2 tablespoons coffee essence with same amount of cold milk, then add this to other ingredients. Coffee ice cream is delicious served with whipped cream and nuts.

Chocolate: Mix 1½ oz. chocolate powder to a smooth paste with a little milk and a few drops vanilla essence, then add to other ingredients.

Raspberry: Add 8 oz. thick sieved fruit pulp to any of the three basic mixtures.

Strawberry: As raspberry.

SWEETS WITH ICE CREAM

Ice cream sundaes

These are quickly and easily made by combining ice cream, fruit, jelly, etc. Serve in shallow sundae (grapefruit) glasses. Try:

Chocolate walnut sundae: Put vanilla, coffee or chocolate ice cream into a glass, top with chocolate sauce and chopped nuts.

Fruit sundae: Put a layer of fresh or well-drained canned fruit into a sundae glass, top with ice cream, a layer of whisked fruit jelly, then whipped cream and a piece of fruit.

Fruit melba

Put a scoop of ice cream into a glass, top with fruit (peaches, strawberries, raspberries, pineapple, pears are the most usual). Coat with Melba sauce (recipe below) and top with whipped cream if wished.

Coupe Jacques

This is similar to a Fruit melba except fruit salad is used.

Melba sauce

4–6 oz. raspberries (fresh or well drained canned or frozen) either 2 tablespoons water plus ½–1 tablespoon sugar or	2 tablespoons sweetened fruit syrup 1 teaspoon arrowroot or cornflour 2 tablespoons redcurrant jelly (4)–(6)

Sieve the fruit if wished (not essential). Blend the water and sugar or syrup with the arrowroot, then put into a saucepan with the raspberries and jelly and stir over a moderate heat until clear and thickened. Cool before using. A larger amount may be prepared and stored in the refrigerator for some days.

Economical recipe: Heat equal quantities of raspberry jam and redcurrant jelly, dilute with a very little water if too thick.

Poires Belle Helene

Top vanilla ice cream with halved dessert or canned pears and hot or cold chocolate sauce (page 148).

Meringues glacés

This is the name given to meringues when they are sandwiched with ice cream instead of whipped cream.

Baked Alaska

1 round or square of sponge cake small can fruit or fresh fruit large block of ice	cream (6)–(8) *Meringue:* 4 egg whites 4–8 oz. castor sugar

Put the sponge into an ovenproof serving dish, then top with the well drained canned fruit or sweetened fresh fruit. Place the ice cream on this. Make the meringue—directions on page 189—tastes vary as to the amount of sugar desired. Spread or pipe the meringue over the ice cream, etc. *It is essential that the ice cream is completely covered*, for the meringue acts as an 'insulation' against the oven heat. Put for 3–5 minutes only in a very hot oven (475–500°F.—Gas Mark 9–10) until tipped with brown. This sweet will stand for about 20 minutes before serving without being spoiled.

18. CAKE AND BISCUIT MAKING

BASIC methods of cake making are in Book 2. The recipes in this chapter are based on these. There are also recipes for biscuits, as these are made by the same methods. Points to remember:

1. Weigh ingredients carefully and do not alter the proportions in the recipe. There must be a balance between the fat, eggs and flour used. In some recipes self-raising *or* plain flour and baking powder are equally suitable but in other recipes, particularly where there is a considerable weight of fruit, it is advisable to use plain flour and little, if any, baking powder.

2. Handle the ingredients as directed in Book 2 —incorrect handling often results in a poor-textured cake.

3. Check (a) oven temperature. The guide on page 48 gives average setting only, and ovens vary; (b) oven position. If a cake should be baked in the centre of the oven and is placed too high (where it is hotter) it will brown too quickly on the outside yet be insufficiently cooked in the middle.

4. Use the size cake tin recommended in the recipe or adjust the cooking time. If the recipe states a 7 inch tin and the mixture is put into a 6 inch tin the cooking time should be lengthened by approximately 20 minutes for a light cake

but considerably more for a rich fruit cake, owing to the greater depth of mixture. If put into an 8 inch tin where the depth is less the cooking time must be shortened.

5. Test the cake carefully *before* removing from the oven (a) by seeing it has shrunk away from the sides of the tin; (b) by pressing firmly on top to see if an impression is left by the finger. Test a very rich cake by listening for a humming noise (page 181).

RUBBING IN METHOD

THIS is used for rock buns, plain cakes— recipes Books 1 and 2.
Fat is rubbed into the sieved dry ingredients, then the mixture is bound with egg, etc.

Eggless fruit cake

8 oz. self-raising flour (or plain flour with 2 level teaspoons baking powder)	or soft brown 8 oz. dried fruit $\frac{1}{2}$ teaspoon bicarbonate of soda $1\frac{1}{2}$ tablespoons vinegar
4–5 oz. margarine or cooking fat or dripping	approximately $\frac{1}{4}$ pint plus
4–5 oz. sugar—white	4 tablespoons milk ⑫

1. Sieve the flour, or flour and baking powder, into a mixing bowl. Rub in the margarine or fat,

add the sugar and the dried fruit. Blend the bicarbonate of soda with the vinegar, then add to the other ingredients together with enough milk to make a slow dropping consistency.

2. Put into a 2 lb. greased and floured, 6 inch round or 5 inch square cake tin. Bake in the centre of a moderate oven (350–375°F.—Gas Mark 4) for approximately 1–1¼ hours.

3. Test by pressing firmly, then turn out carefully on to a cooling tray. Eat when reasonably fresh, although this cake keeps for several days. The vinegar helps to make the cake light—the function normally performed by eggs. Use either brown vinegar for a darker cake or white malt vinegar, but naturally none of the flavoured vinegars or wine vinegar.

CREAMING METHOD

USED for a great variety of cakes from light Victoria sponge to rich fruit cakes. A selection of recipes is given in Book 2.

Fat and sugar are beaten until light and fluffy before adding eggs, sieved flour, etc.

Madeleines

3 oz. margarine	*To decorate:*
3 oz. castor sugar	4 oz. raspberry jam
2 eggs	2 oz. desiccated
4 oz. self-raising	coconut
flour (or plain flour	6–9 glacé cherries
and 1 level teaspoon	little angelica
baking powder)	24

These are based on a plain creamed mixture—or quick creaming method as page 183.

Follow the method of creaming under Cherry cake below. Half fill well greased and floured dariole (castle pudding) tins. Stand on a flat tray and bake above the centre of a hot oven (425–450°F.—Gas Mark 6–7). Bake for approximately 12 minutes until firm. Turn out of the tins and cool.

Look at the pictures on page 174.

Picture 1: Insert a fine skewer or fork into the base of each cake and brush the sides and top with warm but not hot jam.

Picture 2: Roll the coated cake in the coconut and press firmly against the sides with a flat bladed knife.

Picture 3: Top with halved glacé cherries and angelica leaves.

Rich cherry cake

6 oz. butter	8 oz. plain flour
6 oz. castor sugar	1 level teaspoon
3 eggs	baking powder
4–6 oz. glacé cherries	⑩-⑫

Cream the butter and sugar until soft and light. Beat the eggs and add gradually to the creamed mixture. Should this show signs of curdling, fold in a little sieved flour. Halve the cherries and mix with the sieved flour and baking powder or rinse in cold water then dry on kitchen paper to remove the sticky syrup; add to the flour. Fold into the creamed mixture.

Cherry cake

Do NOT add any liquid in this recipe. Put into a well greased and floured 7 inch cake tin, bake for approximately 1¼–1½ hours in the centre of a very moderate oven (325–350°F.—Gas Mark 3).

A plainer cherry cake is given in Book 2.

Almond cherry cake

As rich cherry cake but use 6 oz. plain flour, 1 level teaspoon baking powder and 2 oz. ground almonds.

Battenburg cake

Victoria sandwich mixture:	3 oz. castor sugar
6 oz. margarine	3 oz. sieved icing sugar
6 oz. castor sugar	few drops almond essence
3 eggs	1½ egg yolks to bind
6 oz. self-raising flour (or plain flour and 1½ teaspoons baking powder)	2–3 tablespoons sieved apricot or raspberry jam
few drops cochineal	*To decorate:*
Almond paste or marzipan:	approximately 6 glacé cherries,
6 oz. ground almonds	angelica (10)–(12)

1. Cream the margarine and sugar until soft and light, then gradually add the well beaten eggs. If the mixture shows signs of curdling fold in a little sieved flour. Lastly fold in the sieved flour or flour and baking powder.
2. Put half the mixture into a basin and add enough cochineal to give a pink colour. Either bake in two 1 lb. well greased and floured *straight* sided loaf tins, or line a small Swiss roll tin with greased and floured greaseproof paper and bake the white cake at one end and the pink cake at the other.
3. Allow approximately 25–30 minutes just above the centre of a moderate oven (375°F.—Gas Mark 4–5). Turn the cake or cakes on to a cooling tray and when quite cold cut into 4 fingers—2 white and 2 pink.

4. *Make the marzipan* by mixing all the ingredients together, then roll out to an oblong sufficiently large to wrap round the completed cake.
5. Brush the fingers of cake with the jam and press together so that the bottom layer has a white and pink strip, then put a pink strip of cake on top of the white, and a white on the pink. Make certain that the outside of the cake is well coated with jam, and lift on to the marzipan. Wrap this round the cake, seal the edges and turn the sealed edges to the bottom of the cake. Either flute the two long sides of marzipan or mark with a fork as in the picture, and make a pattern with a knife, taking care

not to cut the marzipan. Neaten the short ends if necessary, and decorate with halved glacé cherries and leaves of angelica. Brush these lightly with jam to make certain they stick to the marzipan.

Variations

Since the Victoria sponge gives a very light cake which must be handled with care, a more economical mixture, i.e. 5 oz. margarine, 5 oz. sugar, 3 eggs, 8 oz. flour, and a very little milk may be used instead.

Chocolate Battenburg cake

(See picture.) Add ½ oz. sieved cocoa to half the mixture together with a few drops of milk.

Rich Dundee cake

6 oz. margarine or butter	2 oz. chopped blanched almonds
6 oz. sugar—castor or soft brown	2 oz. cherries
3 eggs	1 lb. mixed dried fruit
8 oz. plain flour*	2 oz. peel
1½ level teaspoons baking powder	2 tablespoons milk
1 teaspoon spice	*To decorate:* 2 oz. split blanched almonds ⑭–⑯

*With this rich cake, this is better than self-raising flour, or use half self-raising and half plain flour.

1. Cream the margarine and sugar together until soft and light. Gradually add the beaten eggs. Sieve dry ingredients together. Mix the chopped almonds, floured cherries, fruit and chopped peel together. Stir the flour etc. into the creamed mixture, with enough milk to make a slow dropping consistency. Lastly, put in the fruit.

2. Put into a greased and floured 8 inch cake tin. Cover with split almonds (see picture) and brush with egg white from egg shells to glaze.

3. Bake for 2–2¼ hours in the centre of a very moderate oven (325–350°F.—Gas Mark 3). Lower the heat after 1½ hours if wished to cool (275–300°F.—Gas Mark 1–2), and leave to the

end of the cooking time. Cool slightly in the tin before turning on to wire cooling tray. This mixture can be baked in a deep 7 inch cake tin, allow $2\frac{1}{4}$–$2\frac{1}{2}$ hours.

Simnel cake

Ingredients as Rich Dundee Cake (above). The spice may be increased to 2 teaspoons and a little powdered cinnamon and nutmeg may also be added if wished. *Marzipan:* 8 oz. ground almonds	4 oz. castor sugar 4 oz. icing sugar few drops lemon essence 2 egg yolks *To decorate:* egg white apricot jam (optional)

⑭–⑯

1. Prepare the cake. Put half the mixture into a well greased and floured 8 inch cake tin.
2. Make the marzipan (see directions, page 176). Use just under half the marzipan and roll it out to a round approximately 8 inches in diameter. Put over the cake mixture, then top with the remainder of the cake mixture.
3. Bake as the Rich Dundee Cake (above), allowing a little extra time because of the marzipan.
4. Turn cake out when cold, brush top with a little egg white or apricot jam, cover with a round of marzipan. If any is left it can be formed into a decoration to go on to the cake. Brush the marzipan with egg white and brown this either in the oven for a few minutes, or under a grill with the heat turned very low.
Decorate with fluffy chickens or other Easter motifs.
Although a Simnel Cake is generally served on Easter Sunday, traditionally it was a Mothering Sunday cake.

Dark rich Christmas cake

10 oz. butter 10 oz. moist brown sugar 1 level tablespoon black treacle grated rind 1 lemon grated rind 1 orange 5 large eggs 2 tablespoons brandy or sherry 12 oz. plain flour $\frac{1}{2}$ level teaspoon cinnamon $\frac{1}{2}$ level teaspoon grated nutmeg	$\frac{1}{2}$ level teaspoon mixed spice $1\frac{1}{4}$ lb. currants 12 oz. sultanas 8 oz. chopped raisins 4 oz. chopped prunes 4 oz. chopped dates 4 oz. blanched chopped almonds 4 oz. chopped candied peel 4 oz. chopped glacé cherries

㉚–㊱

1. Prepare an 8 inch square or a 9 inch round tin at least 3 inches in depth. Put a double band of greased greaseproof paper inside the tin— cut the bottom so there is a neat fit at the base of the tin. Put a square or round of double brown paper over this covered with a square or round of double greased greaseproof paper.

Tie a deep band of brown paper round the outside of the tin, allowing this to stand 1 or 2 inches above the top of the tin.

2. Cream the butter and sugar with the black treacle and lemon and orange rind. Continue beating until the mixture is soft and light. Whisk the eggs and liquid and gradually beat into the creamed butter mixture, adding a little sieved flour if it shows signs of curdling. Sieve the flour and spices together. In this recipe you do not need any raising agent. Mix the prepared fruit with the almonds, candied peel and glacé cherries. Stir into the cake thoroughly with the flour and spices, but do not over-beat.

3. Put mixture into prepared cake tin and bake in the centre of a very moderate oven (325–350°F.—Gas Mark 3) for 1½ hours, then lower heat to 300°F.—Gas Mark 2 for a further 3 hours.

4. To test this type of cake make certain it has shrunk away from the sides of the tin. Press gently but firmly and if no impression is left bring the cake out of the oven and listen very carefully. A completely cooked rich fruit cake will be silent, but if the cake is even slightly under-cooked there is a faint 'humming' noise, and the cake should be returned once more to the oven.

5. Allow the cake to cool in the tin, for if this type of cake is turned out when hot the weight of the fruit may cause it to break. When quite cold, turn out of the tin, remove the brown paper from the base but store with the greaseproof paper round the cake until ready to ice.

Checking the cake's progress

1. It does not hurt to open the oven door carefully for a rich cake like this, and it is an excellent guide as to whether the particular oven being used is the same temperature as given in the recipe. Half way through the cooking time the cake should be a pleasant golden colour, if it is paler, the oven is lower than average and the cooking time will probably be longer. If it is becoming slightly darker, adjust the oven heat to a lower temperature or mark than given in the recipe and put a piece of brown paper over the top of the cake tin.

2. Never choose too large a cake tin for the size of the oven, for if the tin is over the gas burners or touching the heating elements the cake is bound to become too dark.

A Rich Christmas Cake recipe is suitable for any special celebration, including a wedding. The following gives an idea of how to adapt the cooking time and quantities:

For a 5 inch square or 6 inch round cake:
Use half the ingredients, and bake for 1 hour at 325–350°F.—Gas Mark 3 (temperature A)

and 2 hours at 300°F.—Gas Mark 2 (temperature B).

For a 6 inch square or 7 inch round cake:
Use three-quarters of the ingredients, and bake for 1 hour at temperature A, and 2½ hours at temperature B.

For a 9 inch square or 10 inch round cake:
For a tin not more than 3 inches deep, use 1½ times basic ingredients and bake for 1½ hours at temperature A and 3–3½ hours at temperature B. For a really deep tin use twice the amount of ingredients, and bake for 1½ hours at temperature A, and 4½ hours at temperature B.

Chinese chews

1 oz. margarine or butter	½ teaspoon baking powder)
3 oz. castor sugar	3 oz. chopped dates
1 egg	1–2 oz. chopped walnuts
½ teaspoon vanilla essence	*To decorate:*
2 oz. self-raising flour (or plain flour and	1 oz. icing sugar ⑫

Cream the margarine and sugar, add the egg and vanilla essence together, then the flour or flour and baking powder, dates and nuts. Spread into a greased and floured 8 inch sandwich tin and bake for approximately 15 minutes above the centre of a moderate oven (375°F.—Gas Mark 4–5). Cool in the tin, then cut into small fingers and coat in icing sugar.

Australian honey raisin bars

3 oz. butter	1 teaspoon baking powder
6 level tablespoons honey (6 oz.)	6 oz. stoned raisins
3 eggs	4 oz. chopped hazelnuts or walnuts ⑯–⑳
6 oz. plain flour	

Cream together the butter and honey until soft and light, and beat in the eggs one at a time. Add sieved flour and baking powder, raisins and nuts. Spread in a greased rectangular baking tin approximately 9 by 12 inches, and bake in the centre of a very moderate oven (350°F.—Gas Mark 3–4) for approximately 30 minutes until golden brown. Cool in the tin and cut into bars. Lift out carefully. These bars keep well and are 'chewy' and moist.

3. Blend the sieved icing sugar with the lemon juice and spoon over the cakes. Then decorate as shown to make faces.

Shortbread

3 oz. butter	1 oz. cornflour or rice flour
1½–2 oz. sugar	
3 oz. plain flour	⑧

1. Cream butter and half the sugar, work in the flour and cornflour, then the last of the sugar. Knead well, then press into a good round shape on the back of an ungreased tin, or roll thinly and cut into fingers, or put into a floured shortbread mould. If using a mould, leave the shortbread in this for approximately 30 minutes to form the shape, then turn gently but carefully on to the baking tin.

2. Bake for 40 minutes if $\frac{1}{3}$–$\frac{1}{2}$ inch thick in a slow oven (300–325°F.—Gas Mark 2). Cool on the tin. For thinner biscuits bake for about 20 minutes in the centre of a very moderate to moderate oven (350–375°F.—Gas Mark 3–4).

Basic biscuit dough

12 oz. margarine or butter	1 lb. flour, preferably plain
12 oz. castor sugar	A little milk or 1–2 eggs to mix

Cream margarine or butter and sugar until soft and light. Add the flour and knead very

Funny face cakes

4 oz. self-raising flour, or plain flour and 1½ level teaspoons baking powder*	Soft glacé icing: 10 oz. sieved icing sugar, 3 tablespoons lemon juice
4 oz. castor sugar	To decorate:
4 oz. easy creaming margarine	'Smarties' or 'polka dots', angelica, currants, chocolate
2 eggs	vermicelli ㉔

*This is preferable.

1. Sieve dry ingredients into a bowl. Add the other ingredients and beat together for 2 minutes until well mixed. Spoon this mixture into about 24 cake cases arranged in patty tins to keep their shape.

2. Bake above the centre of a moderately hot oven (400°F.—Gas Mark 5–6) for about 15 minutes. Allow to cool.

well, then gradually add sufficient milk or egg to bind.

If you only wish to make one lot of biscuits or smaller quantities, make only $\frac{1}{2}$ or $\frac{1}{3}$ of this mixture.

Traffic light biscuits

Roll out $\frac{1}{3}$ of the basic dough above to $\frac{1}{4}$ inch in thickness. Cut into rounds and put half on to an ungreased baking tin. Cut three tiny holes from the rest of the rounds and place these on another tin. The dough removed can be kneaded and used for further rounds. Bake for approximately 10 minutes in the centre of a moderate oven (375°F.—Gas Mark 4–5). Cool on the tins, put the biscuits with the holes on top of the plain rounds. Fill the holes with red, yellow and green jam or glacé icing—18 biscuits.

Animal biscuits

Cut $\frac{1}{3}$ of the basic biscuit dough, rolled out as above, into fancy shapes. Bake as above, cool then ice as shown in the picture.

Biscuit whirls

Roll out the remainder of the dough to a neat oblong about $\frac{1}{4}$ inch thick. Cover with chocolate spread, jam or finely chopped dates. Roll as a Swiss roll, cut into slices about $\frac{1}{2}$ inch thick. Bake for 15 minutes at the temperature for the Traffic Light Biscuits. Dust with sieved icing sugar.

MELTING METHOD

Used for gingerbread, etc.—recipe Book 2. Fat, sugar and golden syrup or treacle (if used in the recipe) are melted then added to the sieved dry ingredients.

Canadian cake

11 oz. self-raising flour (or plain flour with 2½ level teaspoons baking powder) 1 level teaspoon spice	½ *level* teaspoon bicarbonate of soda 8 oz. dried fruit under ½ pint water* 2 oz. lard 4 oz. brown sugar

*Measure out ½ pint and take out 1 tablespoon.

1. Sieve the flour or flour and baking powder with the spice and bicarbonate of soda into a

mixing bowl. Add the dried fruit.

2. Put the water, lard and brown sugar into the saucepan. Heat until the lard is melted. Leave the mixture to cool. Pour over the dry ingredients and mix thoroughly with a wooden spoon.

3. Line a 7-inch round cake tin with greased greaseproof paper and pour in the cake mixture.

4. Bake in the centre of a very moderate oven (325°F.—Gas Mark 3), for about 1¼ hours.

For a cake with a little more flavour, use 12 tablespoons water only and add 2 *level* tablespoons golden syrup or honey to the lard and sugar.

Flapjacks

| 3 oz. margarine or fat | 2 oz. golden syrup | |
| 2 oz. soft brown sugar | 6 oz. rolled oats | ⑫ |

Heat the fat, sugar and syrup in a saucepan until the sugar dissolves, cool slightly, mix the rolled oats with the melted ingredients. Spread in a shallow greased 8-inch square tin. Bake in the centre of a very moderate oven (350°F.—Gas Mark 3–4) for 30–35 minutes. Leave to cool a little, then cut into finger-size pieces and leave to finish cooling on a cooling tray.

Brandy snaps

2 oz. butter	2 oz. flour (self-raising or plain)*	
2 oz. castor sugar		
2 oz. golden syrup	½–1 teaspoon	
(2 level tablespoons)	powdered ginger	⑫

*Remove 1 teaspoon flour.

1. Put the butter, sugar and syrup into a saucepan and heat until the butter has melted, then stir in the sieved flour and ginger. Put teaspoons of the mixture on well greased baking trays or sheets, allowing about 4–5 inches between as the mixture spreads out during cooking.

2. Cook for 8–10 minutes as near the centre as possible of a very moderate oven (325–350°F.—Gas Mark 3) until the mixture is golden brown in colour. Since the biscuits must be rolled

while hot it is advisable to time the cooking so one tray only comes from the oven at a time.
3. When the biscuits are cooked, cool for about 2 minutes until sufficiently set to insert a palette knife under them. Take one biscuit and roll it round the greased handle of a wooden spoon. Hold in position until the biscuit sets, then put on to a wire cooling tray. Continue with the rest of the biscuits. If they begin to harden too much to roll return the baking tray to the oven for 2–3 minutes. When quite cold store in an airtight tin.

Variations

Use black treacle instead of golden syrup and 1 teaspoon lemon juice instead of ginger. Allow the full 2 oz. flour (illustrated).

Fill the brandy snaps with whipped cream just before serving.

WHISKING METHOD

USED for the lightest cakes, sponges, etc.— recipes Book 2.

Eggs and sugar are whisked until light and thick, then the sieved flour, etc. is incorporated.

Swiss roll

2 eggs	1 tablespoon hot
2–3 oz. castor sugar*	water ④–⑥
2 oz. self-raising flour	*To fill:*
(or plain flour,	3 tablespoons jam
½ teaspoon baking	*To decorate:*
powder can be added)	castor or icing sugar

* The larger amount of sugar gives a lighter sponge.

This is based on a whisked sponge cake, and having mastered the technique of making a sponge, the Swiss roll is very simple.

1   **2**   **3**

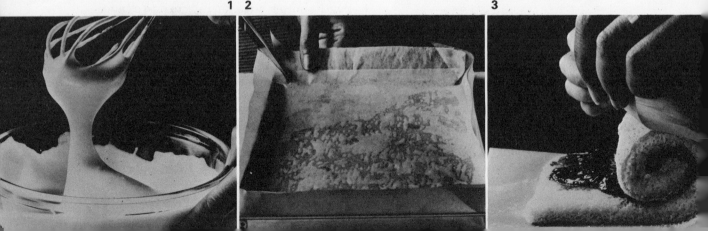

1. Line a small Swiss roll tin approximately 7 by 11 inches with greased greaseproof paper. Cut the paper neatly at the corners so the cake will turn out a perfect shape. Put the jam to warm.

2. Put the eggs and sugar into a basin and whisk until light and thick. If desired, the eggs and sugar may be whisked in a basin over hot but not boiling water.

3. Fold in the sieved flour or flour and baking powder with a metal spoon. Lastly fold in the hot water, for a Swiss roll should flow readily.

4. Pour the mixture into the prepared tin and bake for 7–9 minutes towards the top of a hot oven (425–450°F.—Gas Mark 6–7). Test by pressing gently but firmly with the forefinger, and if no impression is left turn the Swiss roll on to a sheet of sugared paper. Trim off the crisp edges, spread with the warm jam.

5. To roll a Swiss roll make a shallow cut in the roll ½–1 inch from the end nearest to you. Fold this over firmly, lift the paper under the sponge and use this to help form the cake into a neat roll. Cool away from a draught.

Flavourings: Use 1½ oz. flour and ½ oz. cocoa, or add dessertspoon coffee essence to eggs and sugar.

Cream Swiss roll ④–⑥
Make and bake as directions for Swiss roll.

Turn on to sugared paper. Cover with piece of greaseproof paper.
Roll firmly—leave until quite cold.
Unroll gently and slowly, spread with jam and whipped cream or butter icing.
A small roll, as recipe given, needs ¼ pint whipped cream or butter icing made with 2–3 oz. butter, etc.

Genoese pastry

2 eggs	with ½ teaspoon
2–3 oz. castor sugar	baking powder)
2 oz. self-raising	2 oz. butter
flour (or plain flour	

This is an adaptation of a whisked sponge (method given in greater detail in Book 2).

1. Whisk the eggs and sugar until thick and light—see Swiss roll. Fold in the sieved flour or flour and baking powder with a metal spoon, then fold in the melted and cooled butter. This should be done slowly, gently and thoroughly.

2. Either bake in two 6–7 inch greased and floured, or lined, sandwich tins for approximately 12–14 minutes above the centre of a moderate to moderately hot oven (375–400°F.—Gas Mark 5–6), or use one 8 inch sandwich tin, or an oblong tin 8 by 6 inches.

Genoese pastry is ideal for:
(a) cutting into fancy shapes for small cakes. It is lighter than a Victoria sandwich but

firmer to handle than a whisked sponge.
(b) As the basis for gâteaux.

Macaroon biscuits

2 egg whites	5 oz. ground almonds
few drops almond essence	glacé cherries
	almonds
5–6 oz. castor sugar	⑫–⑯

Whisk egg whites lightly. Add almond essence, then sugar and ground almonds. If the egg whites are exceptionally large then work in a little more ground almond. Roll the mixture into rounds and put—well spaced out—on rice-paper. Put a cherry on half the biscuits and an almond on top of the remaining half and bake for approximately 20–25 minutes in the centre of a moderate oven (375°F.—Gas Mark 4–5). When nearly cold, remove from the tin and tear or cut round the rice paper.

Chocolate macaroons

To each egg white allow 1 oz. ground almonds, 1 oz. grated chocolate or chocolate powder and ½ oz. ground rice. Bake as before using same amount of sugar.

Coconut macaroons

Use 1½ oz. ground almonds and 1 oz. desiccated coconut to each egg white, together with 2½ oz. sugar. Proceed as before.

Doughnuts

½ oz. yeast	*Filling:*
1 oz. sugar	3 tablespoons jam
¼ pint tepid milk or milk and water	*For frying:* deep fat or oil
12 oz. plain flour	*For coating:*
pinch salt	2 oz. castor sugar
1 oz. margarine	⑫–⑯

These are made from a yeast dough, which is fried, instead of baked. There is a fuller treatment of yeast cookery, including bread making, in Book 2, Section 33.

Cream the yeast with a teaspoon of sugar, then add the milk and a sprinkling of flour. Put into a warm place for about 10–15 minutes until the surface is covered with bubbles, i.e. the 'sponge breaks through'. Meanwhile, sieve the flour and salt, rub in the margarine, add the rest of the sugar, then bind with the yeast liquid, add more liquid if desired for a pliable dough. Knead until smooth, cover the bowl and allow to 'prove' for 1 hour until double the size. Knead again and form into 12–16 balls, make a 'dent' in each ball, put in a little jam then re-form the ball so the jam is covered with the dough, put these on to a warmed greased baking sheet to 'prove' for 15 minutes. Meanwhile heat the fat or oil and test carefully—it must not be too hot otherwise the doughnuts will over-brown on the outside before being cooked in the centre. A cube of bread when tested should brown within 1 minute if using fat but just over $\frac{1}{2}$ minute with oil. Lower some of the doughnuts into the fat and cook for 2–3 minutes, then turn with a perforated spoon or two large spoons so they brown all over. When brown all over—this should take 6–8 minutes, lift out of the fat, drain for 1 minute on absorbent paper, then roll in the sugar.

Re-heat and re-test the fat or oil and cook the next batch.

Variations:

An egg may be used to bind the dough; in this case use a little less milk.

Ring doughnuts—make a firm dough, roll out after 'proving', cut into rings, 'prove' and fry for about 5 minutes.

Cream doughnuts—do not put the jam in before 'proving'; cook the doughnuts and when cold, split and fill with whipped cream and jam, roll in sugar.

MAKING MERINGUES

MERINGUES are made from a combination of egg white and sugar and form a delicious cake or topping for a pudding. Here are some important points to remember:

1. Egg whites will not whisk if they are too fresh. They must be at least 24 hours old.

2. The bowl should be scrupulously clean. A slight speck of flour or smear of grease will prevent the egg whites being whisked.

3. A good whisk, either hand or electric, must be used.

4. Whisk until the egg whites are so stiff that the bowl can be turned upside down without fear of the egg whites falling out.

5. Add the sugar by one of these methods:

(a) Gradually fold in all the sugar (for a rather soft topping on a pudding).

(b) Gradually whisk in half the sugar then fold in the rest (the method usually preferred).

(c) Gradually whisk in all the sugar (particularly suitable with an electric mixer).

Take great care to add the sugar correctly, or the egg mixture will lose its stiffness.

Meringues

2 egg whites	*To fill:*
4 oz. castor sugar	$\frac{1}{4}$ pint cream or mock
or 2 oz. castor and	cream
2 oz. icing sugar	

*To make 16–20 medium, 6–8 large shapes.

1. Whisk the egg whites until very stiff and add the sugar as described above. Brush the baking tin or sheet with a *very little* oil or melted butter.

2. Either put spoonfuls of the mixture on to the

tray or insert $\frac{1}{4}$–$\frac{1}{2}$ inch plain or rose-shape meringue pipe into a cloth bag and pipe the desired shape on to the tin.

3. Bake the meringues for $1\frac{1}{2}$–3 hours, according to size, in a very cool oven, 225–250°F.—Gas Mark 0–$\frac{1}{2}$. They should be dry but still uncoloured. If there are several trays of meringues, the oven position cannot be determined, but the ideal position is below the centre.

4. Remove the meringues from the baking tray while warm; lift them with a warm palette knife, which has been dipped in very hot water, then dried on a tea towel.

When cold, store in an airtight tin; they keep for weeks if desired.

Brisbane meringue (recipe page 152)

To flavour: Sieve 2 teaspoons cocoa or 1–2 teaspoons instant coffee with the sugar.

To fill meringues: Do this just before serving, as they become soft if stored longer.

Cooking meringues on top of puddings

1. Follow directions for beating the eggs and incorporating the sugar (page 189).

2. If serving HOT you can use the smaller proportion of sugar, i.e. 1 oz. to each egg white.

3. If you wish to serve it COLD, however, the meringue will be much crisper if you allow 2 oz. sugar to each egg white.

4. If the meringue becomes sticky this may be because the egg white mixture did not touch the pastry. Always put it to the very edge of the pastry or the dish for quick baking.

5. The real secret of a good COLD meringue pudding is to set the meringue very slowly indeed, i.e. allow the minimum of 1 hour at 250–275°F.—Gas Mark $\frac{1}{2}$–1. An even longer period at this low temperature will be quite satisfactory and will not harm the filling.

6. If serving HOT you can set the meringue within about 15–20 minutes in a moderate oven.

7. In a Baked Alaska (recipe page 172) the meringue is 'flashed' (just browned) in a very hot oven for a few minutes or even under the grill. This makes certain that the ice cream or filling is not heated.

190

DECORATING CAKES

BOOK 2 gave the recipes and methods of decorating cakes by covering with icing sugar, glacé or water icing, butter icing and marzipan and royal icing.

It is possible to use both butter and royal icing for piping on cakes. Glacé icing is only suitable for a line design as used in feathering.

Feathering

Make up the desired amount of glacé icing and tint a small amount in a darker colour.
Picture 1: Cover the cake with the icing; DO NOT ALLOW TO SET. Use a piping bag of paper or material or an icing syringe and insert a writing pipe No. 1 or 2 in it. Put in the darker coloured icing and pipe lines across the cake.
Picture 2: Take a fine skewer and 'drag' the lines of icing towards one side at regular intervals.
Picture 3: 'Drag' the icing the opposite way between the scallops, so giving the effect of feathers.

Piping with butter or royal icing

The icing should be an easily controlled consistency. If too soft it will not hold a shape. If too stiff it is difficult to handle.

Butter icing is made by creaming 2 oz. butter and 3 oz. sieved icing sugar and colouring and flavouring as desired.

Royal icing is made by whisking 8 oz. sieved icing sugar into 1 egg white and beating until white, then adding 1 dessertspoon lemon juice and colouring as desired.

Equipment

There is no need to buy a great number of icing pipes.

A writing pipe No. 1 is very fine, No. 2 medium, No. 3 thicker.

A star pipe No. 5 or No. 6 or No. 8 will give a great variety of designs—see picture.

For writing or a flowing design hold the pipe at an angle—rather like a pen—and let the icing flow steadily.

For erect shapes keep the pipe upright and press to give the required size, then lift the pipe sharply to break off the icing.

With the exception of cake 1, which has no piping and No. 6, in which a No. 21 (12 star) pipe was used, all the rest have been decorated by using butter icing and a No. 8 (8 star) pipe. The groundwork of glacé icing must be dry before piping.

The form of piping is:

2. Upright stars.
3. First 2 lines then a shell pattern between.
4. First a ring of small stars, then the pipe is held less upright to make the border design.
5. Lines in vanilla then chocolate butter icing.
7. Lines then a flowing shell pattern.
8. A flowing design.

19. FOOD PRESERVATION

IT is wise housekeeping to preserve foods when they are cheap or readily available, for use later in the year when they may be out of season or expensive. There are various ways of preserving food:

1. *Jams, pickles and chutneys*
Simple jams and chutneys were covered in Book 2.

2. *Bottling*
Methods of bottling fruit are given below. Vegetables must only be bottled in a pressure cooker and the manufacturers of pressure cookers give excellent instructions.

3. *Deep freezing*
Home freezers are becoming more plentiful and it is not difficult to preserve food in a deep freeze.

BOTTLING FRUIT

1. It is essential that the fruit should be firm and ripe. Do not choose over-ripe fruit; it will break. Under-ripe fruit, on the other hand, has a poor flavour.

2. Fruit has a much better flavour if bottled in syrup rather than water.

3. It is important to follow the timing for fruit preservation, for if fruit is sterilised for too short a period it will not keep, and if for too long a period it will become over-softened.

Fruit may be sterilised in a deep pan or in the oven. On the whole the deep pan method is preferable, since the fruit is kept more moist by being covered by the liquid during sterilisation. If you have a pressure cooker, follow the manufacturer's instructions carefully.

To prepare jars for bottling
Wash new jars thoroughly. Old jars should be inspected carefully in case there are any chips which would prevent the jar from sealing. Rubber rings should be put into a basin and covered with boiling water to sterilise them and make them more pliable. Replace old rubber rings.

To prepare fruit for bottling
Fruits such as plums will need washing in cold water then drying. Soft fruit should be picked over carefully, rinsed in cold water then left to drain. Gooseberries should be topped and tailed, then washed and dried. Some fruit, however, needs more preparation.
Apples: Peel, core and slice, and immediately drop into a bowl of salted water. (Use 1 level tablespoon kitchen salt to each quart of cold water.) Let the apples stay there for 10 minutes, covered with a plate if desired, but this is not really necessary. This stops them going brown.

Peaches: Lower the peaches carefully into boiling water and leave for ½ minute. Remove with a perforated spoon or tablespoon then lower into cold water. Remove the skins. Leave in cold water until ready to pack the jars, to prevent discoloration. Halve and stone.

Pears: Prepare dessert pears as apples. If using hard pears, simmer in the syrup (below) until nearly tender, then drain if using the oven method or cool if using the steriliser method. A little lemon juice added to the syrup improves the flavour and keeps the pears white.

Tomatoes: Skin, if wished, as under peaches. Although it is not essential, tomatoes are improved if ½ teaspoon salt and ½ teaspoon sugar are added to each 1 lb. tomatoes.

Rhubarb: Wipe and cut into convenient-sized pieces.

Preparing syrup for fruit bottling

People vary in the amount of sugar they like in a syrup. The following gives the approximate amounts to use.

A light syrup: 4 oz. sugar to 1 pint water. This is an excellent amount for quite sweet fruit or when entering fruit into a competition, as there will be little tendency for the fruit to rise.

Medium syrup: 6–8 oz. sugar to 1 pint water. This is the syrup preferred by most people as it keeps the maximum flavour in the fruit.

Fruits may rise a little in this syrup.

Heavy syrup: 12 oz. sugar to 1 pint water. This gives a very sweet taste and fruits are very likely to rise in the jars.

Boil the sugar and water together until the sugar is dissolved. Strain if wished before using.

Bottling in a steriliser

Any deep container can be used, but a proper steriliser with a thermometer is obviously the most efficient.

1. Prepare the fruit and make the syrup. Pack the fruit into the jars, as tightly as possible. Fill to the very top of the jars with COLD water or COLD syrup. Put on the rubber bands and the lids. If using the screw-band jars, turn these as tightly as possible, then unscrew for half a turn, so allowing for the expansion of the glass. If using the clip tops put the clip into position.

2. Put some sort of padding at the bottom of the steriliser. A wooden board, several thicknesses of paper or an old cloth will do. Stand the jars on this, being careful they do not touch the sides of the pan, or each other. It is always preferable to completely cover the jars in the steriliser with cold water, but if this is not possible, fill the steriliser with cold water up to the necks of the jars, then either put on the lid or cover with a board or tea cloth to keep in the steam.

Stuffed eggs and prawn

194

3. Take 1½ hours to bring the water in the steriliser to simmering, i.e. 165–175°F. for all fruits except pears and tomatoes, when the water should be brought to 180–190°F. With pears, peaches and tomatoes maintain the temperature for 30 minutes. With all other fruits, maintain the temperature for 10 minutes.
4. Before lifting out the jars bale out a little water so that it is easier and safer to lift them out. Stand the jars on a wooden surface and in the case of jars with screw bands, tighten these.
5. Leave the jars for 24 hours, then test by removing the clip or band and seeing if the lid is tight. If it is, and the jar can be lifted by the lid, then the jars have sealed.

Bottling fruit in its own juice

The flavour of fruit bottled by this method is much the best, for it is not diluted with water or syrup. Particularly suitable for tomatoes, but can be used for raspberries, strawberries, peaches and halved plums. Do not use other fruits containing less juice. For tomatoes— skin, cut in half if large, pack into jars with ½ teaspoon salt and ½ teaspoon sugar. Other fruit —pack into jars with sprinkling of sugar. Put on rubber rings, tops, etc. DO NOT sterilise in the oven, but follow directions above for bottling in a steriliser.

Pulping fruit

Stew fruit, adding little or no water and sugar to taste. For tomatoes, add ½ teaspoon sugar and ½ teaspoon salt to each 1 lb. If smooth pulp is required, rub cooked fruit through a sieve and reboil. Put tops of jars and rubber bands to boil for 10 minutes. Also put glass jars to get VERY HOT. Pour the boiling pulp into jars, seal down as quickly as possible and immediately stand jars in steriliser filled with boiling water. Boil fruit pulp for good 5 minutes and tomato pulp for good 10 minutes. Screw bands should be loosened half-turn before going into the boiling water and tightened when they come out.

To bottle in the oven

Prepare the fruit as pages 193–4. Pack into the clean dry jars, packing as tightly and neatly as possible. A jar looks more attractive if all the same size fruit is used.
Since the fruit obviously shrinks during sterilising, it is suggested that the jars are filled to just above top. The jars are put into a cool oven (240°F.—Gas Mark ½); where pressure is extra good use Gas Mark ¼.
Stand the jars either on an asbestos mat, several thicknesses of paper or cardboard, or on a wooden board. Cover the tops of the jars with an old, clean tin lid. While the jars are in

Food for a picnic

the oven, put the glass lids and rubber bands on to boil for 5 minutes. If using metal tops, drop these for 1 minute into boiling water.

How long to leave fruit in the oven

Raspberries, Loganberries: 45 minutes
(Do not pack too tightly.)
Rhubarb, Red and Black Currants: 50 minutes
Plums, Apples, Blackberries, Damsons, Greengages and Cherries: 1 hour
Whole Peaches, Whole Apricots: $1\frac{1}{4}$ hours
Halved Peaches, Halved Apricots, Pears, Tomatoes: $1\frac{1}{2}$ hours
Fruit Salad: Give time required by fruit needing maximum sterilising, e.g. peaches, pears.
Have ready a kettle of boiling water or a pan of boiling syrup. Bring the jars one at a time out of the oven. Put on to a wooden surface, pour over the boiling liquid, tapping the jar as you do so, until it completely overflows. If using a screw top type of jar, put on the rubber ring first, put on the top, hold on to this tightly, then either screw down, clip down or put on weight. Do not handle the jars any more than necessary for 24 hours. After this time, remove the screw band or clip and test to see if the lid is firm. It should be possible to lift the jars by the lid. When the jars have sealed there is no need to replace either the clip or screw band. If the screw band is put on the jar, do this only

loosely, and it is advisable to lightly grease the inside of the band. The oven method is suitable for all fruits, but *not for pulping or tomatoes or fruit bottled in its own juice* (see previous page).

HOME FREEZING

The popularity of home freezing is growing enormously and in addition to the separate home freezer, it is now possible to buy ordinary refrigerators with a compartment where you do your own home freezing and can store the frozen foods. Never attempt to freeze foods, except ice cream and iced and frozen desserts, in the ordinary freezing compartment of a domestic refrigerator. The temperature here is much too high and spoils the food.

Only best quality foods should be preserved by home freezing. Fruits and vegetables should be frozen directly they are picked. Meat and poultry, if freshly killed, should be hung for several days to make sure it is tender.

Packaging
Moisture-vapour-proof packaging materials are essential for freezing and storing produce. Food will lose moisture by evaporation unless well packed and sealed, because of the low humidity inside the freezer. The food will become dry, the texture and colour will deteriorate and the flavours will disappear. Badly packaged strong smelling food may spoil other

produce stored in the same freezer. Leave as little air as possible inside the containers before sealing.

Equipment

The quality of frozen foods depends on speed in preparation and quick drop in temperature when in the freezer. For freezing set the home-freezer at −20°F. or −20°C. For storing set the home freezer at 0°F.

Freeze small quantities quickly:

(a) This method, by restricting the size of the ice crystals formed from the natural juices in food, minimises any change in its cell structure.

(b) With the shorter freezing times, there is less time for the separation of water in the form of ice, so less mineral salts are lost through seepage as the foods defrost.

(c) In this rapid freezing process there is quick cooling of the food to temperatures at which bacteria, moulds and yeast cannot grow. Foods are therefore protected from deterioration.

Note: Do not freeze too much food at one time, or you will overload the freezer.

General points on freezing

Detailed instructions for freezing various types of food will be found in a special book, but here are some general points to observe:

Meat and poultry: Use young, tender joints of poultry. Separate chops from each other so they do not stick during freezing. Wrap giblets separately from the bird.

Fruit: Pack the fruit in containers either with a light sprinkling of sugar between each layer or in a cold sugar syrup (page 194). If using syrup, fill the container to within ½ inch of the top to allow for expansion during freezing. Polythene bags may be used, or waxed containers.

Vegetables: Prepare as for cooking, i.e. shell peas, slice runner beans, etc., and then blanch by immersing in boiling water for 1–3 minutes. This time varies according to the vegetable; peas, for example, take 1 minute only. Drain and cool, then pack and freeze.

Cooked foods: Many ready-cooked foods, e.g. bread, sandwiches, meat pies, light sponge cakes, etc., may be frozen. These are extremely useful for emergencies. Follow instructions given by the manufacturer.

DRYING HERBS

Pick the herbs during a dry spell. Wash them. Put on flat baking trays covered with a thick layer of newspaper topped with a sheet of kitchen paper, greaseproof or muslin. Parsley is a better colour if dried for a few minutes in a hot oven; all other herbs should be dried slowly in the airing cupboard or very low oven (with the door ajar), until brittle. Crumble and store in airtight jars.

20. MENU PLANNING

GOOD menu planning means:
1. Considering the tastes and needs of all the family.
2. Giving variety to stimulate the appetite, and to develop a liking for many foods in young children.
3. Using money wisely and cooking with cheaper foods which are often high in nutritional value.
4. Considering the time available. Good meals *can* be prepared in a short time by working wives, business girls, etc.
5. Making use of convenience foods and short cuts when suitable.
6. Making wise use of the cooking facilities available. These may be limited as in a flatlet, etc. (page 210).
7. Considering particular problems, e.g.
   (a) cooking for special diets (page 205–6).
   (b) preparing packed meals (page 224).
   (c) choosing foods for those who need to lose or gain weight (pages 229–30).

When the menu has been chosen, the next important point is to make a shopping list and decide on the quantities of food needed.

Note: Unless stated to the contrary, most cookery books give quantities for four average portions. In this book, and Books 1 and 2, the portions are given in the coloured recipe panels. For special menus, i.e. entertaining, quantities to buy are given on pages 216–17, 219 and 222.

Above all else, meals must be planned to provide the essential nutrients for all the family. A breakfast menu is analysed below. Book 2 analysed menus for a selected family in detail. Family meals must also be planned to provide a time of relaxation for everyone.

DISH	FOOD VALUE
Grapefruit with sugar	Vitamin C and sugar
Fried bacon and egg	Protein in both Fat in bacon, little iron in egg
Fried bread	Carbohydrate, fat and vitamin B
Toast	Carbohydrate and vitamin B
Butter	Fat, vitamins A and D

Family breakfasts

Some people feel that a cooked breakfast is too time-consuming for busy people. It is pos-

Suggestions for breakfast

1st course:

Cooked fruit, prunes, grapefruit, fruit juice
or Cereal with milk and sugar
Porridge with milk and sugar

Main course:

Eggs—baked, boiled, fried, omelettes, poached
    or scrambled
Bacon—grilled, fried, bacon cakes (page 112)
Cold ham
Fish—grilled, fried or baked. Serve white fish,
    herrings, kippers, bloaters, canned sardines,
    smoked haddock—poached or in kedgeree
Vegetables—tomatoes, mushrooms (grilled or
    fried), baked beans, potatoes (fried or as
    potato cakes)
Cheese
Bread, toast, crispbread, starch reduced rolls,
home made hasty rolls
Butter and jam, marmalade, honey
Tea, coffee, or milk for children

sible, however, to have an adequate meal without cooking, e.g. fruit or fruit juice, cold ham or canned sardines, or cheese (this is a particularly good protein food and very popular in Scandinavia); bread or rolls, butter, marmalade or jam; coffee or tea and/or milk.

A good breakfast is an essential start to the day, particularly if the main meal is eaten at night.

Main meals for the family

Generally, the main nutrients of the day are provided at this meal. The choice of menus is limitless—10 are given, each one with a particular advantage, and suitable for a midday or evening dinner.

All recipes are in this book or Books 1 or 2.

Menu 1

Vegetable soup (with cream, see picture)
Cold brisket of beef, salad,
jacket potatoes
Rice pudding and baked fruit

This menu is satisfying and needs little preparation (except for the soup—and this could be canned). It is important that the salad contains tomatoes, to provide some vitamin C.
To save fuel the soup could be cooked or heated in a covered dish in the oven.

Menu 2

Steak and kidney pudding,
creamed potatoes, spring greens or spinach
Fresh fruit salad and custard sauce

This menu is prepared without using the oven. As a substantial main course is prepared the rest of the meal can be light. Small children should not be given too much suet crust.

Menu 3

Roast stuffed chicken, sausages, bacon rolls,
bread sauce, gravy
Roast potatoes, sprouts or cabbage
Fruit pie, cream or ice cream

This more expensive meal is ideal for Sundays when the family have time to enjoy it.
The pie can be prepared beforehand and reheated.

Menu 4

Fish Portuguese, green salad,
scalloped potatoes
Fresh fruit
Cheese and biscuits

This gives a satisfying and interesting way of serving fish and an economical use of the cooker. Small children need to develop a taste for raw fruit and cheese.

Menu 5

Grapefruit
Fried fish, tartare sauce,
chipped potatoes, peas
Jam sponge pudding

This meal avoids using the oven and is the most popular way of serving fish. As little vitamin C is provided, however, it is a good idea to begin with fresh grapefruit. Small children should not be given too much of the coating of the fried fish.

Menu 6

Grilled chops, tomatoes, mushrooms,
sauté potatoes, sprouts
Fruit flan (pastry or sponge) and cream
or ice cream

In this menu the sweet may be prepared beforehand and so the rest of the meal is easily and
quickly cooked.

Menu 7

Lancashire hot pot
Cauliflower or a green vegetable
Lemon soufflé pudding

The main dish uses a cheap cut of mutton or
lamb. As the dish contains potatoes, etc. there
is no need to cook more than one vegetable.

Menu 8

Stuffed marrow, roast or jacket potatoes,
green salad
Honeycomb mould

The main dish may be varied by using either a
meat or vegetarian stuffing and provides an
economical but appetising meal. The green
salad gives a good contrast in texture.

Menu 9

Cheese soufflé,
baked tomatoes, spinach
Baked bananas and cream

This menu is ideal when a light meal is re-

Fried pork chops and fried apple rings

quired. Make sure the family are ready to eat
the soufflé immediately, as it cannot be kept
waiting.

Menu 10

Vegetable platter served with cheese sauce
Fruit jelly

A selection of vegetables: artichokes, cauliflower, beans or peas, carrots, etc., topped with
a sauce containing plenty of cheese for protein
—at least 1 oz. per person—gives a most satisfying meal.

Family tea

There is a great difference in the type of tea that families have. Sometimes it will be rather like afternoon tea (given in the section on entertaining), but probably less elaborate. At other times it will be a high tea. Suggestions for high teas are given below. It is important that younger schoolchildren, who will not stay up late for supper, have some protein at tea time. If a substantial midday and evening meal is given, most adults will only need a cup of tea and a biscuit or piece of cake.

High tea

A high tea is an ideal meal for children, for as it is served at the normal tea time, they can play after the meal before going to bed. At high tea, you could serve:

A savoury main course: something cooked, like fish and chips with salad; sausages, potatoes and tomatoes; something served on toast such as poached or scrambled eggs or Welsh rarebit; cold meat or cheese or hard-boiled eggs and salad, served with bread and butter and tea.

Cake is often served at this meal, but it is a good idea to have fruit or fruit salad, if meals throughout the rest of the day have not included a great deal of fresh fruit or green vegetables to provide vitamin C.

The menus below are also suitable for high tea.

Supper or lunch

The pattern of family eating varies according to whether or not most of the family come home for a midday dinner. If the main meal is served at midday, then the evening meal can be lighter. It may be a high tea or an evening supper. On the other hand, if it is more convenient to serve the main meal in the evening, then the meal in the middle of the day can be lighter.

Menus for light suppers or lunches

Stuffed tomatoes with Russian salad
Jelly cream

Fish au gratin with Lyonnaise potatoes
Fruit Melba

Fishcakes with anchovy or cheese sauce
Fruit shortcake

Cornish pasties with mixed salads
Chocolate mould and ice cream

Fish salad
Fruit cobbler

Liver and bacon with tomatoes,
mushrooms (optional)
Economical soufflé

Buck rarebit with grilled tomatoes, lettuce
Sponge gâteau

Feeding babies and small children

Up to the age of three to six months—this varies according to the particular child and the advice given by the doctor or clinic—a baby lives on milk, plus cod liver oil and orange juice to provide essential vitamins. A routine of feeding should be followed and this again will vary a great deal. The next stage in a baby's development is when weaning begins. This means that new foods are gradually introduced. Never try to introduce more than one new food in any one week, so that the weaning is a gradual process.

The foods are first introduced at the 2 o'clock feed, when bone and vegetable broth or half a lightly boiled egg yolk or $\frac{1}{2}$ to 1 tablespoon of very finely minced meat, liver or fish and creamed potatoes are given. The next stage will be adding prune, apple or apricot purée as a sweet, which can be mixed with some of the milk.

During this period a baby is generally developing its first teeth and needs really hard teething rusks.

As weaning continues, breakfast time will include a cereal—there are special baby cereals available—followed by rusk or toast spread with butter and honey or seedless jam. The main meal will include sieved carrots, green vegetables and, gradually, pieces of raw fruit.

The fruit must be peeled or washed carefully and when a small child is first given apple or any fruit that could lodge in its throat, an adult must be at hand.

After a year, a baby will be able to eat really crisp bacon, eggs cooked in various ways, steamed fish, including herring roes. Meat may be chopped rather than minced and light puddings, i.e. milk puddings, steamed sponge puddings, egg custards, etc. can be given. Tea time should include a protein, e.g. cheese sandwiches, sardine or egg sandwiches, and a light milk sweet such as junket, milk jelly, etc. Fruit containing pips, such as strawberries, raspberries, loganberries, should be sieved; *ripe* bananas should be mashed; stewed fruit may be given.

After two years of age, a small child can have family meals, but should not be given too large quantities or highly spiced or seasoned foods, pastry or very rich puddings.

Many authorities say that food habits are formed by two years of age. So it is desirable that plenty of variety in flavour and texture should be introduced as early as possible.

Feeding the elderly

As people become older they need less food than children, teenagers or active adults. It is essential, however, that they have adequate amounts of protein, vitamins and such minerals as calcium and iron.

Older people often have to manage on a restricted income; or find that certain foods that they have previously been able to eat cause indigestion, so choice of food is often limited. Milk and eggs are relatively cheap, easily digested and give essential nutrients. Cheese is a good protein food and a valuable source of calcium for bones. Doctors are now inclined to feel that the incidence of broken bones in old people might be due to lack of calcium rather than old age. Cooked cheese may cause indigestion in which case use uncooked in sandwiches, with biscuits, etc. Meat—tripe, sweetbreads are easy to digest; choose tender lean meat, which can be grilled, roasted, stewed, but not fried.

Fish is ideal if baked, steamed, poached, etc. but not fried.

Vegetables may need to be mashed or sieved, but freshly cooked green vegetables as well as fruit or fruit juice are important for their vitamin C content.

Vegetarians

Some vegetarians avoid meat and fish on humanitarian grounds but will eat eggs, cheese; other vegetarians prefer to eat no food that has any contact with animal life. This means that nuts must be substituted for eggs, cheese, meat, fish; nut milk is used in place of ordinary milk (although most vegetarians do drink ordinary milk); only vegetarian fats are eaten.

Health food stores provide a range of vegetarian foods, but it is essential that a strict vegetarian has a good protein intake from recipes using nuts and by including plenty of the vegetable proteins, e.g. beans, peas and lentils.

21. STORE CUPBOARD MEALS

CHAPTER Four, pages 33–43, dealt with a well-stocked store cupboard and the following four menus give examples of the kind of dishes that can be prepared quickly from food in stock.

Menu 1

Tomato soup au gratin
Corned beef cutlets with peas and tomatoes
Creamed rice with blackcurrant or rose hip sauce

Tomato soup au gratin

Large can tomato soup	2 tablespoons grated cheese
4 small triangles of bread	④

Heat the soup, toast the triangles of bread. Put the soup into heat-resisting soup cups, top with the toast and grated cheese and brown for 1 minute under the grill.

Corned beef cutlets

12 oz. can corned beef	*To coat:*
1 oz. margarine	1 egg
1 oz. flour	1 tablespoon water
¼ pint milk	2 tablespoons crisp
seasoning	breadcrumbs (raspings)
2 oz. soft	*To fry:*
breadcrumbs	2 oz. fat ④

Chop the corned beef, put into a basin and break with a fork. Make a thick sauce with the margarine, flour and milk (page 101), mix with the corned beef, together with seasoning and breadcrumbs. Allow to cool, divide into four portions, form into cutlet shapes with a palette knife. Mix the beaten egg and water, coat the cutlets with this, roll in the crisp crumbs then fry in the hot fat until crisp and golden brown. Drain on crumpled tissue or absorbent paper. Serve with canned peas and fried halved fresh or canned tomatoes.

Creamed rice with blackcurrant or rose hip sauce

Can of creamed rice
Blackcurrant or rose hip syrup ④

Put the creamed rice into four glasses and top with the syrup just before serving. Allow about a dessertspoon of syrup per person.

This menu and those that follow give quite well-balanced meals.

Menu 2

Salmon crisp crumble
Cheese, butter and biscuits
Fresh fruit

Salmon crisp crumble

2–4 oz. mushrooms	1 oz. flour
1½ oz. butter	7–8 oz. can salmon
2½ oz. (3 individual packets) potato crisps	1 medium can condensed tomato soup
	salt and pepper

Slice and fry mushrooms in 1 oz. of the butter. Coarsely crush crisps. Rub the remainder of the butter into the flour then add the crisps. Flake the salmon and blend with the soup and the cooked mushrooms. Season to taste. Put into a greased 1½ pint ovenproof dish. Sprinkle crisp mixture over the top and bake in a moderate oven (350–375°F.—Gas Mark 4) for 30 minutes.

Menu 3

Ham and vegetable casserole
Lettuce and tomato salad
Canned fruit and cream or evaporated milk

Ham and vegetable casserole

1 medium can chopped ham	2 tomatoes
1 medium can vegetable soup	*To garnish:* little chopped parsley

Cut the ham into neat pieces. Heat the soup, add the ham and sliced tomatoes and heat for a few minutes. Pour into a hot serving dish, top with parsley.
To make a more exciting meal, top with breadcrumbs and a little margarine and/or grated cheese and brown under the grill.
This can be served with heated potato crisps or with creamed potatoes prepared from dehydrated potatoes.

Menu 4

Individual cheese soufflés
Macedoine of canned vegetables
Poor knight's fritters
or
Fresh fruit
or
Sliced orange and nut salad

Individual cheese soufflés

Use the recipe on page 125, but the small soufflés pictured above had 2 tablespoons of milk added to give a softer texture and were baked for 20 minutes only.

Macedoine of canned vegetable

Heat canned vegetables, strain and toss in a little margarine and chopped parsley.

Poor knight's fritters

Make sandwiches of 8 slices of bread and butter and jam or marmalade, cut into fingers. Beat 1 egg, ¼ pint milk and 1 oz. sugar. Dip sandwiches in this quickly, so they do not become too soft, then fry in a little fat until crisp and brown on either side. Drain and sprinkle with sugar and serve with jam sauce (page 152).

Sliced orange and nut salad

Cut away orange peel and white pith, slice oranges thinly, arrange in glasses and top with chopped nuts.

22. MEAL PLANNING WITH LIMITED COOKING FACILITIES

MANY people have a bed-sitting room or flatlet with limited cooking facilities, and tend to plan snack meals only and to eat too many buns, cakes, etc. which need no preparation and are relatively cheap. This is a mistake. It is false economy to try to save time and money by eating inadequate food, for well-planned meals together with fresh air, exercise and adequate sleep are a sound basis for good health. It may well be that a good main meal can be purchased in a café or canteen so that other meals can be lighter and include salads, fresh fruit, cheese, milk, eggs, which are easy to prepare and give necessary nutrients.

The cooking equipment provided is often just a gas ring or electric hot plate or grill-boiler, and it may be worthwhile investing in a 2 or 3 tier steamer or a pressure cooker, as well as saucepans and a frying pan. Do not get into the habit of frying all food. Varied meals can still be prepared without an oven, although a somewhat different technique must be employed.

(a) *Roasting:* Use a strong covered saucepan or pressure cooker for a pot roast.

(b) *Casseroles:* Cook in a saucepan as a stew.

(c) *Vegetables:* Choose vegetables that can be cooked in the same pan—peas and carrots, mixed root vegetables—but do not omit green vegetables, even with one ring. These must be cooked separately, so prepare the main dish, remove from the heat and cover tightly, then cook the finely shredded green vegetables for a few minutes only in a small amount of boiling salted water. To reduce smell—as well as retain maximum of vitamins—cover the pan tightly. A piece of crust of bread in the pan absorbs the smell; flush the sink well with cold water.

(d) Cakes need to be steamed, and special recipes are necessary.

(e) Scones can be cooked in a frying pan.

If time is limited, it is a good idea to prepare a stew or casserole the night before, partially cook this and then continue cooking the next day. This is not safe in hot weather, unless you have a refrigerator.

Caravans

Some caravans are fitted with complete cookers, and normal meals may be cooked. Naturally, on a holiday, these will be simple meals which take the minimum of preparation. The ideas under store cupboard meals (page 207) may be found helpful.

Where a caravan is a permanent home and has limited cooking facilities, it is wise to invest in a pressure cooker for more ambitious meals.

23. ENTERTAINING

SUCCESSFUL entertaining depends on the following:

1. Inviting people who will mix well. It is the job of the host and/or hostess to make sure that guests are properly introduced and have someone to talk to with whom they have a certain amount in common. With young people formal introductions are rarely necessary, but it is important when older people come to a party to appreciate the fact that you introduce a younger person to an older person, for example: 'Grandmother, I would like you to meet a friend of mine, Jane Smith.' Or where the older person is not related: 'Mr. Brown, I would like to introduce a friend of mine, Jane Smith, who has just come back from France. Mr. Brown is my employer.' (Or some indication of what he does, who he is.) You may then go on to say: 'Mr. Brown I know enjoyed his holiday in France last year.'—so there is now an opening for a conversation.

A single girl is introduced to a married woman. A man is introduced to a woman unless there is a big difference in their ages, as assumed above. 'Mrs. Smith, may I introduce Mr. Brown', etc.

2. Pre-planning, both of food and entertainments, if any, so there is the minimum of fuss and last-minute preparations. Work out a complete shopping list and buy as much as possible beforehand.

3. Budget carefully for quantities of food and drink so there is sufficient, but little waste.

4. Each party, e.g. children's party, buffet party, dinner party, needs special planning and this is covered in the various sections.

Sending invitations to a party

Quite often, invitations are given on the telephone, but for a rather special occasion, it is better to write so there can be no misunderstanding about date or time. In most cases, an informal invitation will be sent, for example:

Dear Betty,

   I am giving a record party at home on Saturday 15th April from 8–11 p.m. and I do hope you can come.

Jennifer

A reply to such an invitation would be:

Dear Jennifer,

   Thank you very much for the invitation to your record party on Saturday 15th April and I should love to come.

Betty

The refusal would be:

Dear Jennifer,

Thank you very much for your invitation to a record party on Saturday 15th April. I am so sorry but we are going away for the weekend and therefore I cannot come. I am sure it will be a most enjoyable evening.

Betty

If a formal invitation is to be sent, it is worded in the third person. Here is an example:

Jennifer Smith
has much pleasure in inviting
Betty Green
to a record party at
24 Windsor Street, Brighton
on 15th April 1969, from 8–11 p.m.

R.S.V.P.   Informal Dress

(R.S.V.P. is an abbreviation of the French expression meaning 'Please reply'.)

On either a formal or informal invitation, you can give some idea of the kind of clothes people will wear, e.g. on the invitation above, you will notice the words 'Informal Dress'. Had it been an invitation to a dance, the same words might have been used, or 'Dinner Jackets' or 'Evening Dress'.

A formal invitation needs a formal reply.

An acceptance would be:

Betty Green
has much pleasure in accepting
the kind invitation of
Jennifer Smith
to a record party on
15th April 1969

A refusal would be:

Betty Green
regrets that
due to a previous engagement
she cannot accept
the kind invitation of
Jennifer Smith
to a record party on
15th April 1969

Tea time

Afternoon tea is not served at a table with everyone sitting round, but people have cups of tea and a small plate and serviette either on their laps or preferably on small tables or stools and the food is passed round. The kind of menu to serve would be:

small savoury sandwiches; scones and/or bread and butter with jam; small cakes or a light cake and possibly a fruit cake; pastries such as éclairs and meringues—these are eaten with a small fork.

Cheese men, stuffed eggs and cheese-raf

Menu 1 for special afternoon tea for 8 people

Asparagus rolls (recipe page 115)
   8–10 slices brown bread, etc.
Scrambled egg sandwiches
   8–12 slices bread, etc.
Scones (Book 2, pages 141–2)
   basic mixture made from 6 oz. flour, etc.
   2–3 oz. butter
   4–6 oz. jam
Dundee cake (recipe page 177)
   8 oz. flour, etc.
Orange gâteau (Book 2, page 152)
   8 oz. flour, etc.
Tea—average 2 cups per person
   3 oz. tea, 4 pints water, 1 pint milk, 4–6 oz. sugar

Menu 2 for special afternoon tea

Cucumber and tomato sandwiches
Scones—butter—whipped or clotted cream and jam
Macaroon biscuits (recipe page 188)
Rich cherry cake (recipe page 175)
Chocolate éclairs (recipe page 148) Tea

Menu for economical afternoon tea

Sandwiches of cheese and/or potted meat or potted fish and lettuce
Flapjacks (recipe page 185)
Eggless fruit cake (recipe page 173) Tea

Substantial tea time meals

There are times when a very much more substantial tea is required and after a sports meeting, for example, a menu could be:

   Sausage rolls and/or Cornish pasties; variety of rather larger savoury sandwiches; scones and jam or bread and butter and jam; fruit and iced cakes, doughnuts; tea.

Buffet parties

A buffet party is an excellent way of entertaining the maximum number of people in a relatively small amount of space. For a very large buffet party you can often borrow or hire trestle tables and these should be covered with tablecloths and decorated with low bowls of flowers. If a tablecloth is not available, a well laundered white sheet should be used instead. Food can be already arranged on the tables when guests arrive, with savoury dishes at one end and sweet dishes at the other. Try to plan food that may be eaten with fingers or with just a fork, unless there is room for people to sit down. It is extremely difficult to manage a knife and fork without sitting on a chair at a table. A buffet menu can include:

   Grapefruit, easier to eat if removed from skin and served in glasses.
   Melon, better cut into neat pieces and served in a glass.

Danish party menu

Soup—make sure soup cups or plates are not too full.

Chicken or other meat salad—cut the chicken or meat into neat, small pieces; sausage rolls;

vol-au-vent cases filled with savoury mixtures, page 135;

Cornish pasties;

open sandwiches—these look much more attractive than ordinary sandwiches;

a variety of cold sweets: fruit salad, trifles, ice cream, fruit flans, gâteaux;

cheese, biscuits, rolls and butter.

The cheese may be cut into portions suitable for an individual serving. Jugs of soft drinks, fruit cup or cider cup, tea or coffee should also be served, but it is generally more convenient if someone can pour out the drinks rather than everyone helping themselves.

Buffet menus

The following sample menus give quantities for 25 people for a buffet supper or lunch and also a simple tea menu for the same number.

If a greater selection of dishes is planned, prepare a smaller quantity of each dish.

Buffet for lunch or evening—25 people

Grapefruit

$\frac{1}{2}$ per person or 1 medium can serves 4–5

or

Melon

3 medium sized

or

Soup

Allow $\frac{1}{4}$–$\frac{1}{3}$ pint thin soup per person, i.e. $6\frac{1}{2}$–$8\frac{1}{2}$ pints. Allow $\frac{1}{4}$ pint only of thick soup

Chicken or

cold meat

2–3 oz. *boned* cooked meat per person, i.e. 2 large stuffed chickens *or* 6–7 lb. uncooked meat

Mixed salad

lettuce—3 good sized; cucumber—1 medium; tomatoes—2 lb.; hard-boiled eggs—4–6; watercress—4–8 oz.; mayonnaise—1 pint

Potato salad (Book 2, page 200)

3 lb. potatoes, etc.

Fruit salad (Book 2, pages 216–17)

2–3 large cans fruit (sliced peaches, pineapple, etc.); bananas—4 large; apples—2 large; pears—2 large; oranges—4 large; grapes—medium bunch

Rich trifle (page 155)

Sponge cakes—12, etc.

Ice cream

3 quarts or 1 gallon if buying *or* 6–7 large blocks *or* make mixture to give 6–7 pints

Cheese and biscuits

Cheddar $1\frac{1}{2}$–2 lb; Dutch 1 lb.; Camembert

2 boxes; Danish blue 12 oz.; biscuits 1½ lb.; butter 1½–2 lb.; rolls 30; lettuce or parsley to garnish

Buffet tea for 25 people

Tea (allowing 2 cups per person)
  8 oz. tea; 12 pints water; 3–4 pints milk; 1 lb. sugar
Bridge rolls (approximately 2 each)
  4 dozen or 50 rolls; 6 oz. butter; fillings as required (pages 115–16)
Sandwiches, allowing 1 slice bread per person, 1 large and 1 small sandwich loaf (3 lb.); 6 oz. butter or margarine; fillings as required (pages 115–16). For a more substantial tea, double these quantities.
Scones (1 each)
  Basic mixture made with 1 lb. flour (Book 2, pages 141–2)
Small iced cakes (30)
  Victoria sponge cake mixture, made from 8 oz. flour (Book 2, page 153)
  Rich fruit or Dundee cake (recipe page 177)
  2 cakes, 8-inch, cut into approximately 16 slices each
Swiss roll (recipe pages 186–7)
  2–3 rolls, cut into 10–12 slices each
Cold drinks
  1–2 bottles cordial, each giving 20–25 glasses

Complete meals

One of the best ways of entertaining is to invite people to come to a meal either in the middle of the day or in the evening. You serve the same kind of meal that the family enjoy, but will probably choose rather special dishes or make them look particularly attractive with interesting garnishes. The meal is more enjoyable if the table looks attractive, so plan a pleasant colour scheme. Polish silver and glassware well so they gleam and look well cared-for. Information on correct laying of a table is given in Book 1, pages 112–13. Have a small bowl of flowers on the table. Do not use tall vases which might be knocked over and which obscure vision and make it difficult for people to talk to each other. For a formal party, it is usual to have the most important male guest on the right of the hostess and the most important female guest on the right of the host. In order to make the meal easy to serve, the following hints may be useful:

1. Do not plan too many courses. Most people prefer to enjoy a three course meal plus cheese and coffee, i.e. hors d'oeuvre or soup, main course, sweet and cheese. It is a good idea to serve the cheese at the same time as the sweet, in case some of the guests prefer it. Sometimes a savoury can be served in place of a sweet— see pages 118–21, 125 for suggestions.

For a more ambitious meal, serve hors d'oeuvre followed by soup to give an extra course, or sweet followed by a savoury.

2. Try to plan a cold or very easy first course. This could be either fruit or tomato juice; grapefruit or melon—remember to have sugar on the table, or sugar and ginger with melon; avocado pear, page 159; hors d'oeuvre, recipe page 61; soup which just needs heating at the last minute, recipes page 64 (croûtons can be already fried and kept hot in the oven); a simple fish course such as a prawn cocktail, page 62 or fish salad, Book 2, pages 198–9.

3. The main meal can be either a roasted joint or poultry with correct accompaniments. This is a particularly good choice when entertaining someone who lives alone and who will rarely buy a good-sized joint. If someone can carve expertly, this can be done at the table. If not, carve the joint or poultry just before the meal, arrange it on a hot dish, cover it with foil and keep it warm in the oven. There are, however, many interesting hot dishes which may be brought straight to the table, for example, Chicken Maryland, page 84; Veal and ham pie, page 100; Braised beef. Grilled or fried steaks or chops need last-minute cooking, so are not a good choice unless the guests are very old friends and will not mind the hostess leaving them for a while to stay in the kitchen.

In hot weather or if a hot soup is served at the beginning of the meal, a very attractive meat or fish salad may be served.

If one guest is a vegetarian, it·is important to make a special vegetarian dish.

4. *Sweets:* if wishing to serve a hot sweet, a really good fruit pie served with cream needs no last-minute preparation. It is, however, important not to over-cook the pastry and when entertaining people, it is easy to forget the food is in the oven. It is safer to cook the pie before the meat and then reduce the heat in the oven so the pie is kept warm without fear of over-cooking. On the whole, however, cold sweets that may be prepared earlier in the day are ideal: trifle, page 155; chocolate mousse, page 156; meringue nests; cold soufflé, page 168; etc.

5. *Cheese and biscuits:* arrange an interesting selection of cheese, for example, Cheddar or Lancashire; Camembert or Brie; cream, cottage or processed cheese; Danish blue or Gorgonzola. If you have no cheese board, put these on a large dish or plate or small tray, with butter and biscuits. Garnish with lettuce leaves, sprigs of watercress, washed celery or radishes.

A savoury such as a cheese soufflé (page 125); Welsh rarebit; mushrooms on toast, etc. could be served as well as, or instead of, cheese.

6. *Coffee:* Make coffee and serve with hot and/or cold milk or thin cream and sugar.
7. For wines to choose, see pages 234–5.

Menu 1
Special dinner for 4 people
2 large grapefruit
Cream of tomato soup (can be omitted) (recipe page 65).
   1 lb. tomatoes, etc.
Roast beef
   joint 3 lb. if possible*
Yorkshire pudding
   3–4 oz. flour, etc.
Roast potatoes
   minimum 1 lb. *peeled* potatoes
Sprouts
   minimum 1–1¼ lb. sprouts
Caramel custard (recipe pages 154–5)
   4 eggs, etc.
Cheese and biscuits
   selection of 3–4 cheeses and biscuits; 4 oz. butter
Coffee
   1 pint coffee, etc.

A smaller joint gives less flavour and is more difficult to carve.

Dinner menu 2
   Fruit or tomato juice
   Chicken pie
   Summer pudding (recipe page 155)
   Cheese straws (Book 2, page 181) Coffee

Dinner menu 3
   Melon (can be omitted)
   Minestrone soup (recipe page 64)
   Salmon mayonnaise
   Potato salad
   Rich trifle (recipe page 155)
   Cheese and biscuits
   Coffee

Dinner menu 4
   Hors d'oeuvre (recipe page 61)
   Coq au vin (recipe pages, 96–7)
   New or Duchesse potatoes (page 113)
   Cauliflower with white sauce or
   Cauliflower Polanaise (recipe page 110)
   Chocolate soufflé (cold) (recipe page 168)
   Cheese and biscuits
   Coffee

Dinner menu 5
   Scallops (recipe page 78)*

Prepare, coat with sauce and heat just before the meal.

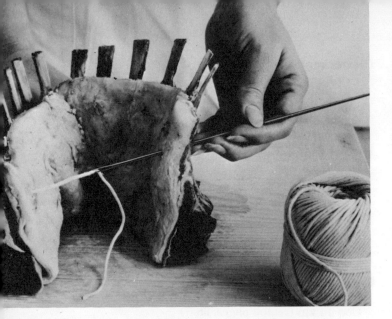

Crown roast of lamb (see below)
Duchesse potatoes (recipe page 113)
carrots, peas
Peach melba (recipe page 172)

Pipe ready to re-heat.

Crown roast of lamb

Buy two joints of best end of neck or loin of lamb in one piece—a minimum of 12 chops are required. Trim, or ask butcher to trim, the ends of the chops and cut between the chops so the meat may be formed into a round. Skewer, tie or sew into a round—see first picture. Place in the roasting tin and fill centre with a stuffing. The meat *and* the stuffing must be weighed to calculate the total cooking time, i.e. 20 minutes per lb. and 20 minutes over in a hot oven (425°F.—Gas Mark 6–7). Protect the ends of the bones and stuffing with foil during cooking. Garnish with cutlet frills (second picture).

Keeping food hot

Try to have all the food dished up or ready to dish up before the guests arrive.

Soup can be kept hot in the saucepan over a very low heat. If it is the type of soup that might spoil by over-heating, transfer to the top of a double saucepan over a pan of hot water.

Roast meat or poultry: Lift from the meat tin on to the serving dish, or carve (pages 89, 238) and arrange on the serving dish and cover with foil to prevent drying. Fried foods and Chicken Maryland may be kept hot for a very limited period on an *un*covered dish.

Vegetables: Put into hot serving dishes, cover with foil and put in the oven or warming compartment, or keep hot over pans of boiling water. Make sure the oven heat is reduced to a minimum to prevent over-cooking or scorching or use the warming compartment of the cooker. It is possible to buy electric warming plates on which food may be kept hot.

Steamed puddings: Turn out on to the hot serving dish; put over a pan of boiling water, cover with the basin. This saves hurried turning out at the last minute.

Custard: Keep hot as sauces.

Coffee: Have everything ready but make the coffee freshly (unless a thermostatically controlled percolator is being used), so the coffee is not over-infused.

To make cleaning up easier

Fill a tall jug with hot water and detergent so that when the dirty knives and forks are brought out from each course they may be lowered into it (keep ivory handles above the water). This makes them much easier to clean. Try to wash up saucepans, etc. before the meal or put them in soak.

Plates, etc. may be put to soak in warm water in the sink.

Sauces should be covered with a round of damp greaseproof paper to prevent a skin forming and put in the oven, or kept hot in the top of a double boiler.

24. PLANNING CHILDREN'S PARTIES

WHERE possible, try to avoid a very wide range of ages, so that games, food, etc. can be chosen to appeal to most of the guests. With family parties this is not always possible, so plan activities for several ages and group the children. For younger children follow a rather boisterous game with a quieter one.

Food for a children's party
(a) Have savoury as well as sweet dishes.
(b) Do not introduce too exotic foods, as most children are fairly conservative.
(c) Make cakes and sandwiches in tiny sizes.
(d) Do not have too elaborate icing or cream-filled cakes, for young children are inclined to be excited and cream cakes could make them ill.
(e) Be careful that the teapot and hot water are kept well away from little children.

Younger children's party menu for 12
Small bridge rolls—left as open sandwiches topped with cheese, eggs, etc.
    18 small rolls; 2 oz. butter; 3 oz. cheese—sliced thinly; 2–3 scrambled eggs; small jar potted meat
Banana sandwiches

24 slices bread; 1–1½ oz. butter; 3–4 mashed bananas
Sausages on sticks
    1 lb. tiny cocktail sausages (32 to lb) or chipolatas (16 to lb.) halved; 32 sticks
Fancy biscuits (recipes pages 183–4)
Little iced cakes—allow 2 per person (recipe page 183)
    8 oz. fat, etc.
Birthday cake (see pages 178 and 181–2)
Ice cream
    2–3 large blocks or about 3 pints
Jelly or jelly novelties (see below)
    3 pints jelly
Milk—6–8 pints
Fruit squash—1 bottle orange squash; 1 bottle lemon squash; water

Jelly novelties
Orange clowns: Cut tops off 8 medium-sized oranges, remove centre pulp and juice. Take away pith leaving an orange case. Dissolve 1 orange flavoured jelly in just under a pint water. Mix juice and orange pulp with jelly, allow to cool and stiffen. Whisk sharply, then pile into each orange case. Put an ice cream cone on top and pipe eyes, nose and mouth with thick cream for clown faces.

Sailing boats: Make up 1 pint green jelly. Pour into 8 saucers and allow to set. Top with an upturned pear and pipe lines of whipped cream on jelly to look like waves. Cut 8 ice cream wafers into triangles, to resemble sails. Press into little cream in each pear half.

Party menu for 12 older children

Hamburgers in rolls
  1½ lb. meat; 12 soft rolls
Sandwiches—ham, scrambled egg, cheese and lettuce. Allow 3 slices bread per person
  2 large loaves; 8 oz. butter or margarine; 8 oz. ham; 4–5 eggs, etc.; 4 oz. cheese; 1 lettuce
Sausages on sticks
  3 lb. large sausages (24); 24 sticks
or sausages and sausage rolls
  Allow 1½ lb. sausages and pastry made with 1 lb. flour, etc. (recipe page 133)
Doughnuts (recipe page 132)
  1½ lb. flour, etc.
Iced cakes—2 per person (page 183)
Chocolate biscuits (buy these)
  1 lb. biscuits
Iced birthday or celebration cake (pages 181–2)
  8 oz. fat, etc.
Ice cream sundae (page 171)
  3 blocks ice cream, etc.
  or Fruit salad (recipe Book 2, pages 216–17)
  2 large cans fruit—sliced peaches, pineapple, etc.; bananas—3 large; apples—2 large; pears—2 large; oranges—3 large; grapes—medium bunch
Milk—6 pints
Squash—1 bottle orange; 1 bottle lemon; water
  or provide ginger beer as a change

223

25. OUTDOOR CATERING

Planning for a picnic

The kind of food one takes on a picnic will vary a great deal according to the travelling facilities. People who are walking or going by train need food that is easy to carry and pack. A simple menu would be:

sandwiches—keep the fillings reasonably moist and wrap them well in greaseproof paper, foil or polythene bags so the bread does not dry;

Cornish pasties, sausage rolls, pork pies, or similar savouries;

lettuce, tomato and fresh fruit—carried in polythene bags;

milk, a fruit drink, tea or coffee may be carried in a vacuum flask.

Take care that this type of menu does not contain only carbohydrate foods. It is important to plan a well-balanced menu which includes adequate protein and vitamins. If travelling by car, however, a very much more ambitious menu may be planned and this can be similar to a cold meal served at home, with pies, cooked meat, salads, etc.

The picture on page 196 shows a menu that would be suitable if travelling by car.

Pasties: Blend 4 oz. diced cooked carrot and 4 oz. cooked peas together with 1 lb. sausage meat. Make 12 oz. short crust pastry, roll out then cut into 4 large rounds. Put the filling in the centre, form into a pasty shape, glaze with milk or beaten egg. Bake for 45 minutes in the centre of a moderately hot oven (400°F.—Gas Mark 5–6). Serve with salad.

Salad loaf: Split a long French loaf, butter then fill with mixed salad.

Apple fool tart: Bake a pastry case 'blind' and carry in baking tin with the apple fool mixture (recipe Book 2) in a screw-topped jar. Fill and then decorate with sliced fresh apple just before serving.

Coffee and fruit drinks can be carried in vacuum flasks.

To avoid having two dishes with pastry substitute fresh apples for the apple fool tart, or eat the filling only.

Always remember to clear away litter from a picnic and never leave glass bottles on beaches.

A barbecue

Cooking food over a barbecue fire is popular in countries where they have long, warm days. It is a very pleasant form of eating and entertaining. Take care that the fire is in a safe position and that small children are kept away. Simple food like sausages, chops, steaks, jacket potatoes, are cooked on a grid over the fire.

26. PARTY DRINKS

BOOK 2 gives a good selection of home-made drinks ranging from the familiar lemonade to less usual appleade, etc.
A fruit or cider cup is a good choice for a party, and it is possible to get non-alcoholic cider.

Fruit cup

2 lemons	*To decorate:*
2 oranges	1 orange
$\frac{1}{4}$ pint water	1 apple
2 oz. sugar	few cherries
1 can pineapple juice	
few ice cubes	
1 pint soda water	

Pare the rind from the fruit and simmer in the water for 5 minutes. Strain the hot liquid over the sugar. Stir until dissolved. Cool. Add the lemon, orange and pineapple juice. Pour into a bowl over ice cubes, then add the soda water. Decorate with the thinly sliced fruit and cherries. This quantity gives 8–10 glasses.

Variations

Use appleade, rhubarbade (Book 2, page 223).
Use ginger beer in place of soda water.

Cider cup

2 lemons	*To decorate:*
2 oranges	1 apple
$\frac{1}{4}$ pint water	1 orange
3 oz. sugar	few slices of
2 pints cider	cucumber
$\frac{1}{2}$ pint soda water	sprigs borage or mint
ice cubes	

Method as fruit cup.

27. COOKING FOR INVALIDS

THERE are some general points to consider when looking after an invalid.

1. Follow the doctor's instructions regarding food, etc. at all times.

2. Keep the sick room well ventilated without being unduly cold.

3. Clean the room as quietly and unobtrusively as possible and before meals make time to straighten the patient's bed and wash their face and hands if they are unable to do it themselves.

4. In the case of infectious illnesses (and this includes colds and influenza) it is very important that all china and cutlery used in the sick-room is washed and stored away from family china. It is also a good idea to wear an overall in the sick-room for added protection against infection.

Providing meals for an invalid

1. Do not ask if your patient is hungry. Assume he *is* and that he *will* enjoy the food. Your attitude will make a great deal of difference to his approach to meals.

2. Make sure the tray is easy to hold and the dishes will not tip easily.

3. Serve small portions—too large an amount of food can be quite overwhelming.

4. Do not have dishes that are too hot.

5. Individual portions look better than a piece cut from a larger portion.

6. See the food is easy to eat. Jellies and moulds should not be too stiff; remove skin from fish and bones from meat.

7. If the meal is not completely eaten, take it away—do not leave it there.

8. Have jugs or containers of iced or cold water, lemonade, etc. beside the bed and keep them covered with a clean serviette. Renew these drinks frequently.

9. A small posy helps to make a tray of food look more attractive, but it must not be too large or it will make the tray tilt.

10. When people have a high temperature they are disinclined to eat. Unless the doctor prescribes otherwise, give plenty of fluids, i.e. tea, milk, fruit drinks, etc. Give frequent sponging and make sure the bed linen is changed often so the bed is as comfortable as possible.

The menus suggested do not include beef tea. Once this was the accepted invalid fare, but now it is realised that while beef tea has a pleasant flavour—which may stimulate the palate like any clear soup—the food value cannot be extracted from the beef.

A yeast extract made into a drink with hot water gives some vitamin B.

Dealing with children who are ill

The same rules regarding food apply to children who are ill. The food should be served in a tempting fashion with as little fuss as possible. In addition, a child must be kept amused with books, coloured pencils and paper and simple jig-saw puzzles which are small enough to be made up on a tray. Try to sit in the room with a sick child for short periods during the day. If the patient has a sore throat, give soothing blackcurrant or lemon and honey drinks or lemonade.

Take particular care that there is nothing which could irritate the throat like sharp bones, etc. Ice cream is excellent as it acts as an astringent and helps in healing.

The following menus are suitable for invalids:

Menu 1

Fish custard (see below) with toast fingers
Simple soufflé (use raspberry jelly)

Menu 2

Fish cream with spinach and mashed potatoes
Fruit fool

Menu 3

Fresh grapefruit
Chicken in white sauce with sieved carrots
Fresh fruit
Cream cheese and biscuit

Menu 4

Baked fish with white or cheese sauce and creamed potatoes
Green salad (if permitted)
Fresh fruit jelly and ice cream

Menu 5

Consommé
Poached egg on spinach
Fresh fruit

Fish custard

Put a small fillet or slice of skinned fish into an ovenproof dish. Beat 1 egg yolk with seasoning and $\frac{1}{4}$ pint milk, strain over fish. Bake for 40 minutes in the centre of a very moderate oven (325–350°F.—Gas Mark 3). Garnish with lemon and parsley.

Cooking for people with ulcers

Many people have to follow a very strict diet for a very long period in order to treat a stomach ulcer, but the same kind of food and rules apply to people with gastric influenza or a temporary gastric complaint.

1. Include plenty of milk in the diet.

2. Avoid all highly spiced and highly seasoned foods, fried foods, pastry and alcohol.

3. Never give food which has been twice cooked, e.g. shepherd's pie made with minced *cooked* meat.

4. Do not allow too long a period to elapse between meals. A day's diet should be rather like this:

Breakfast
  Boiled or scrambled egg, bread and butter
  Milk or milky tea

Mid-morning
  A milky drink and sponge cake

Lunch
  Fish, creamed potatoes, sieved spinach
  Baked custard served with sieved jam or a smooth fruit purée (e.g. apple)
  No coffee or tea to follow—it can cause indigestion.

Tea-time
  Thin bread and butter, honey or sieved jam, sponge cake
  Milk or very milky tea

Evening meal
  Fish or a very little boiled chicken (without skin), sieved carrots, creamed potatoes
  Milk jelly or cornflour mould

Late night
  A milk drink and a plain biscuit

Leave a vacuum flask filled with milk and a tin of biscuits beside the bed, for the pain from an ulcer can often be relieved by having something to eat.

5. As the above menu shows, avoid skins or pips or pieces of vegetable or fruit, which might irritate the ulcer or stomach.

6. Often boiled or steamed fish only is allowed, but after a time chicken or lean minced meat will be permitted.

7. When the diet has to be followed for a long period it is important to try and give variety with milk puddings, etc.

Catering for a diabetic sufferer

It is extremely difficult to give general advice and recipes for diabetics, for each person has different requirements. An individual diet will have been prescribed by the doctor or the dietician at a hospital and should at all times be followed.

The general rules to remember are that people suffering from diabetes have to be particularly careful about their intake of carbohydrates, i.e. starches and sugars.

A great deal of good advice is given by the British Diabetic Association.

Meals for people who wish to lose weight

Serious over-weight spoils one's appearance, places a great strain upon the heart and often prevents people from enjoying any form of physical exercise. When dieting, have as much fresh air and exercise as possible.

No diet as strict as the one given below should be followed without medical advice.

There are many different slimming diets; some authorities believe that unlimited amounts of protein, fruit, vegetables (except potatoes) do not add to weight and that as long as fats and carbohydrates are restricted severely or omitted from the diet, people will lose weight. Another theory is that fat may be included, but carbohydrates omitted.

The third method of dieting is to restrict the calories but to plan a well balanced diet, with a generous amount of protein, a reasonable amount of fruit, plenty of green vegetables, little, if any, carbohydrates and very little fat. On the whole, this is the most satisfactory diet, for it enables people to plan normal meals, though loss of weight may be slower than with some of the rather drastic diets.

A typical day's menu on the third diet would be as follows:

Teenagers must drink a pint of milk a day. Adults should have ½ pint. Any milk used in coffee or tea must be taken from this ½ pint. Butter should not exceed ½–1 oz. All drinks should be sweetened with a sugar substitute.

Breakfast
Fresh grapefruit, unsweetened
or orange juice, unsweetened
Boiled or poached egg, or scrambled egg using some of the butter from the day's allowance
One slice of toast or bread
Tea or coffee

Midday meal
An average helping of lean meat or steamed or grilled fish—no extra fat to be used in cooking; no sauces or thickened gravies
Plenty of green vegetables
One small potato
Limited quantities of peas or beans or carrots
Fresh fruit or a small piece of cheese or stewed fruit cooked with sugar substitute

Evening meal
As midday meal
Starch-reduced bread, rolls, etc. help to reduce weight, as their calorie content is lower than ordinary bread.

Meals for people who wish to put on weight

Many people who appear to be quite healthy are seriously under-weight. This applies to growing children and to adults. It may be that they are too active and need a little more rest or that they have little liking for food and therefore their meals are not the type to add weight. If the doctor checks a very thin person and finds he is healthy there is no need to worry. If the doctor suggests that it would be a good idea to add a certain amount of weight, these are the points to remember:

1. Try to plan meals so that they can be eaten when people are not over-tired.
2. Include foods rich in calories, i.e. fats, carbohydrates, but at the same time do not give such a large quantity of these foods that they spoil the appetite for the more important foods containing protein, vitamins, etc.
3. Serve well sweetened puddings, desserts.
4. People who are under-weight should have as much rest and sleep as possible, but need fresh air and exercise too, to stimulate their appetite.
5. Serve a smaller portion of a variety of dishes rather than two very substantial courses, to add interest to the meal and sharpen the appetite.

A typical day's menu for someone who needs to put on weight would be as follows:

Breakfast
    Well sweetened grapefruit or fruit juice or stewed fruit
    Bacon and egg or cooked fatty fish such as herrings, etc.
    Toast or bread, butter, marmalade, honey or jam
    Tea or coffee served with milk and sugar

Mid-morning
    Milky coffee or milk and sweet biscuits

Midday meal
    A small helping of a thick soup
    An average portion of meat or fish which may be fried, grilled, etc.
    Potatoes, preferably creamed with butter and milk
    A green vegetable plus a good helping of peas or beans or carrots
    Fruit and ice cream or a light sweet

Tea-time
    Cheese and tomato, egg or other savoury sandwiches
    Cake
    Tea with milk and sugar

Evening meal
    As midday meal, or high tea or supper, page 204
    Meal should include sweetened fruit, canned fruit, etc.

Bed-time
    Drink of milk and a sweet biscuit or fruit

A simple breakfast tra
for an invali

28. EATING IN RESTAURANTS

THERE will be many occasions when one wishes to or has to, eat in a café, cafeteria or restaurant. Generally one can base the first assessment as to whether it is good or not upon the cleanliness of the tables, the surroundings, table linen, silver, etc. After that it will be the attitude of the staff—whether they are helpful or not, the price and standard of the food served, that will determine if it is a good or indifferent place in which to eat.

In a café or restaurant sometimes you will be given the choice of a 'Table d'hôte' or an 'A la carte' menu.

'Table d'hôte' means that the dishes have been cooked specially for that day or period of the year, and so are readily available and the complete meal is for a set price.

'A la carte' means you may choose dishes that will, or should be, cooked specially. The meal will generally be more expensive but the portions are usually bigger.

Often the menu in a restaurant is printed in French; the waiter or waitress should be able to tell you what the terms mean. As a guide, the endpapers of this book give a list of the more usual foods (most of them covered in this book and Book 2) that would be served in a typical restaurant, with the French names.

When eating in a café or restaurant there are certain points to consider.

1. Do not hurry over choosing your meal. Ask the waiter to return in a few minutes if you have not decided what to eat—sometimes he may try to hurry you. Ask the waiter's advice, but do *not* let him dictate what you should have. In a busy self-service café one cannot hinder other people for too long, but take sufficient time to *look* at the dishes offered and make a wise choice.

2. *Decide on the main course first* and then plan a first course if having this, e.g. with a substantial casserole dish or pie, choose a light first course or *no* first course at all. If the main dish has a delicate flavour—plaice, chicken, veal, etc.—the first course should not be so highly seasoned or spiced that it destroys the taste for this food.

3. If possible, leave the selection of a sweet until after you have eaten part of the meal.

4. When ordering coffee it is usual to be asked if you would like black or white, i.e. coffee without or with milk.

'White' coffee is an incorrect expression which has become part of common usage. A good restaurant will bring both coffee and milk and ask if you would like milk added.

Scotch pancakes

Using table silver in a restaurant

When the table is fully laid in a restaurant it can appear to have a confusing amount of silver, but this is quite easily sorted out—work from the outside towards the centre.

Melon: Use a dessertspoon and fork or small knife and fork.

Hors d'oeuvre: Generally there is a small knife and fork for this or use the fish knife and fork.

Soup: This is drunk with a soup spoon—and you turn the spoon and sip from the side.

Fish: Use a fish knife and fork.

Main meat dish: Use the large knife and fork.

Sweet course: Use either just the dessert fork (for gâteaux, pastry, etc.) or both the dessert spoon and fork or often a small teaspoon is provided for ice cream.

Cheese: Use the small knife.

Rolls: It is considered correct to break rather than cut these, and the butter is put on the side of the plate, then spread on the pieces of roll.

Fresh fruit is served with a small fruit knife and sometimes a fork too. A small bowl of cold water (called a 'finger bowl) is put on the table in a first class restaurant so you can dip the tips of your fingers in it after peeling fruit.

Tipping in a restaurant

In many restaurants of today, a service charge is included in the bill. This can range from 10% (2/– in the £) to 15% (3/– in the £) of the amount of the bill. For example, a bill which comes to £3 might have a service charge of 6/– or 9/––in this case there is no need to leave a tip. If no service charge is included in the bill, work out the amount for yourself and leave a tip accordingly.

Staff serving in a café or restaurant will naturally appreciate a reasonable tip and welcome the customer on other occasions, but like all busy people they respond to courtesy and consideration. If the service or food is very bad it is wrong *not to complain* for the sake of other people visiting the establishment.

Choosing wines for a meal

Wines come from many parts of the world, the most popular are readily available—coming from France, Germany, etc. but many other countries produce wines—Australia, Morocco, Yugoslavia, etc., in fact any country where grapes grow and ripen. On the following pages is a brief description of some of the most usual wines. The prices will vary according to the vintage, but these can all be termed moderately priced wines.

Vintage wines:

This is a term used to describe wines that are of special value due to a particularly good harvest. If a wine is described as 'vintage' it is an assurance that the wine is thoroughly matured and should be a fine flavour.

Naturally a palate for wine is like a palate for food—it depends on personal taste—some people like dry wines, others prefer a sweeter flavour.

On a wine list you will often see some wines given as vintage and non-vintage, the second wine being cheaper.

Wines to choose

Many people are dictatorial about which wine to choose with which type of food. This is a mistake for while some people like white wine with most foods, other people prefer red.

On the whole, however, it is better to choose a white wine to serve with: hors d'oeuvre; soup; fish; chicken and white meat such as veal. This is because a white wine has a more delicate flavour and will not obscure the taste of these foods.

It is better to choose a red wine to serve with: richer poultry such as duck and goose (although it goes well with chicken) and to have with meat and game. In between red and white wines, you can buy vin rosé (pink coloured), which pleases most palates and saves choosing white wine for some people and red for others. At a very formal meal it is usual to drink white wine with the fish, then follow with a red wine for the main course.

Amounts of wine to allow:

A half bottle of wine serves from two to three people (a glass each). One bottle serves four to six people.

Glasses for wines:

Many wine experts prefer to drink all wines from a tulip-shaped glass for they maintain this retains the 'bouquet' (flavour and smell) of the wine, but most people choose a different glass for each type of wine—illustrated on page 237 are a selection of glasses and the wines with which they are usually associated.

White wine

In order to taste this wine at its best, it should be served slightly chilled. Put it into a refrigerator for a short time, or keep in a very cool place.

If you wish to select a white wine you would look on a wine list under:

1. *White Bordeaux* (called this because the group of wines come from this part of France). Some of the most usual and popular of these are: Graves (fairly dry); Sauterne (rather sweet); Barsac (very sweet).

2. *White Burgundy* (coming from this part of France). Most of these are fairly dry. Popular wines of this group are: Chablis; Macon; Pouilly Fuisse.

3. *Hock* (a German wine). Two of the more popular are:

Liebfraumilch; Niersteiner.

Rosé

This should be chilled as a white wine. One of the most famous in this group comes from Portugal and is called 'Mateus'; there is also a good Graves in a 'vin rosé'; and another good wine in this group coming from France is 'Tavel'.

Red wines

Should not be served chilled. Ideally the bottle should be opened at least an hour before the meal and the wine left in a warm room.

The two main groups of red wines from France are:

1. *Red Bordeaux* (from this part of France), and the choice of wines here is very great. Often you see these listed under clarets. Three popular wines in this group are:

Médoc; St. Emilion; Margaux.

2. *Red Burgundy* (coming as the white wines from this part of France). Well known wines in this group are:

Beaune; Pommard; Nuits St. Georges; Beaujolais.

Sparkling wines

All the wines described above are still wines and do not bubble when opened. There are, however, sparkling wines—the most famous of all being 'Champagne' (often considered the finest wine France produces).

Champagne is generally served for special occasions—weddings, etc. It is possible to buy sparkling red and white wines at a considerably lower cost than champagne.

Sherry

This is another great wine. It is generally served before a meal or with the soup, and although sherry comes from several countries, the most prized comes from Spain. Sherries range from very dry:

Tio Pepe; Fino; Amontillado

to medium:

Oloroso

and so to really sweet brown sherries, the finest coming from France.

Brandy and port wines (from Portugal)

These are wines that are offered at the end of the meal. They, like sherry, are fortified wines and are therefore much stronger than the table wines.

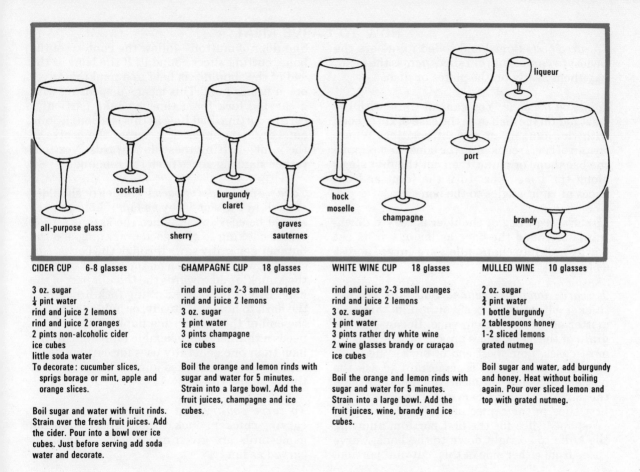

liqueur

cocktail

burgundy
claret

port

hock
moselle

champagne

all-purpose glass

sherry

graves
sauternes

brandy

CIDER CUP   6-8 glasses

3 oz. sugar
¼ pint water
rind and juice 2 lemons
rind and juice 2 oranges
2 pints non-alcoholic cider
ice cubes
little soda water
To decorate: cucumber slices,
   sprigs borage or mint, apple and
   orange slices.

Boil sugar and water with fruit rinds.
Strain over the fresh fruit juices. Add
the cider. Pour into a bowl over ice
cubes. Just before serving add soda
water and decorate.

CHAMPAGNE CUP   18 glasses

rind and juice 2-3 small oranges
rind and juice 2 lemons
3 oz. sugar
½ pint water
3 pints champagne
ice cubes

Boil the orange and lemon rinds with
sugar and water for 5 minutes.
Strain into a large bowl. Add the
fruit juices, champagne and ice
cubes.

WHITE WINE CUP   18 glasses

rind and juice 2-3 small oranges
rind and juice 2 lemons
3 oz. sugar
½ pint water
3 pints rather dry white wine
2 wine glasses brandy or curaçao
ice cubes

Boil the orange and lemon rinds with
sugar and water for 5 minutes.
Strain into a large bowl. Add the
fruit juices, wine, brandy and ice
cubes.

MULLED WINE   10 glasses

2 oz. sugar
¾ pint water
1 bottle burgundy
2 tablespoons honey
1-2 sliced lemons
grated nutmeg

Boil sugar and water, add burgundy
and honey. Heat without boiling
again. Pour over sliced lemon and
top with grated nutmeg.

HOW TO CARVE MEAT

To carve beef: Boned and rolled joints are the easiest to carve; cut thin slices *across* the meat. Lay them neatly on the plates or dish.

Joints on the bone: You can cut these with the meat flat on the dish or in the case of rib of beef, with the joint in an upright position. Where sirloin of beef is cooked on the bone, first remove the backbone or chine, then cut the first slices along the bone. Next turn the joint and cut slices at right angles to the bone.

To carve veal: Leg or shoulder is carved downwards or round the bone as lamb; loin is cut downwards into chops; fillets are carved across as beef.

To carve lamb or mutton: Cut into slightly thicker slices than beef, although this is a matter of personal preference. Because of the grain of the meat, slices are cut downwards, in most cases. Loin, best end of neck—these are cut into chops and it is important to ask the butcher to 'chine' the meat, or chop it through the bone for easier carving. Leg—make the first slice in the centre of the joint and cut a 'V'-shaped slice for the first portion, allowing the knife to go right down to the bone. Carve slices from either side of this 'cut out' portion.

Shoulder of mutton—follow the contour of the bone, cutting slices round it. If the bone at the end of the shoulder is held in a napkin it gives one a firmer hold. This means dispensing with a carving fork for a time, so take particular care in cutting. Saddle—as this is a double loin, cut very long slices first across the centre of the joint—cutting these downwards. Next cut rather slanting slices from the remainder.

To carve pork, ham or bacon: Cut leg or shoulder of pork in the same way as lamb. Loin of pork should be easy to cut, since the skin is scored before cooking to give good crackling, and the butcher generally saws through the bones. Cut slices downwards. Ham on the bone is cut from the knuckle end towards the thicker part of the ham. Either press the carving fork firmly into the flesh to hold this steady, or hold the bone at the end of the ham with a napkin. Ideally one needs a thinner, more flexible knife for carving ham than one generally uses for carving other meats. Boned and rolled joints of bacon are cut thinly across the meat.

To carve poultry and game: Instructions for carving chicken, duck, turkey, goose, hare and game birds are given on page 89. Venison is carved as lamb.

WORDS USED IN COOKERY

Terms used in preparing food

beat, a brisk movement to lighten

bind, blend ingredients together with an egg or a thick sauce (panada), to form the desired consistency. The term often used for the binding agent is 'liaison'

blend, to mix ingredients thoroughly

blanch, some offal, e.g. tripe, sweetbreads, are put into cold water, the water boiled then discarded. The purpose is to whiten or 'blanch'. Vegetables are blanched before freezing
Almonds are 'blanched' when placed into boiling water for a short time so the skins may be removed

chop, to cut food into small pieces with a sharp knife on a chopping board

clarify, to clean. Generally used in connection with dripping or fat (Book 2, page 122)

coat, to cover food with flour, egg and crumbs or batter to encourage browning (Book 2, pages 101–103)

conserve, to retain. Vegetables are cooked in minimum of liquid to conserve vitamins, etc.

consistency of mixture, this means the appearance and texture of the mixture. It is used a great deal in cake-making to describe whether the mixture should be soft, stiff, etc.

cream, to soften a mixture to the consistency of cream, e.g. creamed potatoes; creamed fat and sugar. Use a wooden spoon

decorate, to add extra ingredients to make food look more attractive. The word 'decorate' is generally used for sweet dishes, 'garnish' for savoury ones

dice, to cut into even small pieces

dilute, to make less strong, e.g. fresh lemon juice is diluted with water for lemonade

dredge, to coat liberally, generally with flour or sugar

dust, to coat lightly, generally with flour or sugar

ferment, the chemical change that takes place in bread making, also in wine making

flake, to divide food (fish in particular) into small pieces

fold, to 'flick' an ingredient into others already beaten, to retain lightness, e.g. flour into eggs and sugar (Book 2, pages 165–6). Use a metal spoon or palette knife

garnish, see 'decorate'

glaze, to brush with egg, milk, or liquid and sugar before baking to give a shine OR to cover fruit in a flan.

grate, to rub food against a grater to obtain small pieces, e.g. cheese, citrus fruit (for rind), etc.

knead, a word used in yeast cookery, (Book 2, page 230) also handling some biscuit dough. The ingredients are mixed with the hands, to give an extra texture

knock back, 'proven' or risen yeast dough is kneaded until it returns to its original size

mash, to beat food into a smooth purée, e.g. potatoes. Use a fork or potato masher

pare or peel, to remove the outer skin or rind of vegetables or fruit

pipe, to press a mixture, generally some form of icing, cream, creamed potatoes, etc. through a shaped pipe

prove, the term used in bread making where the dough is put to rise (Book 2, page 230)

purée, see 'mash' and 'sieve'

rise, the word used to describe the change that takes place in certain dishes which swell and become light during cooking, e.g. cakes, due to the action of the raising agent used; or pastry and a whisked sponge where correct handling incorporates air; and bread, where yeast makes the dough ferment and so rise

roll out, dough for pastry, etc. is rolled lightly with a rolling pin to the required shape and thickness

rub in, to mix fat with flour with your fingers until the mixture is like breadcrumbs

season, to add salt and pepper. In many recipes the word 'seasoning' is used to denote these. Mustard and other flavourings are listed separately. It is also the term for preparing an omelette pan (Book 2, page 58)

scrape, to remove peel, etc. by a scraping movement with a sharp knife. Use for new potatoes, new carrots, when it would be wasteful to peel

sieve, to push food, e.g. spinach, fruit, etc. through a sieve to obtain a purée, or to lighten flour, etc. and ensure it is free from lumps

sponging, or to 'allow the sponge to break through', a term used only when cooking with yeast (Book 2, page 230)

strain, (a) to remove food from liquid, e.g. vegetables when cooked; (b) to remove stock from bones, etc.

toss, one method of turning a pancake (Book 2, page 207); or vegetables, etc. are tossed, i.e. 'turned in' hot fat before serving or adding liquid in a stew or casserole

whip or whisk, cream is whipped to thicken it. Care must be taken that it is not over-whipped. A fork or egg whisk is used. Egg whites are whisked to make a meringue. A proper egg whisk is used

work, the method of moving eggs in an omelette (Book 2, page 61)

Terms used in cooking

bake, to cook in the oven without using additional fat. Custard, cakes, biscuits, pastry are baked and so is some meat

bake blind, to bake a pastry case without a filling. When this is done there is a tendency for the pastry to rise. When making a flan, therefore, it is advisable to use plain flour for whichever pastry you choose. Either prick the pastry well with a fork (see picture, page 143) or, better still, put a piece of greased greaseproof paper or foil inside. Cover this with crusts of bread or dry haricot beans to weigh down the bottom of the pastry. In order to make sure a flan case is very crisp cook for approximately 15 minutes, at temperature given in the recipe, then remove the paper, etc. If using a flan ring this may also be removed so the outside of the pastry will brown more easily. Return to the oven for a further 5–10 minutes.

bain-marie, cooking in a container (bain-marie) of water, e.g. caramel custard.

baste, to spoon hot fat over meat, poultry or other food while it is cooking to keep it moist

boil, to cook in liquid at boiling point, i.e. 212°F. (100°C.). Liquid is boiling when it bubbles hard. Many foods are just brought to boiling point and then the heat lowered so the food simmers, see below

braise, to cook foods, generally meat, in a rich brown sauce, above a mirepoix of mixed vegetables, etc. (page 98). Wine is often added

casserole, a baking dish with a tight-fitting lid, used for cooking stews and vegetables in the oven

coagulate, to allow mixture to thicken or to set

curdle, when the ingredients separate and look lumpy instead of smooth. This can happen in egg dishes cheese sauce when adding eggs to a creamed mixture see pictures page 155

fry, to cook in fat; sometimes a very small amount is used, sometimes a larger amount. The correct temperature fat must be used

grill, to cook under the grill, generally a quick process

par-boil, to cook partially in boiling salted water, e.g. parsnips before roasting (Book 2, page 82)

poach, to cook slowly in liquid. Eggs, fish, etc. are poached in salted water

roast, to cook in the oven in extra fat; some fat meat can be roasted in its *own* fat

'roux' making a, to cook fat and flour in the first stage of a sauce

season, this is already covered in Book 2. See pages 6 and 58 on the preparation of food and omelette pan

simmer, steady cooking in liquid. You should see an occasional bubble on the surface. The temperature is 180–190°F. Cover pans when simmering for a long time, otherwise the liquid evaporates.

steam, to cook in steam rather than liquid. A proper steamer which is put over a pan of water is ideal. Otherwise use a small quantity of water so the food is not immersed (completely covered)

stew, to cook slowly by simmering in a little liquid in a closed pan or casserole

INDEX

Figures in italics refer to coloured pictures

LES LÉGUMES—VEGETABLES

Pommes de terre	potatoes, but generally the method of cooking is given. Often shortened to pommes, e.g.
Pommes frites	fried potatoes
Pommes de terre naturel or	boiled potatoes
Pommes de terre à l'anglaise	boiled potatoes
Pommes de terre persillées	often used to describe roast potatoes
Purée de pommes de terre	creamed or mashed potatoes
Petits pois	peas
Oignons	onions
Navets	turnips
Épinards à la crème	creamed spinach
Choux verts	cabbage
Chou-fleur au gratin	cauliflower with browned topping
Chou-fleur Mornay	cauliflower in cheese sauce

MENU

The dishes mentioned are those usually found on the menu of a good average restaurant. Most of them will be found in this or earlier books.

LES VOLAILLES ET LE GIBIER —POULTRY AND GAME

Poulet grillé	grilled chicken
Poulet frit	fried chicken, but sometimes given as:—
Poussin	very young chicken
Poulet rôti	roast chicken, but sometimes given as—
Chapon rôti	capon (very large chicken)
Canard rôti	roast duck or
Caneton	duckling, very young bird
Dindon rôti	roast turkey, or often given as—
Dindonneau	young turkey
Oie rôtie	roast goose
Caneton à l'orange	duck and orange
Dindon farci	stuffed turkey
Faisan rôti	roast pheasant
Fricassée de lapin	rabbit fricassée*
Civet de lièvre	dish like jugged hare

*these French words have become the usual term in any language

LES SALADES—SALADS

Salade verte	green salad
Salade variée	mixed salad
Salade russe	Russian salad
Salade de pommes de terre	potato salad or often called
Salade Parmentier	